THE
VISUAL ARTS
AS
HUMAN
EXPERIENCE

DONALD L. WEISMANN

University Professor in the Arts
The University of Texas at Austin

PRENTICE-HALL, INC., ENGLEWOOD CLIFFS, NEW JERSEY

THE
VISUAL ARTS
AS
HUMAN
EXPERIENCE

To
HOWARD THOMAS
and
ROBERT von NEUMANN

THE VISUAL ARTS AS HUMAN EXPERIENCE
by Donald L. Weismann

13–942367–2

13–942375–3

Library of Congress Catalog Card Number: 74–90765

Printed and bound in Switzerland

Designed by Marvin R. Warshaw

Current printing (last number): 10 9 8 7 6 5 4 3 2 1

Preface

The writing of a foreword, a preface, or an introduction almost invariably comes *after* the book is written. It is by virtue of the actual writing of a book that the author discovers what it was that moved him to write it in the first place. In Chapter 1, "Introduction," I have taken several pages to tell why I wrote this particular book and why I feel it was a good thing to do. Still, in fairness to the prospective reader, it may be in place to say something about what he can expect of this volume.

The reader of this book can expect to be introduced to the visual arts in very much the same way that two people are introduced by a third person. I, as the introducer, have done what I could to make this a graceful, open sort of introduction which, it is hoped, will lead to continually rewarding interchanges between the reader and the visual arts. And since this is only an introduction to an unbelievably rich and complex phenomenon, I have had to choose what I would talk about. In all cases I have chosen to speak about what my experience has shown me to be of most importance. And I chose to do this in a direct way, free of excessive technical nomenclature and modish art-jargon. My aim has been to introduce the reader to the visual arts in a way that diminishes the importance of traditional categories and helps bring the art back into the lives of living people. I feel it is of real importance, for instance, that each of us—in his own way—now re-experiences the excitement and extraordinary value of the young Masaccio's adventure in painting *The Holy Trinity*. After almost five and a half centuries it still waits for us in the church of Santa Maria Novella near the railroad station in Florence. It waits ready to enliven and inform us. And so does Jackson Pollock's painting, the one he called *Number 1,* wait for us—on a wall in a museum in

Manhattan—even as all the numberless works of men wait for us all over the world.

My aim has also been to introduce the reader to significant concepts that have to do with the visual arts—with the forms they take, the visual elements, unity, proportion, space and space illusion, form and content, and the creative process. And in all cases I have tried to get at what lies behind the names of these phenomena by encouraging the reader to allow the experiences of his day-to-day life—no matter their kind or quality at the outset—to function as a basis for his own growing awareness and understanding. A basic tenet of this book is that art is part of life, not some abstruse activity carried on outside of life, and that art is produced by human beings fundamentally like you, the reader, and like me.

As one would expect, my personal experience and preferences have functioned in choosing the means that I would use to make this introduction to the visual arts. As it turns out, it is painting, sculpture, and the graphics which are emphasized—not architecture, urban planning, industrial design, or the film. However, most of what is discussed in this book is of such a nature that it is negotiable in those other areas. This is true, for instance, of what is said in the chapters concerning language and visual form; total configuration; three kinds of seeing; the visual elements; expression; unity; visual forces and balance; tension; cohesion and closure; proportion; space and illusion of space; and in other chapters.

In writing this book I have called upon everybody and everything that might help me. It would be impossible to acknowledge in any specific way the debts and the thanks I owe to others. So instead of trying the impossible, I mean to acknowledge all by thanking the man to whom, of all persons I have known, I am deepest in debt, Alexander D. Tillotson. It was he who, when I was twelve years old, introduced me to the visual arts and to that world in which I have ever since lived.

Donald L. Weismann

Table
of
Contents

THE
VISUAL ARTS
AS
HUMAN
EXPERIENCE

CHAPTER ONE

Introduction

It is mainly my high regard for the role that the visual arts have played in my own life that motivates the writing of this book. A kind of common good fortune that was as casual as happenstance began working for me as early as I can remember. From the first, it seems, I was taken by the world as it came through my eyes. And then, as now, I looked at the life and objects of this world as if they were given as clues to my own identity.

Something in the very act of visual perception makes the world ours and, in turn, makes us integral parts of that world. If we are fortunate, this feeling of being naturally at home in the world goes unquestioned for a good part of our childhood. For a while it is enough merely to point at what commands our attention and to call out its name to whomever might be close enough to hear. Later, we find that mere pointing and the simple call are not sufficient. We begin to ask questions about our relation to the world, and to expect answers.

At a point, in whatever ways are opened to us, we become concerned with formulating our experience—with making sense of our life in this world. And it is at this point that the attempts of other men become crucially important to us. It is then that we recognize in art its power to give shape to human experience and to present it in eloquent objective form. Art becomes significant for us as we appreciate more and more how it differs from direct visual perception of the actual world. More and more, we come to value what another human being has done with what he has seen and felt about the world. This book is concerned with some of the ways and means by which the artist formulates his experience and makes images of it for us to see and be affected by.

It is a curiously simple fact that whatever each of us knows has had to be learned or experienced by each one of us separately—each in his own way according to his own lights and shadows. And if someone says, yes, but I have learned a great deal from others, from the Brothers Grimm, from Cervantes, the sculpture of Michelangelo, and Delacroix's *Journal,* it is still true that one learns only to the extent that the experience of other men becomes, somehow, one's own experience. Whatever went into Goya's *Disasters of the War* (Fig. 1–1) was related to his actual and imaginative experience of Napoleon's Peninsular Campaign of 1808. And now, more than a century and a half later, these etchings stand as prime experiences for us. Insofar as we are affected by them, they become part of our own experience, part of us. And just as with our experiences of ordinary daily life, experiences of art have a way of funding in us, of storing up, of patterning and contributing to whatever sense and form our life assumes from hour to hour and year to year.

Fig. 1–1. *FRANCISCO GOYA.* Why? (Disasters of the War). c. 1820. *Intaglio,* $5^7/_{16} \times 7^7/_{16}''$
National Gallery of Art, Washington, D.C. (Rosenwald Collection).

It is a help and often a comfort to remember the simple stubborn fact that art is made by human beings, more like us than any other phenomenon in the world. The unknown creator of the *Venus of Willendorf* (Fig. 1–2) must have been a live human being some twenty-five thousand years ago. The anonymous sculptor of the *Poseidon* (Fig. 13–1) was no less a live human being in fifth-century Greece than was the creator of the *Shiva Nata-raja* (Fig. 14–3) in eleventh-century India. And whether it was Masaccio in

Fig. 1–2. Venus of Willendorf. *c. 15,000–10,000 B.C. Stone, height 4³/₈". Museum of Natural History, Vienna.*

Italy, Pieter Brueghel in Flanders, Velasquez in Spain, Rodin in France, or Pollock in the United States, we can be assured that as they created their works they were more like us than they were unlike us—that, in fact, each one of them worked within a degree or two of 98.6, your own body temperature, even as you read these words.

Like all human beings, artists are born, live out their lives, and die. They experience joy, boredom, ecstasy, terror, despair, frustration, and ful-

Poseidon (Zeus?). *National Museum, Athens. Photo: Hirmer, Munich. Figure 13–1 repeated*

Shiva Nataraja. *Cleveland Museum of Art. Figure 14–3 repeated.*

fillment not totally unlike ours. The telling difference between our experience and the experience of a Rembrandt, a Goya, a Cézanne, or a Picasso is not so much in kind as in how its quality and intensity are faced, felt, acted upon, contemplated, and finally manifested in a work of art. And in a real sense this work of art is a deed which is witness to the man's life and worth, and it is there for us to see.

Not all of one's life is spent in concern for keeping the daily routine. In the busiest of lives, moments come when one is confronted by more than just another operational task, another deadline. Sometimes it comes at the airport when the plane is delayed and nothing is demanded but waiting. Sometimes it comes in the pause afforded by our helplessness in the dentist's chair, and sometimes it comes into the middle of a busy day, unbid but decisive in its stripping away of everything but what one feels essential to the continuance of an aware good life. These moments, familiar to all of us, feel like moments of truth in which, for a little while, we face our condition in this life. We sense that our deepest yearnings and anxieties are being clearly addressed; and now and then we have the feeling of almost grasping the pattern of the whole and our part in it. Material things and thoughts limited to them fall away. We sense and savor the qualities of love, fear, sympathy, sorrow, admiration, and spirited action. More and more, in our impersonal culture, we live these moments alone, or almost alone. Our time and place give no billing to the man who allows himself to be peeled in the sight of other men; we peel down or are peeled down in seclusion, and we wrap ourselves back up before the delayed airplane taxies up and we rejoin our fellows. We may guess that the man in the safety belt next to us has also experienced these moments of truth, but it is a rare event indeed when two persons make this evident to each other.

The artist has always been one who manages to formulate something of these moments in durable images which long outlast his simple time. Courageously, perhaps, he makes these images available to others. We see them in the exhibition hall, in the art museum, and in their reflections afforded by reproduction in books and magazines. Not all of these images are of the highest order, just as not all men or all moments are of the highest order. But the artist puts them out in the world for us to see or ignore and we are often touched by them. Sometimes they analogize something of our own experience; other times they induce new imaginative experiences with the force of directly perceived reality. When this happens, conversation of a valuable sort takes place—a kind of dialogue between persons is made possible. The spectator's experience is helped toward formulation in terms of the presented image, and the image is found to be meaningful in terms of the spectator's experience.

Art is a way of knowing. This way of knowing is capable of a kind of knowledge of which, for instance, the way of science is not capable. Instead of the scientifically abstracted ideas *about* things and conditions, art *presents* those things and conditions. Our experiencing of them heightens our sense of them, and we can come to a fresh, full, and intimate awareness as we are confronted by them in relation to ourselves. This cohabitation in time and place of the live human being and the thing itself allows us to know it as itself. And in this situation, it is we who are required to know this thing by finding or creating a place for it within our experience of the world. It is essential that we keep ourselves in the act, for if we are out of touch with our own experience, we are out of touch with ourselves—our quality and identity are lost, no matter the level of our intelligence or our capacity for abstraction. Art is a means for reaching into our experience of the world, of revivifying it as the relation between reality and ourselves. This is true for the artist who "realizes" his experience in a work of art, and it is true for all those who subsequently find in it an "experience of art."

In a life spun of statistics, formulae, and quantitive measure there is often a deep denial of the very world out of which these have come. Where in such a life does one man's experience meet another man's experience face to face? Where is the reassuring shock of knowledge by recognition? Such knowledge can come by way of art, by way of Donatello's *St. Mary Magdalen* (Fig. 19–11), Brueghel's *The Blind Leading the Blind* (Fig. 5–10),

DONATELLO. St. Mary Magdalen. *Photo: Alinari-Art Reference Bureau. Figure 19–11 repeated.*

PIETER BRUEGHEL THE ELDER. The Blind Leading the Blind. *National Museum, Naples. Photo: Alinari-Art Reference Bureau. Figure 5–10 repeated.*

Rembrandt's *Saul and David* (Color Plate 1), Bernini's *The Ecstasy of St. Theresa* (Fig. 5–11), Chardin's *Kitchen Still Life* (Color Plate 2), de Kooning's *Woman I* (Color Plate 3), and all the heritage of art that we as latest comers can claim as ours.

So what we are saying here is that art is part of life, not some abstruse activity carried on outside of life, and that art is produced by human beings like you and me. We are saying that the artist is concerned with making sense of his life, with formulating his experience in persuasive durable images, just as we are. It is by way of these images formed in stone, wood, steel, paint, or whatever other material he might employ, that we as viewers can share the experience of the artist. And not only can we share his experience in this way, we can revivify our own experience and, in the best moments, witness the excitement of new imaginative experiences that become our own with the undeniable quality of personally experienced reality.

REMBRANDT. Saul and David. *Mauritshuis, The Hague. Photo: A. Dingjan. See Plate 1.*

GIANLORENZO BERNINI. The Ecstasy of St. Theresa. *Photo: Alinari-Art Reference Bureau. Figure 5–11 repeated.*

JEAN-BAPTISTE SIMÉON CHARDIN. Kitchen Still Life. *Ashmolean Museum, Oxford. See Plate 2.*

WILLEM DE KOONING. Woman I. *The Museum of Modern Art, New York (Purchase). See Plate 3.*

CHAPTER TWO

The Visual Arts and Language

It has often been said that art is a language, but unless one can think of language as much more than a verbal means of communication, it is not so. If art were a language, it would have its dictionary and its grammar by this time. There is no such dictionary or grammar published or passed on like ancient sagas or legends. There is no source book that will tell the meaning of the color red, the preferred connotation of a polished surface, or the meaning of a gently curving line 30 inches in length. These elements of the visual arts take on specific and often widely differing, if not opposing, significations in each separate composition, in each unique work of art. It is the whole, the complete work, which determines the role and significance of each of the visual elements employed. There are real and crucial differences between what is generally accepted as language—the whole body of words and methods of combining them used by a nation, people, or race (a tongue) —and the means by which a work of visual art assumes its character or communicates is meaning.

Since most of us have attained the high degree of literacy required by contemporary culture, it will be convenient to use it as a foil against which to point up the quite different character of the visual arts. But just in case we might feel that we have not attained this high degree of literacy, let us remember that long before we entered kindergarten we were speaking. We commanded a vocabulary, and although no rules of grammar and syntax had yet been formally taught to us, we were already proficient in their use. All but the most private games and dances of kindergarten were, for all of us, called for, permitted, and directed by language. From a very early age we live language-oriented lives. For, after all, our *culture* is language-oriented. It is not by accident that there are no paintings or sculpture in the

Declaration of Independence or the *Bill of Rights*—none even in the *Lord's*
Prayer or the *Scout's Oath*. All of them are formed in words; they make
sense in language, and we understand them.

Now, what are some of the most important characteristics of this language that has been part of each of our lives for so long? And how does it
differ from the form that the visual arts take?

Let us begin by considering a simple experience, first as verbally formulated in language, and then as that experience appears when given visual
form in a painting. In this particular case, both the writing and the painting
were accomplished by the same person who, because of this, could base his
work in an identical personal experience. The results are independent
entities; one is not an illustration of the other. The experience which is basic
to both of these formulations has to do with a young boy entering the darkened hallway of a house. The language version is as follows:

> Going to Henry Cranshaw's rooming house on Sycamore Street was like going
> to another city. It wasn't far away, just five blocks, but when Richard turned
> off from the sidewalk, went up the worn wooden steps and through the tall
> brown door, he felt that he had gone out of his hometown and into another
> place on the other side of the earth.
>
> No matter if it was noon with the sun high and bright in the world outside,
> it was always dark inside Henry Cranshaw's rooming house. The little yellow
> electric light bulb with the green lampshade wired on top was always burning
> above the black table in the hallway. The hall was long and dark, with the
> door to Henry Cranshaw's room at the end always open. The noises of the
> traffic in the street would suddenly stop as Richard closed the tall brown door
> behind him, and the light he had let in would be gone. He would stand on the
> rug just inside the door, look at the little yellow bulb, then down to the top of
> the square black table where a letter or two usually lay. Everything else would
> be dark and uncertain as if floating before him in a slowly revolving pool.
> For a while he would stand there waiting for his eyes to see the rest of the
> hall. Gradually it would come around him; first the weak light from another
> bulb burning in the hall above as it reflected from the pink and green wall-
> paper along the stairs; then the rail and spindles of the banister showing
> darkly against the wallpaper; then the stained ceiling above the little black
> table growing from a small spangled patch into a bigger and bigger patch
> extending to the edges of the ceiling, then more slowly to the tops of the wall
> and down. The deep colored floor lay beneath his feet and he knew it was
> there, first by the feel of the little rug, and then by a long strip of carpeting
> that ran way back to Henry Cranshaw's door. And beyond that door it was
> always black, even for that little time when the light from the street fell in
> the hallway as Richard entered and departed.[1]

Now, since all of us are seasoned readers, we did not hesitate for a
moment before we began reading this passage *from left to right*. This is one
of the basic conventions of the English language. And we started with the

---

[1] Donald L. Weismann, *Language and Visual Form: The Personal Record of a Dual Creative Process* (Austin and London: University of Texas Press, 1968), pp. 69–70.

highest line of the passage and moved, *in sequence,* to the next *lower line* on the page. In English we read from left to right and from top to bottom, and the sense or meaning of a statement is not completed for us until we reach its end. We read along in a unidirectional manner according to the rules of grammar and the conventions of syntax. In turn, we interpret groups of letters as words that stand for objects, such as *house, street, city, sidewalk, steps,* and *hallway.* We interpret other groups of letters as words that stand for actions of various sorts, such as *going, turned, went, burning,* and *floating;* and we know how we should combine all of these nouns and verbs with other groups of letters we call adjectives, adverbs, and prepositions, and with the accompanying punctuation. This characteristic of language—how it courses along like a train on a track or a river in its bed—is what we call its *discursiveness:* we say that language is *discursive in form.* Its stimuli and the responses they elicit are strung out in *time.* We say, therefore, that language is *temporal in form.* And because the stimuli of language are *words,* and because words are a special kind of sign, we say that language depends upon signs as means for communication and expression.

Without stopping to consider such means afforded the writer by onomatopoeia, alliteration, metaphor, and simile, let us move on to a consideration of the painting (Color Plate 4). You will remember that this painting was not developed as an illustration of the written passage just quoted. Instead, this painting came about as the result of a separate attempt to formulate in visual terms the same *experience* that motivated the writing. The result is, of course, a very different phenomenon.

DONALD L. WEISMANN. Henry Cranshaw's Rooming House. *Collection of the artist. See Plate 4.*

Obviously, we do not begin to "read" this painting from the upper left and proceed to the bottom by a series of eye fixes progressing from left to right. We do not read this painting at all: we *see* it, and we see it first as a *whole*. And unlike a page of writing, which, it is true, can also be seen as a whole, the painting reveals its subject matter as well as its essential form, its total configuration, in an instant. In looking at the painting, we are not required to follow any directional course from beginning to end in order to grasp its subject and be affected by its total form. The form of this painting is not discursive. The painting, with all the clues to its import, is presented to our eyes totally and all at once—immediately. We say that the form of painting is *presentational*. Time, of the considerable amount required to gain the form, or logic, of the written passage, is not required to gain the same of the painting. Whereas the form of language is temporal, the form of the visual arts is *spatial*. With certain exceptions (due to actual movement, as in the film, and to very large size and multidimensionality, as in murals and sculpture-in-the-round), the work of visual art is presented immediately and completely in space—right there in the space in front of our eyes. And just what is it that is presented to us? What are the stimuli of the visual arts? We said that the stimuli of language are words, or signs. In the visual arts, in architecture, sculpture, painting, drawing, and the graphics, the stimuli are *visual qualities* and *visual images*. In the painting under consideration we are presented with visual images; we see images of doorways, an electric light bulb, a lampshade, table, banister, letters, rug—each presented with particular qualities that contribute to the one overall effect of the visual configuration.

Now, it is not our intention to suggest that the visual arts offer "better" means of communication and expression than language, nor that language is "better." What we mean to make clear is that the forms of each are quite different and that we should not expect language to function in the manner of the visual arts, or vice versa. Because of our early indoctrination into the ways and means of language, because our culture transacts most of its experience in the medium of language, many of us erroneously, if unconsciously, expect the visual arts to function in ways similar to those of language. And yet each of us knows that often enough words have failed us in our desire to give expression to our experience: there we stand, wanting to share with another the great good feelings we are experiencing—and all we seem able to do is smile, reach for a hand, or embrace. And just as often, the visual arts fail to give form to our experience. Human experience is, after all, not simple or poor; it is rich, multidimensional, and multifaceted. It would be most unreasonable to expect that any one of our imperfect forms of communication and expression could ever adequately embody the fullness and variety of our experience. Different forms have different advantages and different limitations, and it is essential that we have some understanding of what the advantages and limitations of the visual arts are.

To come back to language, in the passage concerning Richard and the rooming house the natural propensity of language to intimate a linear passage of time by its consumption of *actual* time (as in speaking or reading) is a welcome one. The inevitable consumption of actual time in reading about Richard's turning off from the sidewalk, going up the worn wooden steps and through the tall brown door, standing on the rug inside the door, and waiting for his eyes to see into the dark hallway—all this contributes to an imaginative experiencing of the time quality of the incident. In a real way this discursive, temporal form of language works to give analogical significance to the episode. Yet, if examined more closely, the language employed to tell of Richard's going to the rooming house, entering, waiting, and observing does not build successively and unidirectionally as do seconds toward the minute and minutes toward the hour. For although words may be strung like beads on a string, one after another in discrete succession, the actions with which they deal, the propositions they construct, and the moods and meanings they impart do not follow likewise.

In the sentence, "The noises of the traffic in the street would suddenly stop as Richard closed the tall brown door behind him, and the light he had let in would be gone," we have occurring in *actual* time (our reading time), first, the stopping of the traffic noises, then Richard closing the door, and then the disappearance of the light. To all of us disciplined in the conventions of English grammar and syntax, the sentence tells something about what took place when Richard closed the rooming house door behind him. We understand all this to be part of a simultaneous occurrence: the traffic noise and the light were cut off at the very same moment that the door closed. However, our language makes it impossible to write, read, or speak in simultaneous groups of words. It requires that we name one entity, then another and another, and that other words that are not names, but signs standing for specific functions, be slotted between or placed before or after —all according to convention. Language requires that we name relationships existing between entities, and that names of objects and entities and names of relations be strung out one after another. Further, it requires that our *ideas* also be strung out end to end, even though those ideas convolve, one within others. This characteristic of language, which is an advantage in giving form to discrete temporal succession and in producing suspense by virtue of withholding key names or relation signs (as in some detective stories), is a distinct disadvantage when simultaneity of various ideas, actions, or opposed qualities is desired. The unilinear, successive order which characterizes language limits our speech and writing to expressions of thoughts and concepts which can be disposed only in this peculiar order. All other thoughts, ideas, and especially feelings which do not lend themselves to this kind of order must be called, in fact, ineffable; they are inexpressible, incommunicable by means of words.

In the written version of Richard's experience upon entering the rooming house, there exists no way to *present* the fact that almost everything mentioned is part of a *single event.* Many of the successively named objects were, in fact, present *all at once* in the hallway, and Richard responded to this "dark and uncertain" complex as if it were "floating before him in a slowly revolving pool." This simultaneous presence of the light bulb and shade, the rug, the table with letters lying upon it, the long hallway, and the open door at the end is impossible to symbolize or express directly in language. And it is impossible with words to *show* how all these quite different things exist together in a particular pattern having a particular quality as a whole.

How different this is with the painting. In it we have presented to our eyes, all at once and immediately, *images* of the many things which make up this particular situation of the hallway. At one and the same time we see the separate shapes, colors, lines, and textures which make up the hallway situation as perceived by Richard. And more than that, we are shown how these visual elements form images of things which appear to interpenetrate each other in a "dark and uncertain way." For instance, it is not clear where the rug in the lower left ends and the floor begins to show; it is not architecturally clear how the door to the staircase in the left center is related to the hallway, and we cannot be sure on what the black table in the lower right rests. Yet, this precisely analogizes the quality of the hallway situation as it comes to Richard's eyes and affects his feeling—even to the extent that an implied motion is set up by the irregular placement of the images around a relatively blank central area. To some extent, the disposition of the visual elements in this painting suggests the pattern of objects, or flotsam, turning on the surface of an eddy. The structure of the painting presents us with qualities suggestive of "floating . . . in a slowly revolving pool."

In the painting, the various components of the hallway situation are presented all at once, as a totality; and we can perceive this as one configuration of visual elements. Opposites such as black and white, rough and smooth, clarity and obscurity, line and area are visually perceivable at the same instant of time. This is impossible with language. It may be the principal difference between the form of language and form in the visual arts. It is important that we recognize this, since it is crucial to our seeing, and hence to our experiencing, the visual arts.[2]

---

[2] For a detailed, comparative treatment of the forms of language and the visual arts, see the author's *Language and Visual Form: The Personal Record of a Dual Creative Process.*

CHAPTER THREE

Total
Configuration

In the recent past we used to refer to the work of art as a *composition*. More recently we have been calling the composition the *structure* of the work. Some people refer to it as the *pattern* or *design* of the work. In any case, it is necessary that we have a satisfactory descriptive term for referring to the whole work of art. More and more the term being used for this is *total configuration*. It is both inclusively descriptive and generally satisfactory. It designates the prime characteristic of visual form: the immediate and simultaneous presence of all the elements and how they are disposed in relation to each other and to the whole.

A simple and dramatic way to demonstrate the rapidity with which the total configuration comes through to us is to have a slide of a totally unfamiliar work flashed on a screen for a fraction of a second. In that little time our eyes are denied an opportunity to explore the work. When the dark screen suddenly lights up with the image, there is no time to move one's eyes before the screen is again dark. In that single fix of the eyes there is time only for the whole image, the total configuration, to register on the retina. And yet, even though the image may have been available for only a half or a fifth of a second, the least experienced viewers will be able to report on the kind and quality of that image. What will have come through strongest will be the basic structure of the image: whether it is based on a right-angle grid, a pattern of acute angles, interwoven curves, a spiral, or whatever. And for most viewers there will be a surprising memory of their responses to the particular qualities of color, shape, size, and line and their relative disposition in the total configuration.

Since it is in the nature of the visual arts to present this total configuration first and immediately, it follows that as viewers of art we ought to allow it to have its maximum impact on us. Our way into a work of visual art

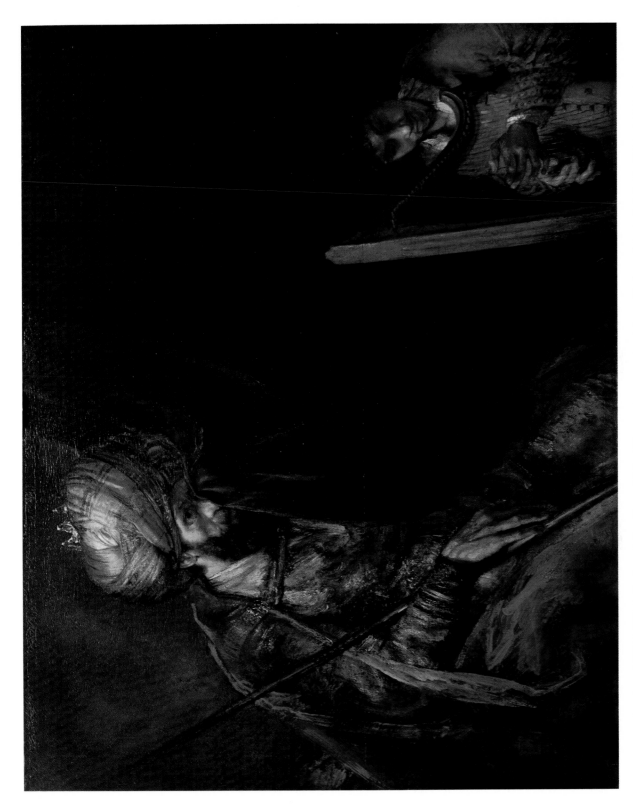

Plate 1. REMBRANDT. Saul and David. c. 1660. Oil on canvas, 51½×64½″. This painting, like so many painted late in Rembrandt's life, attests to his remarkable capacity for experiencing the stories of the Old Testament as direct accounts of how God works among men. Here, across a darkly painted depth, the favored young David makes music speak to the troubled old king. (Mauritshuis, The Hague. Photo: A. Dingjan.)

Plate 2. JEAN-BAPTISTE SIMEON CHARDIN. Kitchen Still Life. c. 1730–1735. Oil on canvas, 12¹/₂×15¹/₄″. With a reserved and steady straightforwardness, Chardin presents these ordinary kitchen objects in a way that they appear both utterly common and extraordinarily impressive. He has a way of showing us a very well known world as if we were seeing it for the very first time. (Ashmolean Museum, Oxford.)

Plate 3.   WILLEM DE KOONING. Woman I. *1950–1952. Oil on canvas, 75⁷/₈×58". The experience of men can be shared through the work of art. In this transaction we, the viewers, when touched by what we see, must make a place for the new experience within our total experience of the world. (The Museum of Modern Art, New York. Purchase.)*

Plate 4.   *DONALD L. WEISMANN*. Henry Cranshaw's Rooming House. *1948. Casein on composition board, 14¹/₂ × 11³/₄″. In the painting, the various components of the hallway are presented all at once, and we can perceive them as one configuration of visual elements. Opposites, such as black and white, line and area, clarity and obscurity, are visually perceivable at the same instant of time. This is impossible with language. (Collection of the artist.)*

Plate 5. PETER PAUL RUBENS. Battle of the Amazons. c. 1618. Oil on wood, 47⅝×65″. Before we have had the time necessary to recognize and examine individual images of human figures, horses, the bridge, and the landscape, we are made aware of a swirling mass of rounded, warmly colored shapes all within a horizontal rectangle. The controlling shape of this mass is spiral. (Bayer. Staatsgemäldesammlungen, Munich.)

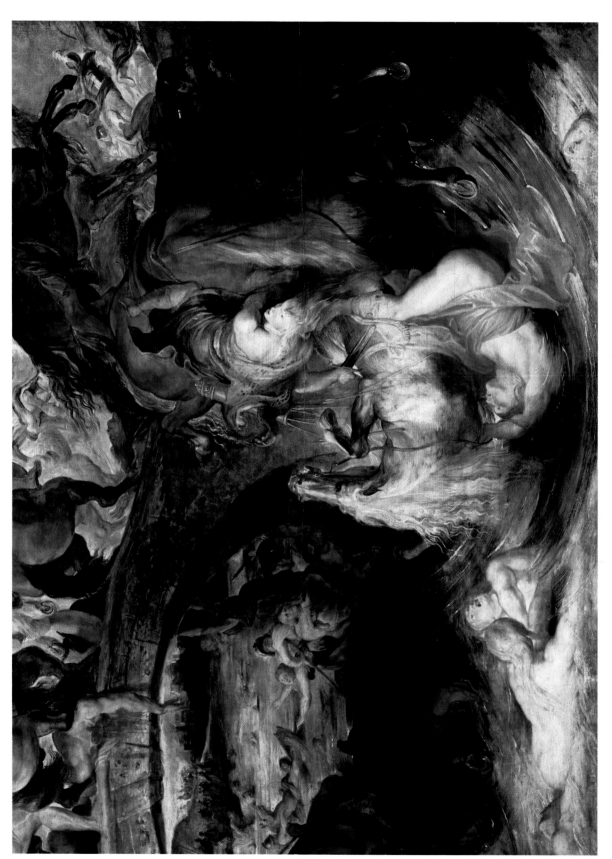

Plate 6. PETER PAUL RUBENS. Battle of the Amazons, detail. Once we have been impressed by the particular character of the total configuration of the painting, that impression remains with us. Our sub- sequent perception of individual parts is oriented according to the lasting impression made in us by the impact of the total configuration. (Bayer. Staatsgemäldesammlungen, Munich.)

Plate 7. PIETRO PERUGINO. The Delivery of the Keys. 1482. Fresco, c. 11' 5" ×18'2". Before we recognize the images of Christ and Peter, before we become engaged with the forms of architectural structures or the meanings of gestures, we are impressed with the overall regularity of this painting. It is the clear bisymmetrical plan of the work that immediately comes through to us and that significantly affects our subsequent seeing of the painting. (Sistine Chapel, The Vatican, Rome. Photo: Scala, New York and Florence)

Plate 8. AUGUSTE RENOIR. The Luncheon of the Boating Party. 1881. Oil on canvas, 51×68″. Much of the sheer visual joy we feel in looking at an Impressionist painting such as this is generated by the rich interplay of color values and color intensities. Along with all the other components of the painting, they work to describe and heighten the images of this place, these people, and this special moment in the year 1881. (The Phillips Collection, Washington, D.C.)

starts at the very same point at which the artist declared to himself that the work was complete—when he stepped back from it, viewed it as a whole, and found it satisfactory. In order to pick up where the artist left off, we must approach any new or unfamiliar work in an attitude of open receptiveness. One would like to be able to say that we should approach such works with an "innocent eye." However, it is too late for that; we know that we lost that so-called "innocent eye" long ago, and that there remains for us only a trace of its function in moments of sudden and great surprise, shock, and high ecstasy. What we mean is simply that we should allow the work a full opportunity to present itself as it is; we should approach it with a minimum of prepossessions, a minimum of any kind of *specific* expectations.

Once having perceived the total configuration of a work, we are affected by that particular overall organization. It does something to us. And in the event that our interest continues beyond this first split-second encounter and we begin to look closely and in detail, the effect of the total configuration still remains with us. In fact, it is the impact of the total configuration and its remembered character which conditions our subsequent perception of the individual parts of the work—no matter how many minutes or hours we may continue looking. It is the total configuration which sets the stage, so to speak, and suggests or engenders the range of expectations suitable to the work. Then, within this range of expectations, the work of art goes on, with time, to fulfill them. This is why we say that the total configuration is a key to the relevance of its individual parts. And unless the work of art is what we might call a sortie in visual irony, or an out-and-out visual joke, it appreciably fulfills the promises first held out to us by the total configuration.

Now, when we first look at Rubens' *Battle of the Amazons* (Color Plate 5), what do we see? Before we have had the time necessary to recognize and examine individual images of human figures, horses, the bridge, and

PETER PAUL RUBENS. Battle of the Amazons. *Bayer. Staatsgemäldesammlungen, Munich.* See Plate 5.

the landscape, we see a swirling mass of rounded, warmly colored shapes all within a horizontal rectangle. The controlling shape of this mass is spiral. It appears to have been compressed to fit within the confines of the rectangular format, much as if a steel clock spring had been forced into a box, the dimensions of which could not easily accommodate the spring in a relaxed state. And more than this, the inner end of the spring, located near the center of the painting, appears to have been pushed deeper into the box. This is one of the principal devices employed by Rubens to create an illusion of space or depth. It lends to the total configuration the characteristics of a vortex or a corkscrew—and it is to this that we first respond.

No matter if we are not entirely conscious of the affect on us of this mass of warmly colored shapes which are both described and defined by the spiral configuration, it still functions in us as a unifying force in our perception of the painting. Once the character of this total configuration has impressed itself on us, it remains with us. Our subsequent perception of individual parts is oriented according to the lasting impression made by the total configuration. Images of separate encounters of horses and riders (Color Plate 6), the giving and taking of blows, the drama of life and death in open battle have been conceived by Rubens as parts of a dynamic overriding design which, in this case, he gives us in the form of a distorted spiral.

PETER PAUL RUBENS. Battle of the Amazons, detail. Bayer. Staatsgemäldesammlungen, Munich. See Plate 6.

How different is our first instantaneous response to Perugino's *The Delivery of the Keys* (Color Plate 7). Before we recognize the images of Christ and Peter, before we become engaged with the forms of architectural structures or the meanings of gestures, we are impressed with an overall regularity. The clear bisymmetrical plan of the painting, whether or not we are immediately aware of it intellectually, comes through to us and affects all of our subsequent seeing.

The organization of the images into three horizontal bands—the lower band of large figures, the central band of much smaller figures, and the upper band formed by the architectural structures and the connecting land-scape—imparts a quality of direct confrontation. We are not drawn into a whirling, expanding spiral, as we are with the Rubens. Rather, we are presented with this mathematically ordered total configuration as if through an open window, and it lies out there, stable and wholly sufficient unto itself. We feel that we ourselves are centered in relation to this configuration and that we are experiencing the ideal unchanging view of it. Our succeeding perceptions of the constituent parts of the painting are conditioned by its generally cool color and clear contours, its rectangular, gridlike structure, and its bisymmetrical organization of masses centering not in either Christ or Peter, but in a point on the doorway of the middle building.

Works of art are more than mere collections of parts, just as we ourselves are more than mere collections of arms and legs and eyes and hands. Each single one of us is a unique configuration of interrelated and interdependent functions as well as parts. Our special patterns of bodily attitudes, our gait, our voice, all our special dispositions go to make up what we still call our personality. It is this larger inclusive quality in each of us that informs the whole and gives relevance and significance to our separate parts and functions. We value the personality of an individual as a phenomenon in itself, as a means to our understanding of that particular human being—and even ourselves. And just as we recognize the crucial importance of personality in people, we also value the total configurations of works of art.

PIETRO PERUGINO. The Delivery of the Keys. *Photo: Alinari-Art Reference Bureau. See Plate 7.*

CHAPTER FOUR

Three Kinds
of
Seeing

In talking about the phenomenon of total configuration we have been concerned with seeing—visual perception. So far, we have touched on only the very first phase—the split second—of the visual perception of works of art. More must be said about the act of seeing, and in order to get at this it may be helpful to speak, somewhat artificially to be sure, of three kinds of seeing.

Everyone who can read these lines is richly experienced in seeing the objects around us and the environments in which they find a place. Not all of us by any means, however, look in the same way at the world, nor do we all see exactly alike. The simple fact that no two people can stand in exactly the same spot at exactly the same time precludes the possibility of anyone seeing exactly what another one sees. The rich variety among individual testimonies concerning just what happened when two cars collided at an intersection is simple proof of this. And these differences between what one individual can swear under oath he saw, and what another, also under oath, can swear he saw, may be simple evidence of the multiple and changing faces of visual reality. Moreover, this does not mean that we do not have a great deal in common in the matter of how and what we see. The world may be less of a twilight jungle than some would have it seem; and people see more like each other than not. Yet, for all this, we still can speak of different kinds of seeing. Perhaps what we mean to talk about is not so much the differences in the very act of seeing, but the almost immediately concurrent series of closely related events. For convenience of reference let us call the three kinds of seeing by the names "operational," "associational," and "pure."

Now, let us imagine that we place the object pictured in Fig. 4–1 directly in the line of traffic of people entering a classroom. No one will be able to avoid seeing it. We have purposely chosen this object for its commanding size—it stands five feet above the floor on its pedestal—and for its attractive nonutilitarian character. It is, in fact, a sphere measuring 18 inches in diameter. Its surface is of a bright blue velvet.

The first person to come into the path of this object is one whose seeing is characterized by an emphasis on the practical or instrumental functions of vision. He is on his way to the classroom. He knows that class will convene there in about four minutes. He is prepared for today's lecture. He has done the preparatory reading. He has his notebook under his arm and a brand-new ballpoint pen ready to swing into action. He knows that he belongs in seat number 230, and he means to get there. As he approaches the velvet sphere and pedestal, he veers easily to one side, skirts the unidentified, almost unnoticed, obstacle and proceeds to seat number 230.

Fig. 4–1. Velvet Sphere. *Diameter 18".*

In a way, this person was, for a moment, visually aware of the object, but only to the extent that allowed for his avoiding it. His vision proved instrumental in getting him past the object and on to the completion of his mission. If, after he had gained his seat, we had asked him about the sphere and pedestal, he more than likely would have had almost nothing to offer in the way of its description. Nor would he have had any remembered feelings or ideas concerning it, except that, whatever it was, it had been in his way and he had walked around it.

This is, of course, a very uncomplicated example of what we are calling "operational" seeing. All of us see and act in this practical way during much of our day and throughout our lives. This is how we get safely across streets, up stairs, and through doorways. This may be the way we manage most of the acts we perform, from seating ourselves in chairs to driving cars and eating breakfast. There is nothing "wrong" about this kind of seeing, but it is a fact that it leaves much of the world and its objects unexplored, barely experienced, almost unknown. How long has it been, for instance, since you really looked at the doorknob on your own front door, or the inside of your own right hand?

Now let us have the next person approach the object. He, too, is on his way to class and he, too, means to get there on time. As he comes upon the object he slows down a little, sees that it is a *ball* of some kind, and walks on. But as soon as he has named the object with the word *ball,* then that *word,* not the object, proves a trigger for a chain reaction of associations. "Ball," he says to himself; and he thinks of the basketball season about to open in a week, and back to his last game in high school when he missed the free-throw that might have won the game; and he is reminded of the girl who comforted him afterwards, and her father—she called him Tom— who, as a boy of 17, had gone up the Amazon to help a herpetologist catch snakes, and how he could never quite understand how anyone would want to be around snakes that much, especially when he remembered little Dave almost dying of snakebite over in San Antonio and how great the doctor was reciting comical lines from Leacock and Aristophanes . . . and so, on and on—a reverie, a chain reaction of associations.

Again we can say that all of us experience this pattern of visually triggered associations. It is a common experience. There is nothing "wrong" about it. In fact, the literarily inclined person, the writer, finds this kind of almost free association especially rewarding. But the fact is obvious that the velvet sphere was never experienced, *for itself,* by this person. Its role was that of a trigger for something else. The velvet sphere *as an object* was deserted as soon as it was named *ball.* Whatever of interest it might have held for this person was never given a chance. It was abandoned on sight.

So, our third person comes along on his way to class. Instead of avoiding the sphere and pedestal as the "operational" type did because it lay in the way of his immediate goal, and instead of employing the name of the object to trigger a chain reaction of associations to the neglect of the object itself, as in the case of the "associational" type, this person stops and looks at it. For lack of a better designation of what he does, we are calling it "pure" seeing.

He observes the shapes of both the sphere and the pedestal, and the way in which the sphere rests. He sees how the curved surface turns back the light, how the color varies from the top to the under side of the sphere, and how the texture of the velvet contrasts with that of the pedestal. He moves around the sphere, looks at it from high and low points of view, and he sees how its appearance changes with his own movement. He experiences the perfection of the spherical shape, how it always turns back into itself, never leading to anything beyond itself except at the point of tangency with the top surface of the pedestal. He is inclined to touch the sphere—to test, as it were, his visual response against the tactile, or touch, response. He is not primarily interested in determining *what* this object is or for what it might be used. He is interested in *how* it is. He is not primarily concerned with the cost of this object, nor is he, in this early stage of seeing, concerned with where it came from or why it happens to be standing in his path. First and foremost, the person who exercises his vision in this "pure" way is taken up with the specific qualities of the particular objects before him. He may even become interested in the temperature of the velvet surface as compared to the temperature of the harder, more closely textured surface of the pedestal. He may wonder how heavy this never-before-seen velvet sphere is, and he may lift it, or try to.

To this person, this object is worthy of his sight, worthy of becoming known to him—for whatever reasons or non-reasons. He discovers the object, as it were, in looking at it. Instead of projecting his biases or preferences into the object, he makes himself available to the specific set of conditions which make up the particular object. In a broad sense he is learning from the object; he is not committing the folly of trying to teach the object what he thinks he already knows. His expectations follow along with his deepening discovery of the quality of the object and they are largely determined by that quality. And so, if he is looking at a velvet sphere, he does not expect the conflict of hard right angles; nor does the absence of a glossy surface disappoint him or make him melancholy.

For the visual artist, the world—whether it be the two rooms of Jan Vermeer or the infinite space of Giovanni Battista Tiepolo—is a boundless place filled with objects, no two of which share identical conditions. And though he indulges in all manner of seeing, it is something like the "pure" type which prevails for the painter, the sculptor, and the graphic artist. For the person at all interested in experiencing works of art *as* works of art, it is this kind of "pure" seeing that must be exercised and strengthened.

CHAPTER FIVE

The
Visual Elements

With all our talk about seeing we still have not asked a fundamental question: what, in the simplest terms, do we see? When we open our eyes to the summer morning and know that sleep is over once more and that we are seeing again—what is it that we see then?

Is it the old brass light fixture hanging from the ceiling by the eleven-link chain we counted years ago? Is it the window with the blinds carefully parted the night before? Is it the table? The clock? The chair?

In the first instant it is none of these—it is simply and wholly *light.* It is light, in waves or corpuscles or charges, that delivers the world to our eyes. But to see light it must be obstructed; it must trace itself on and among the stuff of this world—over the bed, the table, the chair. For we know that up beyond the earth's atmosphere, beyond friction and obstruction, the sky is always black-blue. But put a moon or even your bedroom chair out into that space and it will shine out day and night in the light of the sun.

So first it is just light we see, but light as it is caught by the substantial stuff around us. Ordinarily we say that we see things, objects. We say we see the book before us, our hands and the table. But do we? When we look toward the kind of thing that is known by the name *table,* do we see immediately that it is, in fact, a table? Or do we know that this is a table only after something else has taken place? The fact of the matter is that first we look, and having seen light in some configuration we go on to *interpret* that configuration. In this case we interpret, or recognize (*re*-cognize), it as some kind of table.

Now if we do not see books and chairs and tables, but light in some configuration, what is it that we do perceive in such configurations? Before we recognize, before we *know* that the configuration we are looking at is a

nameable thing, we become aware of its visual qualities. We respond to the
visual elements which go to make up that specific pattern; and we respond
to their particular qualities and interrelationships. This direct acquaintance
with anything through the eyes is properly referred to as an experience of
visual perception. Whatever follows this, whether it be calling out the
accepted name of the object perceived, or generalizing successive perceptions into an idea or *concept* of the object, is properly known as an experience of *conception*. Our aim at this point is to keep the experience of
visual perception foremost in our considerations. Simply, we visually perceive only what is seeable. And although there is some difference of opinion
as to just what can be seen, it may be possible to describe visual phenomena
in terms of seven visual elements: *position, size, color* (or *hue), shape, line,
texture,* and *density*. We can consider them in that order.

POSITION

When we look into any field of vision, we perceive that different things are
located in different places in reference to where we happen to be. Things
are located far from us, or near; they are in positions to our right or left;
they are high or low, or in line with our eyes; and some are in motion, changing position. We perceive and are affected by the positions of things in
relation to ourselves and in relation to each other. We respond differently
to things close to us and to things at some distance from us. We respond
differently to things in motion, whether objects are moving from position
to position or whether light is moving over stationary objects. Things centered in our field of vision affect us differently than those located at the
periphery. We are sensitive to the relative positions in actual, three-dimensional space of the constituent parts of sculpture and architecture; and we
are sensitive to the relative positions of elements on flat surfaces as we find
them in painting, drawing, and prints. Our point here, however, is merely
that the phenomenon of position is visually perceivable and that we are
calling it one of the visual elements.

SIZE

Things and intervals between things can be large or small or equal in size,
and our eyes are sensitive to these magnitudes and their relationships. We
measure and compare with our eyes. In a given field of vision we become
engaged with the size relationships of things—one to another and all to our
own physical, bodily size. Just as with the element of position, the factor of
our own physical presence as a body of some size functions as one of the
terms affecting our visual awareness of sizes of things outside ourselves. In
the simplest terms, then, we visually perceive the element of size—bigness
and smallness and a great range of intervals between.

COLOR

Of all the visual elements, color may be the most pervasively significant and the one most difficult to deal with in words. Many elaborate "color systems" have been devised and published, such as the Munsell[1] and Ostwald[2] systems, each of which is useful in its own way. But color as a functioning visual element in works of art must be experienced in the specific contexts of such works. In a real sense it is nearly meaningless to talk of blue or red or violet as if these qualities of light could be isolated and entertained. And even though the various color systems are true or consistent within themselves, they still have the same limitation that symbolic logic has in philosophy—it will not help the lost wayfarer find his way back to an actual home. Still, there are many things we can say about color which will help appreciation of it as one of the visual elements.

Color, we say nowadays, is a property of light. Differences of color are determined by different wavelengths. Red is characterized as being of long wavelength. It is said to travel more rapidly, for example, than blue, which is of short wavelength. The range of the *solar,* or light, spectrum includes violet, indigo, blue, green, yellow, orange, and red. The primary colors in this spectrum of light are red, green, and blue (or blue-violet or violet). The combining of these *light* primaries is described as "additive" which is to say that the sensations produced by different wavelengths of light are added together. However, in only a few areas of the visual arts do we work exclusively with light in this way. Rather, we work with *pigments*—colored paints instead of light. And when pigments are mixed, the resulting visual sensations differ from those of the "spectral," or light, colors. Even the primary colors of pigment—red, yellow, and blue—are different from those of light —red, green, and blue. Producing different colors by mixing differently colored pigments is called a "subtractive" process since the absorption of some wavelengths of light occurs.

In the visual arts we are principally concerned with what we call the *local color* of objects. Local color is the name given to the apparent color of surfaces—the color of the light that is reflected from the surfaces of paintings, prints, sculpture, and the whole range of objects. When spectral light strikes an obstruction, certain wavelengths are absorbed, others reflected. We see only those which are reflected and are registered on the retina of our eyes. A red surface reflects only the long wavelengths which give us the sensation of color we call red; a blue surface reflects only the short wavelengths, and we see blue. In each case all the other wavelengths are lost to our vision. If all wavelengths are absorbed, the surface appears black; if all

[1] Albert H. Munsell, *Atlas of the Munsell Color System* (Malden, Mass.: Wadsworth, Howland & Co., 1915).

[2] Wilhelm Ostwald, *Colour Science* (Secaucus, N. J.: Winsor & Newton, Inc., 1931). Cf. Egbert Jacobson, *Basic Color, an Interpretation of the Ostwald Color System* (Chicago: P. Theobald, 1948).

wavelengths are reflected, the surface appears white. Strictly speaking, black is considered the absence of all color, and white the presence of all color. However, in speaking of color in the context of works of art, we generally refer to both black and white as colors, since they function as such.

We speak of color as having two attributes known as *value* and *intensity* (sometimes called *saturation*). When we look at any area of color, we are made aware of its yellowness or greenness or redness—its color, or as some say, its *hue* or *chroma*. Now, besides being yellow or green or red, every color is either a lighter or darker *value* of that color. Some blues are lighter than other blues; some yellows are darker than other yellows. When we refer to the *value* of a color we are referring to its relative lightness or darkness on an ideal scale which ranges between white and black. Such an ideal scale is reproduced here as Fig. 5–1. Every color is of a *value* which matches some interval on this scale of lightness and darkness. To illustrate this we have placed some sample blocks of red, yellow, and blue next to their equivalent grays on a value scale (Color Plate 9). Colors equivalent to the central section of this scale, such as the middle block of red in our diagram, are known as *middle value* colors. Colors above this are known as *high value* colors, while those below are known as *low value* colors. Another way of designating high and low value colors is by the terms *tint* and *shade*, respectively.

Besides differing in value, colors differ in *intensity*. The term *intensity* refers to the *brilliance* of color. When a color is pure and at its highest saturation of pigment, we refer to it as being at maximum intensity. It is then as bright as that color can be; it cannot be further heightened, but it can be made duller by mixing it with colors of less intensity or with white or black.

The intensity of a color is often confused with its value; lightness and darkness are often confused with brightness and dullness. It must be understood that the value and intensity characteristics of color can operate independently of each other. For instance, it is possible to have a color which is *dark in value* but *bright in intensity;* and it is just as possible to have a color which is *dark in value* and *dull in intensity*. By the same token, a color can be *light in value* and *dull in intensity,* or *light in value* and *bright in intensity.* Many of the subtleties of color to which we respond are due to the artist's creation and manipulation of color values and color intensities. Much of the sheer visual joy we feel in looking at a painting such as Renoir's *Luncheon of the Boating Party* (Color Plate 8) is generated by the rich interplay of color values and intensities working to describe and heighten this place, these people, and this special moment in the year 1881. We can see that Renoir has employed different colors of similar values, as well as similar colors of different values and intensities. He has intermingled dark, bright colors with dull, dark ones, and light, dull colors with light, bright ones.

In order to point up some of the operative characteristics of color value and color intensity, let us look at some isolated comparisons. In the first

Fig. 5–1.

AUGUSTE RENOIR. The Luncheon of the Boating Party. *The Phillips Collection, Washington, D.C. See Plate 8.*

pair of color blocks in Color Plate 9 the color is the same—red. However, block *a* is lighter in value than block *b;* and block *b* is more intense than block *a*. The degree of pigment saturation is greater in *b,* and as a result we see *b* as brighter than *a*—even though *a* is lighter.

In the second pair of color blocks in the same Color Plate, the color is the same—in this case, blue. But block *c* is lighter in value than *d,* while at the same time *c* is more intense, or brighter, than *d*.

The fact that with color we always have these three variables—the color or pigmentation itself, the value, and the intensity—and that these variables function in any combination of degree, make of color the richest of the seven visual elements. And this richness is further enhanced by the fact that color has certain physical connotations, the simplest of which is *temperature.* Some colors connote warmth to us, others coolness or cold. Colors which are predominantly yellow or red "feel" warm to us, while predominantly blue colors such as blue-green or blue-violet "feel" cool to us. These are what we call "warm" and "cool" colors, and besides connoting degrees of temperature they suggest distance or intervals in space. For most of us the warm colors appear to advance; the cool colors appear to recede. And, as we shall see later, these suggestive powers of color serve the artist in constructing illusions of depth, or space, on a flat surface.

SHAPE

When we speak of *shape* as one of the visual elements, we refer to the external form or contour of any material object or geometrical figure. In this respect, the term is used similarly in the context of art and in the context of human experience in general.

We visually perceive the limitless variety of shape in both two and three dimensions. By a two-dimensional shape we mean a shape which exists in a single plane, just as the shapes pictured in Fig. 5–2 exist in the single plane of this page.

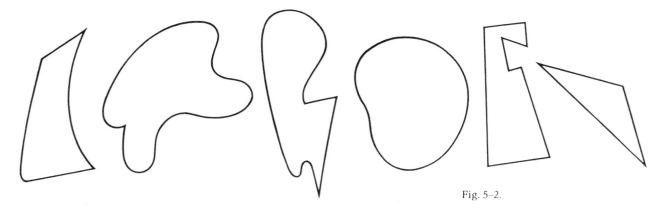

Fig. 5–2.

By a three-dimensional shape we mean one which occupies more than one plane; a shape which has depth as well as length and width (Fig. 5–3). In sculpture and architecture we are engaged by three-dimensional, or solid, shapes; in painting and the graphic arts we are largely concerned with two-dimensional, or flat, shapes.

Fig. 5–3. *Stone relief, nave of St. Patrick's Cathedral, Rock of Cashel, County Tipperary, Ireland. 13th century. c. 14×30".*

27

In the visual arts our concern is always with the total configuration of the work. This means that we are as much aware of what lies *around* a given shape as we are of the *surrounded* shape. Or, to put it in the language of the psychologist, we are about equally affected by the *figure* and by the *ground* on which it lies. The shape of this ground or field is referred to as the *negative* shape. The figure which lies in or upon this field is said to occupy the *positive* shape.

In the red-figured Greek ceramic *Lapith Killing a Centaur* (Fig. 5–4), the generally light area occupied by the images of the lapith and the centaur is referred to as the *positive* shape. The contours of this complex but continuous shape create several dark shapes which lie between the man and animal shapes and the outer boundary of the circular format. These darker shapes are referred to as *negative* shapes. It appears that the unknown creator of this Greek cylix was sensitive to the visual relationships of positive and negative shapes, and part of our enjoyment of this piece is due to just that.

Fig. 5–4. Lapith Killing a Centaur *(Attic red-figured cylix). c. 490–480 B.C. Ceramic. Staatliche Antikensammlungen, Munich. Photo: Hirmer, Munich.*

In the case of sculpture and architecture we deal with three-dimensional shapes, or volumes. All those shapes composed of the material substance of the work—the stone, clay, glass, steel—we call *positive* shapes. All those other nonmaterial shapes—the rectangular air spaces or voids called rooms in architecture, the air space around the building or sculpture—we call *negative* shapes. All the space around Henry Moore's *Reclining Figure* (Fig. 5–5) is known as negative space, and the particular shape of this space is called the *negative* shape. Since Henry Moore's design includes openings, or "holes"

Fig. 5–5. *HENRY MOORE. Reclining Figure. 1945. Bronze, length 17¹/₂". Private collection.*

through the stone, these, too, are properly known as *negative* shapes. These negatives are as functionally important to this piece of sculpture as are the positives, and both have been composed with their combined visual effects in mind.

There remains just one other aspect of shape about which we must speak. This is the phenomenon of *implied* shape as distinct from *actual* shape. Up to this point we have been speaking of shapes which are clearly and directly presented, whether in two or three dimensions and whether of a positive or a negative sort. These are *actual* shapes. They exist by virtue of continuous and closed contours as we saw in the shapes given in Fig. 5–2.

Now, an implied shape is one which is not clearly or directly presented. Rather, it is involved as a consequence of what is shown without being expressly presented. A simple example of this is given in Fig. 5–6. *Actually,* all we have presented here is a number of dots. Except for the individual

Fig. 5–6.

shapes of the dots themselves, no other *actual* shape or shapes exist. However, a circular shape is involved here by virtue of the relative positions of these dots. The circular shape which is *not* positively asserted is logically comprised by what *is* presented. We call this circular shape an *implied* shape.

In the context of works of art, the role of implied shapes is often subtle and complicated. In the work of a man like Piero della Francesca, however, the visual strategy afforded by the employment of implied shapes is often quite clear. In his fresco (watercolors painted into wet plaster) *The Resurrection* (Color Plate 10) we are impressed by a quality of carefully organized stability. Even though the images of the soldiers are presented in a variety

PIERO DELLA FRANCESCA. The Resurrection. *Photo: Alinari-Art Reference Bureau. See Plate 10.*

of positions we sense the presence of a single horizontal line which ties them together at the very bottom of the painting. Then from the bent back of the figure at the furthest left we sense a line or a direction that leads to the elbow of Christ, up his upper arm, to the top of his head. And from the head of Christ we sense a line leading down the upper part of his left arm and along the heads of the two soldiers in the right half of the painting. These three *implied* lines suggest the sides of an equiangular triangle which encloses all the figures. It is this *implied* triangular shape that establishes and supports the quality of stark confrontation and stability of the whole configuration. And this large triangle is powerfully echoed in another implied shape—the equiangular triangle which includes the image of Christ down to the edge of the tomb upon which his foot rests.

The phenomenon of implied shape occurs in sculpture as well as in painting. One obvious example may serve to illustrate this.

(a)　(b)

(c)　(d)

Plate 9.

Plate 10. *PIERO DELLA FRANCESCA.* The Resurrection. *c. 1460. Fresco, 7′ 8″ × 6′ 6″. In the work of Piero della Francesca the visual strategy afforded by implied shapes is clearly evident. Here he employs an implied triangular shape to enclose all the figures and to establish and support the quality of stark confrontation and the stability of the whole configuration. (Pinacoteca Comunale, Borgo San Sepolcro. Photo: Art Reference Bureau.)*

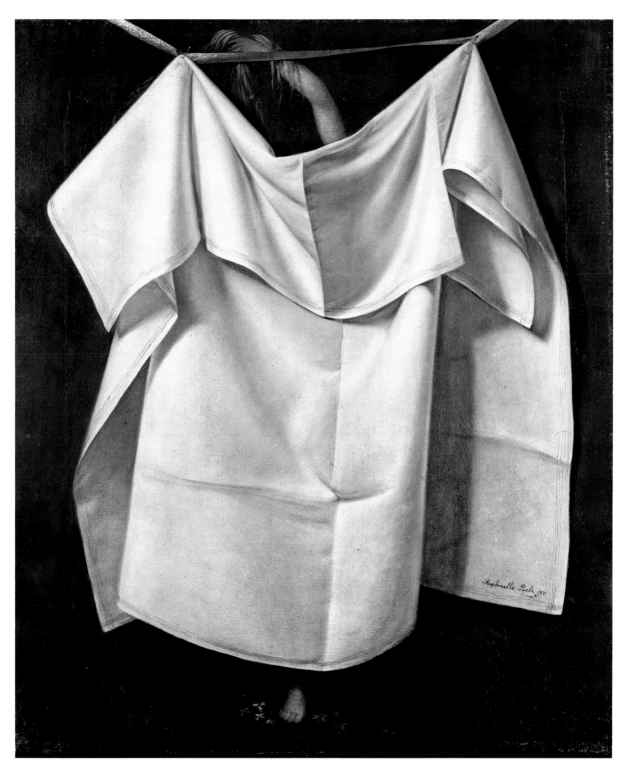

Plate 11.   *RAPHAELLE PEALE*. After the Bath. *1823. Oil on canvas, 29×24″. Unless we check what we see against how it feels to the touch, we can never be absolutely certain of the actual textural quality of any surface. It is this deceptive character of vision that makes possible our seeing Peale's hard enamel-like painted surface as the yielding surface of a bed sheet hanging from a line. (William Rockhill Nelson Gallery of Art, Kansas City. Nelson Fund.)*

Plate 12. DUCCIO. Maesta, or Madonna in Majesty. 1308–1311. Tempera on wood, height 6' 10½". We are visually sensitive to varying degrees of density in works of art—density that is measured by the degree of occupancy of the format. This painting would be charac-terized as being rather dense because there is so little space showing between the figures. We do not have a feeling of looking through or beyond the surface of the painting. (Opera del Duomo, Siena. Photo: Scala, New York and Florence.)

Fig. 5-7. Dionysus, *from the east pediment of the Parthenon. 438–432 B.C. Marble, over life-size. British Museum, London.*

With all the subtleties of bodily attitude and carving evident in the Greek figure *Dionysus* (Fig. 5-7), we are still made conscious of a large controlling shape to which all parts of this figure owe their structural logic. That shape is an *implied* triangle, the apex of which falls in the head of the figure. In this particular case, we know that the sculpture was, in fact, designed to fit rather snugly into an architectural framework—the triangular shape of the east pediment of the Parthenon in Athens.

LINE

Even though it long ago became axiomatic that no lines, as such, exist in nature, line is considered one of the most telling of the visual elements.

We usually think of line as a threadlike mark produced with a pen, a pencil, a fine brush, or any one of a variety of engraving and marking tools. We speak of the lines in a painting such as those used to designate the papyrus stems in the left of the *Fowling Scene* from an Egyptian tomb (Fig. 5-8). And we speak of the lines cut into the marble surface of the sculptured *Hera of Samos* from Archaic Greece (Fig. 5-9). Ordinarily we think of these as *actual* lines. But just as we speak of *actual* and *implied* shapes, we also speak of *actual* and *implied* lines.

Fig. 5-8. Fowling Scene *(fragment of a wall painting), from the tomb of Amenemheb, Thebes. c. 1450 B.C. Distemper. British Museum, London.*

Fig. 5-9. Hera, *from Samos. c. 570–560 B.C. Marble, 76". The Louvre, Paris.*

31

Fig. 5–10. *PIETER BRUEGHEL THE ELDER.* The Blind Leading the Blind. *1568. Oil on canvas, 34×66". National Museum, Naples. Photo: Alinari-Art Reference Bureau.*

Thinking back to our Fig. 5–6 in which the series of dots *implies* a circular *shape,* we could say that that same configuration of dots *implies* a line which turns back on itself, thus suggesting the shape of a circle. Whenever elements or images are found close to each other in rows or in paths, a *direction* is established and this is often spoken of as a line. We speak of a *line* of people and *lines* of objects on the supermarket shelves. These are, precisely speaking, *implied* lines. We are impressed by such an implied line created by the row of heads and shoulders of the men in Pieter Brueghel's *The Blind Leading the Blind* (Fig. 5–10). This downward curving direction is a crucial characteristic of the painting; by its very quality this *implied* line analogizes the consecutive experiences of walking, stumbling. and falling down.

The Brueghel painting can serve us further in pointing out another way in which the visual element of line can be implied: by the abutment of one color area against another. In the lower right corner of this painting we see three shapes which are very light in value. These shapes are descriptive of the stockinged legs of two of the figures. If we look closely at these shapes, we will see that they are not outlined; there are no boundary lines around those light areas. They are clear to us because the light areas are surrounded by other areas which are much darker in value. But even though *actual* lines do not bound these shapes, we *feel* that they do. This is what we continually experience in looking at objects in the world around us. The white pages of a book seen against a dark table top, for instance, are defined by

32

their edges or contours; these edges imply lines much as lines are implied in the Brueghel painting.

Line as a visual element, then, is more than just a continuous thread-like mark made on a surface by some pointed tool. It is also the visual phenomenon produced by the proximity of elements or images which by their closeness and sequence establish a direction that in turn *implies* line. And line is also implied by the edges of shapes and by the boundaries of areas of color. With this broad concept of line as one of the visual elements, we may better appreciate its wide and complex function in all the visual arts.

TEXTURE

Were we to speak of texture in the inclusive sense, we would have to concern ourselves with the very structure of all physical bodies. We would have to take into account the manner of disposition of the particles throughout a given substance, as well as the specific character of those particles. In the visual arts, however, we deal with the *appearances* of things; we are concerned with how light is caught and given back from the *surfaces* of things; and so it is the perceived *textures of surfaces* which engage us in the visual arts.

Most simply, texture refers to degrees of smoothness and roughness. We say that the polished marble tabletop is smoother than the plaster wall, and the inside of our hand rougher than the outside. The textural quality of anything comes through to us visually and tactilely—by means of sight and touch (it may even be true that all our visual perception of texture is pre-conditioned by our past tactile experiences). But no matter how this is, we still do *look* at surfaces and respond to different degrees of smoothness and roughness. And not only do we visually perceive such differences, we also perceive qualities of softness and hardness—the yielding quality of flesh and fabric, the resistant quality of steel and stone. The visual perception of qualities of hardness and softness is based in our prior tactile experiences of those qualities in objects.

It should be clear at this point in our discussion that we are considering the visual element of texture both in its *actual* and *implied* manifestations. And if we hold rigidly to the concept of texture as a visual element, then we must say quite clearly that its more important role is as an *implied* phenomenon. Unless we check what we *see* against how it *feels* to the touch—either at that moment, or how it felt to us in some past experience—we can never be certain of the actual textural quality of any surface. In fact, it is this very deceptive quality of surface as it comes to our eyes that makes possible so much of the illusory in art. It makes possible such a *tour de force* as Raphaelle Peale's *After the Bath* (Color Plate 11) in which a large part of the hard, enamel-like surface of the painting is made to *look like* the yielding surface of a bed sheet hanging from a line. From a short distance our eyes can fool us into thinking that this is actually a draped fabric surface. The

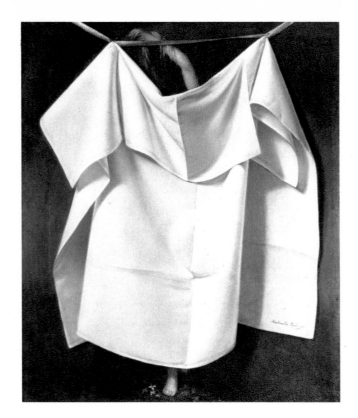

RAPHAELLE PEALE. After the Bath. *Collection of William Rockhill Nelson Gallery of Art, Kansas City, Missouri (Nelson Fund). See Plate 11.*

Fig. 5–11.
GIANLORENZO BERNINI. The Ecstasy of St. Theresa. *1645–1652. Marble, life-size. Cornaro Chapel, S. Maria della Vittoria, Rome. Photo: Alinari-Art Reference Bureau.*

particular *visual* quality of this "bed sheet" is illusory; its texture is an *implied* texture.

The same holds true for Bernini's *The Ecstasy of St. Theresa* (Fig. 5–11). This is, in actuality, a large sculpture in white marble. It is cold and unyielding to the touch. Yet, by Bernini's artistry this stone is caused to *look like* the rippling surface of cloth and the smooth warm texture of flesh. So, whatever we say about texture as one of the visual elements, we must give special emphasis to the fact that the textural qualities of surfaces are implied rather than directly presented to our eyes. By the same token, however, we must know that the artist works with these *implications* as basic facts of his craft.

In looking at the world around us we are made conscious of objects and of intervals between them—the trees, shrubs, rocks, roads, and houses in a landscape; the dishes on a table, the books on a shelf in a room. Some landscapes and bookshelves are densely occupied, others sparsely, and we are visually aware of this—and we are affected by it. We can see and distinguish degrees of denseness, so we speak of dense fog, dense crowds, and sparsely populated neighborhoods.

Likewise, we are visually sensitive to varying degrees of density in works of art—density as measured by the degree of occupancy of the format by the visual elements. We say that the front of Duccio's *Maestà* (Color Plate 12) is a denser work than Turner's *The Fighting Téméraire* (Color Plate 13). There is a greater feeling of openness in the Turner; we sense the *intervals* between positive shapes more strongly than we do in the Duccio.

DUCCIO. Maestà, *or* Madonna in Majesty. *Photo: Alinari. See Plate 12.*

J. M. W. TURNER. The Fighting "Téméraire." *National Gallery, London. See Plate 13.*

There is little *ground* in the Duccio; it is composed mostly of the *figures* which block out the ground. In the visual arts this simple connotation of the term density, which alludes to the degree of "emptiness" or "fullness" of a configuration, is extended in the direction of the meaning given the term by photographers. They speak of degrees of *opacity, translucency,* and *transparency* of photographic negatives. Certain areas of the developed actinized film offer no more obstruction to light and vision than does a clear glass window. These are the transparent areas. Those which allow generous amounts of light, but not vision, to pass through are known as translucent areas, while those which obstruct most light and all vision are known as opaque areas. Of all these, the opaque areas are, of course, the densest. Now, while in photography this use of the term density is descriptive of an actual set of conditions, its use in connection with painting and the graphics is metaphorical. Strictly speaking, light does not pass *through* paintings in varying degrees, or perhaps at all. Still, we are visually sensitive to certain phenomena in painting and the graphics which do have something of this quality of screening light. And thinking of density in this way—as well as in the fullness-emptiness way—we can say that *The Fighting Téméraire* is less dense (or more transparent) than the Duccio.

It is in three-dimensional configurations that we come very close to experiences of density in the photographer's meaning of that term—actual visual perceptions of opacity, translucency, and transparency. For example, when we look through the dense network of very thin branches at the top of

Fig. 5–12. Gautama Buddha in Contemplation. *c. 1st–3rd century A.D. Black schist, height 28³/₄". Yale University Art Gallery, New Haven (Anonymous gift through Alfred R. Bellinger).*

a leafless tree, we experience something very close to translucency; closer to translucency, shall we say, than what we experience when we look through the filigree of an iron fence. The side of a wooden house is certainly opaque; but the finely woven cotton curtains at the window screen the light and vision to a degree midway between translucency and transparency.

Our main reason for mentioning this is to bring our eyes and our thoughts to the phenomenon of density as perceivable in sculpture. In Fig. 5–12, *Gautama Buddha in Contemplation,* we have a piece of sculpture of very dense visual quality. Our eyes are stopped at its surface, and stopped quite abruptly. We are not encouraged to try to look through or beyond it. It is opaque. Figure 5–13, the *Laocoön,* affords us the experience of looking through because it is pierced. From this view the sculpture reveals twelve negative shapes or spaces exclusive of the total surrounding negative. This sculpture is less dense than the figure *Gautama Buddha in Contemplation;* its opacity is relieved. The welded sculpture *Twenty-seven Files,* by J. Coleman Akin, (Fig. 5–14) is more open than closed. The total area of the positive

Fig. 5–13. *AGESANDER, ATHENODORUS, and POLYDORUS OF RHODES. The Laocoön Group. Late 2nd century B.C. Marble, height 96". Vatican Museums, Rome. Photo: Hirmer, Munich.*

Fig. 5–14. *J. COLEMAN AKIN. Twenty-seven Files. 1961. Steel, copper, brass, height 24", radius 18". Collection of the artist.*

shapes is less than the total area of the negative shapes, and their combination creates a rough screen for both light and our vision. This sculpture occupies space in a sparse way, not densely. It is similar to our earlier examples of tree branches and the iron filigree fence. It creates visual qualities—by how it modulates both space and light—which are comparable to something between translucency and transparency. It is far from opaque.

There are, of course, actually translucent and transparent materials employed in creating sculpture and architecture as well as painting. It should go without saying that cast or blown glass sculpture, sculpture carved from materials that transmit light, stained glass windows, the glass "curtain walls" of present day architecture, and paintings made with various transparent media manifest less dense visual qualities.

So, it is these seven visual elements—position, size, color, shape, line texture, and density—coupled with effects created by their combinations, that are the constituents of every visually perceivable configuration. And even though we have been speaking of them as if they exist separately, these visual elements necessarily work together and upon each other like charges in an electric field to give us the specific configurations of any moment of our vision. It is the visual artist working with these elements who gives us some of the most rewarding of those moments in which we can celebrate the marvel of vision.

Plate 13. *J. M. W. TURNER. The Fighting "Temeraire." 1839. Oil on canvas, 35³/₄×48". With many of the works of Turner, we experience a quality of open-ness. We sense very strongly the intervals between positive shapes and as a result we have a feeling of looking beyond or through the sparsely occupied surface of the painting. (National Gallery, London.)*

Plate 14.   WASSILY KANDINSKY. The Black Circle. 1924. Watercolor, $14^{1}/_{2} \times 14^{1}/_{4}''$. It is obvious that Kandinsky had no intention of creating anything as specific as a portrait, a landscape, or a still life when he did this painting. It is entirely fair to assume that he was concerned in this painting with the creation and manipulation of visual qualities for purposes of a very generalized sort of expression. (The Museum of Modern Art, New York. Acquired through the Lillie P. Bliss Bequest.)

CHAPTER SIX

The Visual Elements
and
Expression

The inexhaustible variety of our visual world attests not only to the infinite possibilities for combination of the visual elements, but also to the great range of quality within the limits of any one of the visual elements. Something of this range can be suggested by imagining graduated scales for each element. These scales would range between extremes of specific qualities of these elements. For instance, we can imagine a graduated scale of *shape* which would range from the rounded shape to the most angular, as indicated in Fig. 6–1. At each perceptible interval along this scale the quality of the shape can be imagined as becoming less round as we move from *A* to *B*. At the midpoint, *X*, the shape would partake equally of the qualities of both *A* and *B*.

This rich but relatively simple range of shape quality can be extended by thinking in terms of other graduated scales, still concerned with shape.

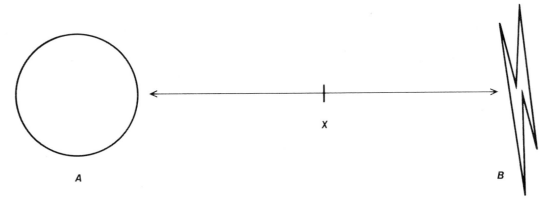

Fig. 6–1.

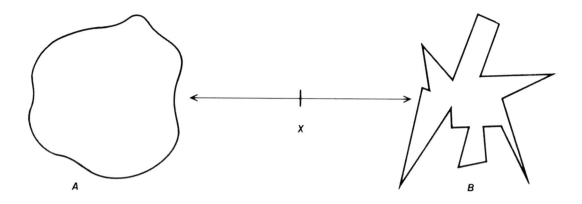

Fig. 6–2.

In Fig. 6–2 and 6–3 we are dealing with a range in shape from roundness to angularity as well as with a range from *simplicity* to *complexity*. In each case these scales are intended to suggest the range of shape from *A* to *B* with the midpoint, *X*, being the interval at which the shape quality would be as much like *A* as *B*.

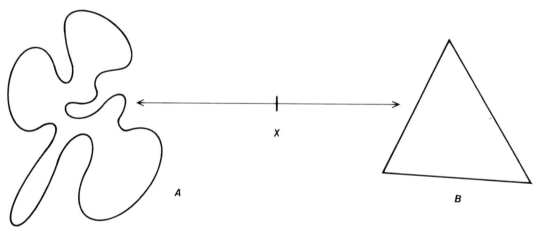

Fig. 6–3.

This same kind of graduated scale can be easily imagined for *position* (highest to lowest, farthest to nearest, etc.), for *size* (largest to smallest), for *line* (most curved and simple to most angular and complex), for *texture* (most smooth and simple to most rough and complex), for *density* (transparent to opaque), and for *color*. With color, because of its three variable attributes—pigmentation, value, and intensity—we have the richest range possible within any scale of the visual elements.

Let us imagine a graduated scale of a color and its attributes of value (lightness and darkness) and intensity (brightness and dullness), as suggested in Fig. 6–4. Even when we limit ourselves to only two colors, red and yellow, the range on such a scale approaches infinity. Along the triple set of hori-

40

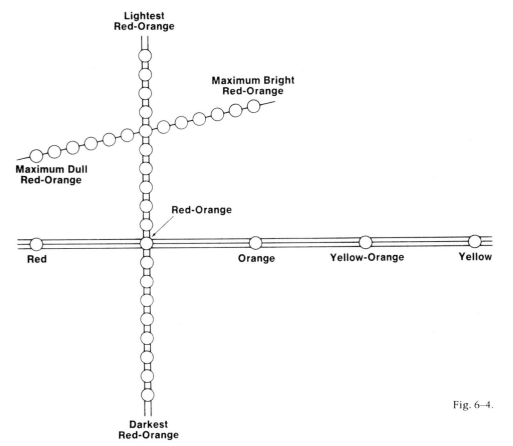

Fig. 6–4.

zontal lines we have a graduated scale ranging from red to yellow. With each visually perceptible interval from red on the left to yellow on the right, the *color* becomes less red. Each interval already represents a considerable shift of color. In the center of the scale where red and yellow are equally asserted, we have the color orange. Between red and orange we have red-orange. Between orange and yellow we have yellow-orange.

Now, if we take any interval along this horizontal scale of color, we can construct a value scale running vertically through that particular interval. In our diagram we have constructed such a scale, indicated with double lines, through the color red-orange. Assuming that this red-orange on the horizontal scale is of a *middle* value, then all intervals above it on the vertical scale would be lighter values of that color while all intervals below it would be darker in value. Similar ranges of value could be constructed at every interval on the color scale. And if we could perceive just 30 intervals of color from red to yellow and a mere ten intervals of value from white to black, then already we would have 300 colors based on the logic of this simple diagram. However, as if that were not sufficient, we can construct another scale—a scale of *intensity* (represented by the slanting single line) through any interval on this value scale. In our diagram such a scale has been constructed through a high value of the red-orange color. Along this scale would be intervals of *intensity* ranging from maximum dullness on the left end to maximum brightness on the right. Such scales of intensity could be constructed through every interval on the value scale of every interval on the color scale. And even if we could perceive no more than ten intervals of intensity, we would have at this point in our discussion 3,000 colors. Still, the possibilities do not end here: we could construct a *second set of value scales* through every one of the intensity intervals we have just located! This would give us 30,000 colors. And through this second set of value scales we could construct a *second set of intensity scales* giving us 300,000 colors! The actual range of color is infinite. It is only our own power of visual perception —our capacity to distinguish intervals in the imperceptibly subtle gradation of one color into another—that is limited.

We have been discussing the visual elements as if it were possible for us to perceive them singly, in isolation. This is impossible. When we look at a line, we are also aware of its length, or *size,* its *color,* and even its *texture.* And so it is with all the visual elements: they involve each other. This is why we spoke earlier of the crucial importance of the total configuration— the whole affective pattern of any visual complex. And now that we have begun to appreciate the immensely rich variety possible within the ranges of the separate visual elements, it is natural and unavoidable to recognize a kind of universe of possibility existing among the visual elements and their qualities. It is a universe in which all of us move, some more knowingly than others. This is the universe that most engages the visual artist. He experiences it as nature, coextensive with himself, and he looks on it as means for creating configurations which embody his own responses to the world. We say that the artist "expresses" his feelings or thoughtful convictions by way of creating patterns of visual qualities. If he does so, there is no other way for us, as viewers of his work, to get what he has expressed except by direct response to what he has given us to look at.

It appears that different visual configurations affect us differently. This is demonstrably true, at least among people somewhat contemporaneous in time, tradition, and place. It appears true, also, that different qualities of the visual elements *themselves*—when separated from the complex configurations of works of art—affect us in quite different ways. We are not always able to say in words just how a particular line or shape affects us or what it tends to "communicate," but we sense its bearing on us in tacit ways. In fact, it is more often the case that we cannot exactly say, or say at all, just how we are affected by visual stimuli. It may be enough, however, to know that we are moved and to value this as evidence of our contact with qualities outside ourselves.

A simple example may suffice to make evident the fact that we are affected by qualities of the visual elements themselves. The shape presented in Fig. 6–5 is not meant to represent anything in particular. It is not intended to make specific reference to any object in the surrounding visual world. It is meant to be only this shape, but that does not mean that we do not respond to the particular quality of this shape when we look at it. Unless we are so fatigued or otherwise incapacitated that we cannot, in fact, see what we are looking at, then we do respond—even to a simple visual phenomenon such as this angular shape. And each of us responds, we presume, in a some-

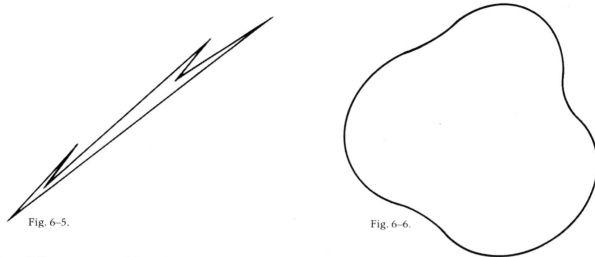

Fig. 6–5.

Fig. 6–6.

what different way, although, as we shall see, there is a generous area of overlap in our individual responses.

Without trying to describe in words just how each of us is affected by Fig. 6–5, let us turn our attention to Fig. 6–6. Now, whatever our response to the first figure was, there can be no question that it was different from our response to this second figure. These two shapes, by their quite different visual qualities, become known to us by our quite different responses to them. The first shape almost immediately suggests a whole range of relevant responses which are not relevant to the second shape; the second shape sets up its own range of relevant responses in us. What these responses are, specifically, is difficult, if not impossible, to say, but they do take place and with considerable definiteness.

Because we respond differently to these two shapes, we often say that they express different feelings or moods. This expression is accomplished solely by the particular visual characteristics of these shapes, not by reference to any actual objects.

The same kind of expression of generalized feelings or moods is also possible with mere sounds—sounds which are not words. Such nonsensical arrangements of sounds falling against our ears have the same power to affect us as the qualities of nonobjective shapes coming into our vision. For example, when we pronounce the following set of letters: M O O M A H B A H L O O M, we hear a particular set of prolonged, low-pitched, heavily undulating sounds which are suggestive of, or which may actually create, a certain kind of mood. This mood is unattached; it is free of any specific alignment with particular things or particular situations. In this regard it is analogous to the mood set up by the shapes of which we have just been speaking. And although we may not be able to describe this mood in any specific or propositional way, we know that mood to be very different from the one created in us when we pronounce the following set of letters: E E K N E E P I N S K E E. This nonsense word is not heavy and undulating in our ears as is M O O M A H B A H L O O M. It is sharp and pinched; it squeaks its way through.

Here, then, are examples, from both visual form and from language,

43

of the potential of nonobjective shapes and nonsense sounds to express generalized feelings or moods. And it is a fact that as human beings our responses to these moods have a good deal in common. The truth of this can be pointed up by simply asking which of our two shapes (Fig. 6–5 or Fig. 6–6) is more like M O O M A H B A H L O O M and which is more like E E K N E E P I N S K E E. There is bound to be just about perfect agreement that our first shape (Fig. 6–5) "matches" E E K N E E P I N S K E E and that our second shape (Fig. 6–6) pairs with M O O M A H B A H L O O M. So, even though we cannot say in words what these shapes or groups of letters mean to us, we still do respond to them; the moods they set up in us are quite real, and we can define such moods by comparison and contrast with other expressive phenomena. We might even go so far as to say that after our little discussion here, all of us would know what was meant by such statements as these: "She went on a diet right after her doctor said she was too moomahbahloom" and "They said he made a good City Treasurer but a poor dinner host because of his eekneepinskee habits."

Whether we know it or not, all of us are continually responding to the special qualities of the visual elements. Our minds may be focused on other more "practical" matters as we move from place to place with great efficiency during our working days. We may be keeping our "eye on the ball" and getting the job at hand done with little or no thought—or knowledge— of the elements which together make up our visual world. At any given moment we may be able, quite automatically, to sort out of our total visual field just those clues required to do a certain job—like crossing a street or returning a book to the shelf. But what many of us do not realize is that the pattern of the whole visual field is working on us all the time. Not only what we are momentarily focusing upon, but the entire surrounding field, to the limits of our peripheral acuity, is continually making its impressions on us. And, most often without our knowing this at all, we respond to this total configuration of visual stimuli.

What else is it but the effect of the whole visual field that causes us to feel at ease in one house and uneasy in another? True, the inhabitants of the houses, by the particular quality of their presence, may contribute in one way or another to an overriding degree; but what if the houses are without occupants? Then it is the composite effect of colors, sizes, shapes, and textures in relation to ourselves which either invites or turns us away. And the same is true for landscape. We are caused to experience feelings of one sort when what lies around us are the huge, jagged, pyramidical shapes and the blue-gray color of the High Sierras, and feelings of quite another sort when we find ourselves to be the most vertical shape on the almost unbroken tan-white flatland of the Gulf coast of Texas. In either case these special configurations of visual qualities get to us. So long as our eyes are open, they work to activate us in mind and body and thereby let us know in tacit ways where we are and *how* we are in relation to what is around us. We can say that the visual elements, in and of themselves, play this expressive role in all of our lives.

CHAPTER SEVEN

Expression:
GENERAL AND SPECIFIC

In giving form to feelings, emotions, and ideas, the artist has recourse to at least two very different modes which result in two very different kinds of emphasis in his art. He may choose or be led, whichever case it might be, to make his expression in general terms or to specify it within quite particular terms.

In our previous discussion of the visual elements and expression, we were concerned with the affective potential of those elements whether they occur in nature or in art. In either case, we were considering the role of the visual elements in expressing—or inducing in us—feelings of a very generalized sort. In making such expressions the artist depends upon his own sensitivity to the strength and quality of lines, shapes, colors, sizes, and all the visual elements. He remains in contact with, and acts with regard for, the deep lying and unspecified associations called up by these elements separately and in combination. With something like what we used to call instinct, the artist fashions sharply edged shapes bristling with acute angles when what he wishes to express is related to hurtfulness and danger. And when he seeks to express warmth, invitation, and fulfillment, he is likely to create rounded, organic, full-bodied shapes. For the qualities of rest, repose, or uneventful movement in a single plane, the artist is likely to depend upon the horizontal line. For a feeling of balanced stability and implied movement up or down, he will depend on the vertical line. And if what the artist seeks is an expression of strong movement or a generally dynamic situation, he will rely upon the diagonally running line—either separately or as part of the contours of shapes. He is sensitive, for instance, to the power of the diagonal line or direction to suggest falling, to the power of the curve to suggest movement in the direction of its bulge, and to the almost universal

WASSILY KANDINSKY. The Black Circle. *The Museum of Modern Art, New York (Acquired through the Lillie P. Bliss Bequest). See Plate 14.*

power of the color red to suggest heat and close proximity to the viewer. In short, the artist who is intent upon making expressions of this general sort will employ the visual elements for their own inherent power to suggest such broad qualities of feeling and emotion.

In modern times it may be Wassily Kandinsky who first produced completely nonobjective paintings. Many of his paintings dating from early in the second decade of this century are records of his concern for the functions of the visual elements themselves. In his watercolor painting *The Black Circle*, reproduced in Color Plate 14, it is obvious that Kandinsky had no intention of creating a portrait, a landscape, or a still life. From the evidence before us it is entirely fair to assume that he was concerned with the creation and manipulation of visual qualities. With the special qualities of the visual elements given us here, he has achieved an expression of a very general sort—of an almost cosmic sort.

On the flat surface of an almost square piece of paper, Kandinsky has constructed two principal areas of interest: the flat black circle in the upper left quadrant and the sharply angular mass in the lower right quadrant. By and large, it is this dramatic contrast of shape qualities, this expression of shocking difference, with which the artist appears to have been concerned. It is true that the combination of variously angular shapes amounts to an area somewhat larger than that of the circle. And it is true that the angular mass is rendered somewhat less dense than the circle. But these differences

46

serve mainly to support the stark presentation of radically opposing qualities of shape.

Now we can ask the question: Is this all that Kandinsky cared to express in this watercolor? It would appear not. For, besides giving us something like opposites simultaneously in one painting, he has presented them in a way that causes them to coexist with ease and grace. For one thing, he has created an illusion of infinite space and light in which the darker shapes appear to float. They give the feeling of having plenty of room; there appears no danger of collision. Also, to bridge the gap between the calm circle and highly active angular mass, the artist has given us what amount to visual stepping-stones. One of these is the small vertical rectangle in the lower left quadrant. It partakes of qualities common to both the circle and the angular mass, and by virtue of this it induces in us a feeling of the *possibility* for arbitration of their differences. The fact that this little rectangle lies isolated in a neutral space between the large opposing shapes brings to it a degree of functional importance which far exceeds its size.

Another of the stepping-stones is the small circle made to appear as if we were seeing through it to the extreme lower right section of the angular mass. This circle, divided exactly in half by a severely straight edge of a diagonally placed trapezoid, also partakes of qualities common to both of the large masses of the painting. Its position—overlapping the angular mass and almost as far from the large black circle as possible—serves to introduce the quality of circularity where it is most lacking. The isolation of the small, seemingly translucent circle in a matrix of opposite qualities gives it a degree of visual importance roughly equal to that of the small vertical rectangle. And, by and large, this circle functions in much the same way as does the rectangle.

So what does Kandinsky's painting express? Whatever it expresses is related to the kind of observations we have just been making. Certainly it is more than a merely interesting configuration of visual elements. We could say that by analogy with the character of its own organization and its own kind of coherency, it expresses potential compatibility among disparate qualities—even opposites. In any event, *The Black Circle*, by Wassily Kandinsky, serves excellently as an example of *general* rather than specific expression. For if we are anywhere near the truth when we observe that his painting is saying something about opposites and graceful compatibility, it must follow that Kandinsky has given us no clue whatsoever concerning specific terms or specific contexts in which he would like to have us experience this. He has given us an example of the compatibility of opposites in terms of the visual elements much as a mathematician gives us examples of the theory of sets by formulae and graphs. We understand that both Kandinsky and the mathematician mean to make their points in the abstract—ideally and in general, unhedged by any considerations except those inherently required by their chosen media.

Much of what we have said about Kandinsky's mode of expression would also apply to the sculpture of Hans Arp. His limestone carving titled

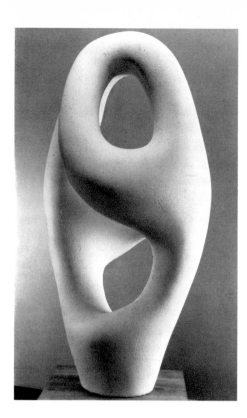

Fig. 7–1. *HANS ARP.* Ptolemy. *1953. Limestone, height 40 $^1/_2$". Collection The Museum of Modern Art, New York (Gift of Mr. & Mrs. William A. M. Burden, donor retaining life interest).*

Ptolemy (Fig. 7–1) is obviously not intended to be a portrait of that Greco-Egyptian mathematician, astronomer, and geographer whose name it bears. It is intended to be nothing so specific. Its expression is of a general kind.

Hans Arp, similar to Kandinsky in this case, is working with the visual elements without concern for employing them to represent any particular object from the visual world. His prime concern is for the potential of the evenly textured limestone to hold and present this particular configuration of three-dimensional shapes. He has worked with both solids and voids to arrive at a sculptural unity. Whatever it expresses of a continuous rhythm, a doubling-back of forces upon themselves, is kept free of any specifiable context. Even if Arp had been motivated by an appreciation of Ptolemy's discovery of the irregularity of the moon's motion, his sculpture makes no such definite a reference. It sets up a powerfully enchanting, self-enclosed rhythm which depends only upon itself and our own deep-lying associations of rhythmic movement for its full realization. Hans Arp's *Ptolemy* is indeed a work realized in the mode of general, rather than specific, expression.

It is quite a different matter, however, when we look at a painting such as Caspar David Friedrich's oil *The Wreck of the "Hope"* (Fig. 7–2). For one thing, we are almost immediately made aware of images of objects and situations from the actual, visible world. The shapes, colors, lines, sizes, and implied textures are of such character and in such relationships to each other and to the whole that they create an illusion of a frozen seascape. Specific qualities of the visual elements are so ordered that in combination they remind us of the sky, jaggedly broken ice, snow, and the disappearing hull of a ship. The visual elements are, however, just as much part of this painting as they are part of Kandinsky's *The Black Circle,* and they function in much the same way. The difference is that Friedrich has chosen to employ them for a specific rather than a general kind of expression.

It is still true, however, that the basic force of Friedrich's expression is generated by the configuration of visual elements. We respond to the long, dark, irregular shapes which run in rising diagonals from left to right. We sense the force of collision between these shapes and those of opposing angles higher in the painting. The strong contrasts of light and dark heighten the drama which is focused on a kind of pitched battle between strongly pressing and strongly resisting wedge shapes. This kind of generalized expression of force and resistance was, it goes without saying, not enough for Friedrich. He wanted to use all the power that the visual elements—in his hands—could generate; he wanted us to feel the crushing drama of opposing shapes and directions. But he worked to have the visual elements express this in such a way that it could be directed into a very specific context—the destruction of a small wooden ship by the action of huge masses of ice. This he managed by making certain wedge shapes look like fractured sections of an ice-covered sea; by heightening the quality of sharpness of edge by playing it against fluffy-appearing light areas that remind us of frozen spume, and by burying in the masses of solid-appearing shapes the dark stern and six toothpick-like masts and spars of the disintegrating ship "Hope."

All of us would perhaps agree that it is a very different thing whether what we see is a small dark shape being battered by much larger dark and light shapes, or what we see is a small dark area *in the shape of a ship* being battered by much larger dark and light areas *in the shapes of broken ice.*

Fig. 7–2.
CASPAR DAVID FRIEDRICH.
The Wreck of the "Hope." *1821.
Oil on canvas, 38¹/₂ × 50¹/₂".
Kunsthalle, Hamburg.*

When we see these images of the broken ship, the ice and the sky, and the distant horizon, hosts of specific associations are called up. Whatever we know of these things from past experience, real or vicarious, are rapidly floated up into our consciousness. This may mean, of course, that we, as viewers of this painting, may indulge ourselves in chain reactions of associations, and in the process may move *away* from Friedrich's expression instead of coming closer to it. This is one of the risks the artist must take in both the general and specific modes of expression. For whenever the artist seeks to *involve* the viewer in his work, rather than merely *impress* him, then he must expect the viewer to respond as an actively engaged human being—with all that that may mean in a free society.

Perhaps the crucial point here is that in *The Wreck of the "Hope"* Friedrich *has* created an expressive configuration of the visual elements. The basic structure of his painting—even without the telltale marks of objective reality—is strongly expressive of contending and powerful forces. It could stand alone as an expressive configuration of the *general* sort. However, by his specification of this basic structure into terms that create images of objects, Friedrich has *transferred* much of the purely structural drama to those images. He has succeeded in associating the powerful mood generated by the visual elements themselves with the objects represented. As a result, the force and quality of that mood becomes lodged in "masses of ice," "frozen spume," and the "disintegrating ship." To all evidences, this is precisely what Friedrich wished to do; he works in the *specific* mode of expression.

For some of us it may be easier to see in the work of a man like Vincent Van Gogh how the artist accomplishes this kind of focusing of expression. His drawing *Starry Night* (Fig. 7–3) is characteristic of much of his work in both drawing and painting. This drawing should come with something of a shock after looking at the work of Friedrich, and mainly for two reasons.

Fig. 7–3.
VINCENT VAN GOGH. Starry
Night. *1889. Pen and ink.*
Formerly in the Kunsthalle,
Bremen (destroyed?).

One quite obvious reason that they look so different is based in the fact that one is an oil painting on canvas, and the other is a much smaller drawing made in pen and ink on paper. The second reason is that Van Gogh did not go nearly so far as Friedrich in the direction of photographically fixing the visual characteristics of the objects he represents in this drawing. In this regard, it is still customary to say that a work such as Friedrich's is more "realistic" than Van Gogh's. It is also customary to describe Van Gogh's drawings as more "abstract" than Friedrich's painting. And since the verb form of the adjective "abstract" means such things as "to draw out from; to separate from the concrete; to reduce to a summary," we can say that Van Gogh's work is further from the specific and the concrete than is Friedrich's. But all this notwithstanding, it is still a fact that this drawing by Van Gogh accomplishes an expression which is more specific than it is general. In its mode of expression it is closer to *The Wreck of the "Hope"* than it is to Kandinsky's *The Black Circle.* Specificity and generality in works of art are comparative matters; they are matters of degree.

One of the reasons why we are so strongly affected by a work such as this by Van Gogh is that it is virtually impossible for the viewer to escape the quality of sinewy turmoil which pervades it. From top to bottom and from side to side, this drawing is filled with hundreds of short, curved lines of varying thickness and value. Strictly speaking, it does not contain a single straight line, nor is any straight line or direction implied. Instead, masses of animalcular lines are mustered into a variety of meandering, undulating, spiral, and concentric patterns. For the most part, it is these composite patterns which form the images of objects in this drawing. And even though these images of houses, hills, and trees are at considerable variance with their concrete prototypes, they still serve admirably as unmistakable clues to a quite specific context—the countryside of the south of France. The images of stars and of the moon are further removed from actuality just as all heavenly phenomena are, in fact, further removed from our actual experience of them. Still, they, too, make clear enough reference to stars that seem to twinkle and move across the sky in galaxies like the curving Milky Way; and to the moon that "shines," "wears silver and golden rings," waxes and wanes, and seems to travel the inside of a darkened bowl.

The swirling, bubbling craters of the upper two-thirds of this drawing and the flamelike shapes that lick up from the chunky, rocking, lower part all serve to suggest a commotion—a turbulence that is more violent than simply dramatic. This almost distraught lyricism is what gets expressed by the structure of the visual elements. It is this general mood with which Van Gogh has infused specific objects. The craterlike shapes are images of stars and the moon; the flamelike shapes are the contours of a huge, heavily drawn cypress tree, a church steeple, and smoke from three chimneys. The chunky, unstable lower part is made of images of houses, the church, and scrubby trees.

Perhaps Van Gogh himself had an ecstatic reaction to an actual situation in nature and then heightened the experience of that situation in the formulated images we see here. But no matter how he came to this finished work, it is clear that Van Gogh creates the volatile and ecstatic mood through a configuration of recognizable specific images. With all the cosmic, ideal, psychological, and generally abstract qualities of this drawing, it is still an excellent example of what we are calling the *specific* mode of expression.

And what about the specific mode of expression in sculpture? As we would expect, it is in as commanding a role there as it is in the other categories of the visual arts.

Earlier, it will be recalled, we looked at a sculpture, *Ptolemy* (Fig. 7–1), by Hans Arp. We said this was, quite clearly, a very good example of the *general* mode of expression. Now, with that sculpture in mind, let us consider the life-size statue *David,* by Gianlorenzo Bernini (Fig. 7–4).

After the first split second required to recognize that this piece of marble is in the shape of a man, we become more and more aware of *how* this figure is. As human beings most interested in ourselves and other human beings, we are naturally more completely engaged by a figure such as this than we would be by a figure of a gnu or a whale. We can identify ourselves with this *David* rather more easily than with those other mammals. We take special interest in seeing how this image of a man holds his head and his hands; how his weight is carried by his right leg and only steadied by his left; how well he is muscled, and how strangely he is draped. We become

Fig. 7–4. *GIANLORENZO BERNINI. David. 1623. Marble, life-size. Borghese Gallery, Rome. Photo: Alinari-Art Reference Bureau.*

so interested in such specifics—and understandably so—that we are hardly aware of Bernini's phenomenal success in organizing them. It is when we begin to respond to Bernini's skill in seeming to catch an actual man in the act of winding-up before firing the rock from his sling, that we sense the sculptor's strategy.

The complete sculptural mass, including David's drapery, equipment, and the accouterment at the base, has been conceived in reference to a spiral. Starting from a fairly flat base, which itself seems to be turning, the figure of David twists upward like a very steep spiral staircase. The twist is equal to more than a quarter of a full turn: if the line connecting David's feet was facing west, the line across his shoulders would be past north and toward the east. And then to counter the force of this twist and bring a strong emphasis to David's face, Bernini turns the head back against the direction of the spiral.

A spiral construction with a certain subdominant countermovement informs all the parts of this sculpture with qualities associated with an elongated coil spring. We feel this spring to be under a tension that will soon be released. This general expression is largely accomplished by the visual elements alone. And thinking of Bernini's *David* in this way, we discover a remarkable similarity existing between it and Hans Arp's *Ptolemy*. Both sculptors are concerned with purposeful organization of volumes as revealed in light. Both are concerned with playing voids against solids. Both are partial to giving form to a rhythmic twisting and interlocking of sculptural volumes. But we must make no mistake: the *David* is a very different kind of thing from the *Ptolemy*. To speak about these two sculptures—the *David* completed over 300 years before the *Ptolemy*—as if they were closely comparable would be misleading, if not ridiculous. For Hans Arp, the whole of the sculptor's art has meaning in its potential for expression of *general* qualities, feelings, and concepts. For Bernini, the art of sculpture includes much of what Arp would have it include, but Bernini would go on from the general to the specific expression. For him, it is essential that the indeterminate power of such a form as the coiled spring, which acts like an armature inside the figure of David, be made precise—the coiled spring must *be* the coiled David. In fact, all evidence points to the possibility that Bernini never thought separately of the general and the specific in matters of his sculpture; his figure of David came right along with the spiraling spring. His art aims at expression of a specific sort, and it succeeds eminently.

To be sure, all this talk about general and specific expression intends no preference for one or the other. Different concepts, feelings, or fantasies require different means of formulation and expression. One means or mode would not suffice for all. What is important is that we recognize what is relevant to each work of art, and not expect a generally expressive piece to be specific, or vice versa. After all, we have learned not to expect the cat to bark, and we have also learned that it is not required that we dislike potatoes just because we like meat.

CHAPTER EIGHT

Monotony, Harmony, Contrast, and Discord

Since we have been discussing the role of the visual elements in expression, it appears in place to say something about the qualities of monotony, harmony, contrast, and discord. These terms are often used in describing the effects of visual situations or complexes upon us. When configurations of visual elements appear harmonious or discordant to us, we can say, quite correctly, that those configurations are expressing those general qualities.

At this point there is much room for discussion of just what is meant by terms such as monotony and harmony. It would be in place to ask such questions as whether what affects us as harmonious will likewise affect people much older or much younger than we are; and whether harmony is very much the same for the contemporary continental Chinese, the Congolese, and for us. These are good, solid questions which deserve serious and extended entertainment—not only in the context of art, but also in the whole context of living. However, we will not attempt to meet these questions at all directly. Something of the variety of the "answers" to such questions has been indicated as we have gone along, and more will be offered by implication in the pages ahead. All that will be attempted here is a presentation of a very simple means for both recognizing and creating configurations of visual elements which have characteristics generally agreed to be monotonous, harmonious, markedly contrasting, and discordant. It should be borne in mind that the simple system to be presented is of a most usual and limited sort; we should think of it only as one way in which these concepts may be entertained.

Before giving any dictionary definitions of monotony, harmony, contrast, or discord, let us go back to the visual elements themselves. We said that we recognize seven of them: position, size, color, shape, line, texture,

Plate 15.   *MATTHIAS GRÜNEWALD*. The Crucifixion, *closed wings of the* Isenheim Altarpiece. *c. 1510–1515. Oil on wood, 8′ 10″ ✕ 10′ 1″. The particular range of visual qualities made use of by Grünewald works to produce the generalized feelings of dread mingled* *with veneration that pervade this painting. And it is these general feelings that he has made undeniably concrete in the specific terms of this crucial act of the Christian drama. (Unterlinden Museum, Colmar, France. Photo: Art Reference Bureau.)*

Plate 16. LYONEL FEININGER. The Glorious Victory of the Sloop "Maria." 1926. Oil on canvas, 21½×33½". In this painting, the artist gives us clear evidence of a unity based on repetition. This unity does not depend upon the simple repetition of an image, but rather upon certain qualities of the visual elements that pervade the entire area of the painting. (City Art Museum of St. Louis. Eliza McMillan Fund.)

and density, and that their various qualities can be thought of as ranging over graduated scales. For each of the visual elements, then, we can imagine scales which are graduated from one extreme quality to its opposite extreme. In words, these scales would be something like the following table.

ELEMENT	FROM	TO
POSITION	High	Low
	Far	Near
	Left	Right
SIZE	Large	Small
COLOR		
From one to any other color	Red	Green
Value	White	Black
Intensity	Bright	Dull
SHAPE	Round	Sharp angular
LINE	Straight	Curved
TEXTURE	Rough	Smooth
DENSITY	Transparent	Opaque

Let us put one of these scales, that of line, into diagrammatical form (Fig. 8–1). It should be understood that this is not the only graduated scale of line that could be made. This is a very simple one which runs from a straight vertical line to a cleanly curving one. Many more intervals than are shown between these extremes could be distinguished, but this diagram will help to clarify our comments about monotony, harmony, contrast, and discord.

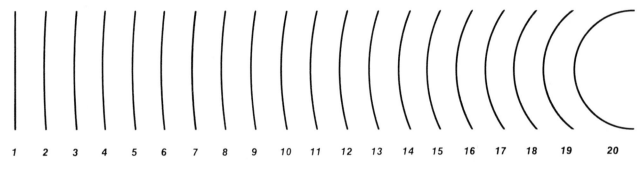

1   2   3   4   5   6   7   8   9   10   11   12   13   14   15   16   17   18   19   20

Fig. 8–1.

Taking any *single* line from this scale and repeating it, without relieving that repetition with other qualities of other elements, will result in monotony. In other words, if we took line number *6* from this scale and simply repeated it over an area, the resulting group of lines would strike us as being monotonous, since monotony is a quality which refers to sameness, repetition, and lack of variety in a composition. This kind of unrelieved repetition of the same quality of the same visual element results in a tiresome and uninteresting effect.

The same unrelieved and boring effect would be produced by repeating *adjoining lines* from such a scale as this, if the difference in the characters of those lines was so slight as to *appear* the same. Repeating lines *9* and *10*, for instance, would produce monotony so long as no other visual elements with quite different qualities were introduced.

Now, let us say that from this same scale we select two or three or more lines which are separated by small but noticeable intervals. Lines *4, 6,* and *9* will serve as a good set. If these were extracted from the scale and brought together in a separate combination, we would perceive their differences. The eye has a special penchant for comparing such qualities, especially when the units observed are close enough together to make comparison possible with a single fixation of our eyes, or with very few fixations. Perceiving these differences is what lends interest to what the eye sees. In this case the differences are not great, and as a result we sense a quality of agreement working among these differences. These lines are something like children of the same family: each is unique, but each bears what we call family resemblances. These lines, we say, are harmonious. This kind of agreement which embraces compatible differences is generally pleasing to us.

Selecting and bringing together lines which are more widely separated on this scale increases the quality of contrast. Lines *7, 10,* and *14,* if excerpted and brought together, would produce a feeling of contrast considerably stronger than that produced by either of the two preceding selections. They would still be harmonious, but the quality of their harmony would be less of a "close harmony" than that set up by lines *4, 6,* and *9.*

It becomes evident as we try to separate harmony and contrast by means of definitions in words that we are engaged in a largely artificial task. Of course, the quality of contrast exists in any visually harmonious configuration. This is how it avoids being monotonous. And, of course, rather strongly contrasting qualities can still be brought together in ways that achieve harmony. It may be that the best we can say about these two terms is that when we describe a composition as harmonious, we are recognizing, rather especially, the quality of agreement which is working among differences. When we describe a composition as exhibiting contrast, we are recognizing the rather forceful differences, even when those differences are still compromised enough to allow a kind of rugged harmony to prevail. Whereas harmony is a quality resulting from agreement among the parts of a composition which embraces compatible differences, contrast is a quality which results from diverse or easily noticeable differences brought into close combination which accentuates those differences. Both are pleasing to the eye.

When we use the word *discord* in the context of the visual arts, we use it in terms of its first connotation: "absence of harmony; diversity." Any discordant visual configuration would be one in which the visual elements and their attendant qualities were so diverse that little or no agreement was apparent.

Thinking again of our diagram (Fig. 8–1), the greatest possibility for discord would exist in a combination of lines from the extremes of this graduated scale. Lines number *1* and number *20* in combination would have this possibility. However, we could be all but assured of discord if, along with line qualities *1* and *20,* we combined similarly extreme qualities from other graduated scales of such visual elements as shape, value, and texture. These extremely diverse qualities, separated by maximum intervals on the graduated scales, create uncomfortable feelings of "gap." These qualities are set off so far from each other that they have great difficulty in conversing, as it were. In looking at a composition made up of such widely separated visual qualities, we sense disagreement and conflict rather than agreement and concord. In general, the final effect on us is one of unpleasantness.

As we said several paragraphs back, this means for thinking about monotony, harmony, contrast, and discord is most elementary. Still, nothing that we have said is not true; it is just that this sort of truth has interest only in a rather limited field. It provides little help, for instance, for the creative individual concerned with constructing compositions of a quite personal kind. Such a person, unusually sensitive to visual phenomena, might not be challenged by any system which appears to reduce concepts of monotony, harmony, contrast, and discord to matters of formula and procedure. However, some of the most extraordinarily expressive works of art can be shown to rely on such rudiments of visual compatibility and incompatibility as this simple system suggests.

In all of the history of art, the most impressive painting of the Crucifixion may be that of Matthias Grünewald (Color Plate 15). There is no question that it draws much of its awesome power from allusion to the event given visual form here: the protracted murder of Jesus Christ. But *how,* in what particular *environment,* Grünewald presents the images required for his highly individual expression of the Crucifixion makes of this painting the extraordinary work of art that it is.

MATTHIAS GRÜNEWALD. The Crucifixion, *closed wings of the* Isenheim Altarpiece. *Photo: Marburg-Art Reference Bureau. See Plate 15.*

In speaking of this painting, H. W. Janson points to "Christ's unbearable agony and the desperate grief of the Virgin, St. John, and Mary Magdalen." In a way that attests to both the expressive force of this painting and the sensibilities of Professor Janson, he goes on to observe

> ... the pitiful body on the cross, with its twisted limbs, its countless lacerations, its rivulets of blood, is on a heroic scale that raises it beyond the merely human, and thus reveals the two natures of Christ. The same message is conveyed by the flanking figures: the three historic witnesses on the left mourn Christ's death as a man, while John the Baptist, on the right, points with a calm emphasis to Him as the Saviour. Even the background suggests this duality: this Golgotha is not a hill outside Jerusalem, but a mountain towering above lesser peaks. The Crucifixion, lifted from its familiar setting, thus becomes a lonely event silhouetted against a deserted, ghostly landscape and a blue-black sky. Darkness is over the land, in accordance with the Gospels, yet brilliant light bathes the foreground with the force of sudden revelation. This union of time and eternity, of reality and symbolism, gives Grünewald's *Crucifixion* its awesome grandeur.[1]

Professor Janson's observations serve to analogize in words what Grünewald accomplished in visual form: an awe-inspiring harmony of powerfully contrasting visual qualities. This potent and precarious harmony maintains itself halfway between victory and disaster.

And of what purely visual qualities does this extraordinary harmony exist? The strongly contrasting colors, whether blue-whites or deep red-browns, are kept high on the scale of intensity. It is, along with other functions of the visual elements, this common quality of high intensity which bridges the gaps between opposing colors and values that range from near white to near black. And if the generally constant quality of high intensity is not enough to keep the colors in harmony, the much greater surface area of dark values keeps the light ones from any serious challenge.

Most shapes within the painting are of a complex and irregular quality, and sharing this, they appear compatible. There are almost no gently rounded shapes. The closest we come to such are those describing the horizontal member of the cross, a few of the distant ridges, and the back of the lamb. The Mary group at the left is irregular while suggesting a triangular enclosure. The figure of St. John with the lamb comprises a series of highly irregular shapes. The attenuated figure of Christ is composed of a series of shapes that defy regularity and symmetry. And the great ominous areas that lie around these images, the "background" or landscape, are all quite irregular. Part of the feeling of calamity and terror emanating from the painting is generated by this rather narrow range of shape quality—by this particular harmonizing of shapes.

---

[1] H. W. Janson, *History of Art* (Englewood Cliffs, N.J.: Prentice-Hall, Inc., and New York: Harry N. Abrams, Inc., 1962), p. 389.

Pointing out such characteristics as Grünewald's "close harmonies" of line and shape, and the highly contrasting harmonies of color, value, and implied texture, will not "explain" this painting. But it may serve to underline the fact that even in so highly individual a masterpiece as this, the visual elements appear in sets or ranges related to our concept of the graduated scales. It is the particular ranges of visual qualities made use of by Grünewald which work to produce the generalized feelings of dread mingled with veneration which pervade this painting. And it is these general feelings which he has made undeniably concrete in the specific terms of this crucial act of the Christian drama.

CHAPTER NINE

Two Ways
to
Unity

No matter what else a visual configuration may have, it must possess *unity* or fail as a work of art. By unity we mean the quality or condition of being one in feeling or purpose. By unity in a work of art we mean that the work affects us as a thing complete in itself: a homogeneous configuration in which elements not only are compatible, but caused to unite in what we sense as an inseparable whole. In this latter sense, unity is more than harmony. We can have harmony with simple agreement among easily noticeable but compatible differences. But when the component parts of a given harmonious configuration fuse into a single cohesive image, we have what we call unity. With such an image we have the feeling of indivisibility. We are made aware of the fact that any change in any part of such a unified whole calls for compensatory changes throughout the structure. And if such changes are made, the result—even if a unity—is another thing from that with which we started.

Artists, I am sure, often arrive at unity in their work by ways so indirect that they defy description. Much of what the painter, sculptor, or designer does to make unity manifest in his work is done unconsciously, or at least without placing any special value on the separate operations themselves. As the artist works, he is constantly measuring his growing visual configuration against the still unformed unity he seeks. His eye is continually searching for evidences of the coherent whole which, with good fortune, he will ultimately be able to describe and present to us. All the clues to *how* he arrived at unity in his work are usually only tacitly known to him, for he attends *from* those subtle clues *to* his goal of unity. We, however, are going to try to be more explicit than some artists in our attempt to describe how unity may be achieved.

If we can settle for rather large categories, then we can say that there are two principal ways to unity. The first is *by repeating elements and qual-*

ities which are similar. We often refer to this as "unity by dominance." The second way is *by counterbalancing the influences of elements and qualities which are not similar.*

Let us take an extreme example of the first way: by repeating elements and qualities which are similar. If we were presented with an empty pail and a pile of sand and asked to put into the pail an amount of sand that would relate harmoniously the sand and the remaining emptiness of the pail, we would have a problem. Our task would be to put in just so much sand in relation to the total capacity of the pail that the sand and the remaining void would fall into a harmony. But if our assignment did not specify a relationship of sand to void, it would be almost no task at all to *unify* the volume of the pail with sand: simply fill the pail to capacity with sand. It is then as unified as when it was completely empty. This is an extreme example of unity by dominance. In one case it is the common element of sand that dominates; in the other, when the pail was empty, the common element was air. In both cases the volume of the pail is a unity because it is so much like itself all over and through and through. This is the simplest way—and maybe the most ideal way—of achieving unity: by filling the given measure with similar or identical stuff, by saturating it.

But, we can argue, this sort of unity is monotonous. Certainly the mass of sand in the pail would present an unrelieved and fatiguing sameness. And we would be correct: unity by dominance can be highly monotonous when the dominant elements and qualities are very similar or identical. The fact of the matter is that variety and charm are not required by the first connotation of the word *unity*. It may be that the *ideal* unity is a monolithic one, "the condition of the unit or number one." And as an ideal that may be quite appropriate. But in our regular, less than ideal, existence, we long for relief from boredom; we long for the charm that comes with subtle and even gross varieties. Few of us, it would seem, long for the homogeneity of Egypt of the Old Kingdom, some 5,000 years ago—or for that of several more recent and monolithic societies.

In the context of the visual arts, as well as in the context of the life we actually live, we think of unity as existing among appreciable differences. In the case of unity being achieved by repeating elements and qualities which are similar, we usually avoid identical repetition in any configuration that is to be looked at for more than a few seconds at a time. Some things, like simple border designs for playing cards, allover patterns for grills on air conditioners or drains, and the like, are often unified on the basis of identical repetition of visual elements and qualities. These would be, by all precise definition, monotonous. However, such configurations or "designs" are usually not intended to hold our attention or to be objects of any particular concern. Most often they are intended to "decorate" a surface or to "relieve the plainness" of some object, which usually means that they merely achieve innocuousness.

Something of the difference between a unity achieved by repeating elements and qualities which are *identical* and one achieved by repeating elements and qualities that are merely *similar* can be indicated by a dia-

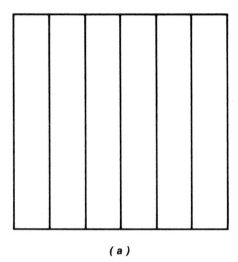 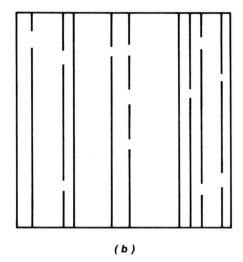

(a)   (b)

Fig. 9–1.

gram. Figure 9–1 *(a)* shows a rectangular area which has been unified by repetition of vertical lines of the same length, equally spaced. Figure 9–1 *(b)* shows the same rectangular area unified by vertical lines, not the same length and not equally spaced. Both of these have been unified in our first way: by dominance. And in this case the dominant element is the same: the vertical line. But in Fig. 9–1 *(b)* these lines are similar, not identical; and by this fact they work to create unequal areas between the lines. There is no question that Fig. 9–1 *(b)* is the more interesting.

Again, in Fig. 9–2 *(a)* and *(b)* rectangular areas have been unified by repeating smaller rectangular shapes. Figure 9–2 *(a)* repeats identical shapes. Figure 9–2 *(b)* repeats shapes of different sizes and different proportions, but they are rectangles also. We know which is the more engaging.

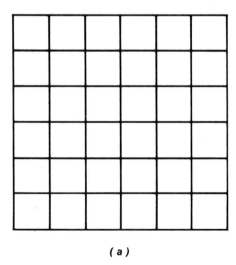 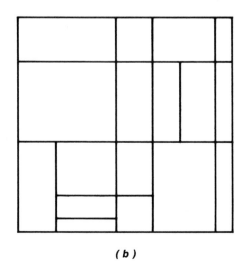

(a)   (b)

Fig. 9–2.

When we look at a group of numbers such as 63, 27, 39, 15, 84, they have interest for us partly because of their considerable differences. Yet they comprise a special sort of family of numbers. Something unifies them: the fact that all five numbers are divisible by the number 3. In some arithmetic and algebra we still call this 3 the "least common denominator"—the smallest whole number by which all other numbers of a set are divisible. It is this "threeness" present in all these numbers that lends to them a special kind of relationship—one to another, and each to the entire group. We can say that there is a unity (as well as a harmony) here, and that it is a unity by dominance—a dominance of equal potential for tripartite division.

Returning to the visual arts, we can say, for instance, that the dominance of a single color will work to unify a group of colors. This will be so, no matter the number or the range of colors in the group. Such unity can be accomplished by giving over to one color the maximum portion of the entire color area. In other words, if we were to paint the color yellow over 60 to almost 100 per cent of a given area—no matter how many other colors were part of the total area—yellow would predominate. And this would be true even if the other colors included broad ranges of reds, violets, purples, greens, blues, and even black and white. It would be the preponderant yellow *surface area* that would catch and hold our attention. The mere *size* of the yellow area would make the color yellow dominate and unify the total configuration of colors.

And since we have used color as our example here, it may be in place to note that this is not the only way to unify groups of color. We can cause a single color to dominate, even though that color does not appear, as such, in the group of colors. Let us say that we have ten or fifteen colors of paint in jars or pails. And let us say that these colors range from dark to light values, from bright to dull intensities, and from the most violent pinks and magentas through the hottest reds and bluest violets to chrome yellow and white. These colors can be harmonized and brought to a unity simply by adding an amount of one color to each of the other colors. It does not matter which color is added, just so it is added to all the others. When this is done, every color takes on something of the quality of the color that is added. If it is red that is added, then the blue-violets move closer to red-violets, yellow moves toward orange, greens toward gray, and so on, each color showing its new affinity with red.

In the case of our numbers we had a "least common denominator" of three, and it was this "threeness" that lent to them a special kind of relationship. In the case of our colors our "least common denominator" is red, and it is this "redness" which unifies the entire group of colors.

Perhaps one of the most dramatic present-day examples of unity achieved by repeating elements and qualities which are similar is Andy Warhol's painting *Black and White Disaster* (Fig. 9–3). The basic unit of this work is an image of an overturned automobile. It is contained in a rectangular format about half again as high as it is wide. Besides the automobile

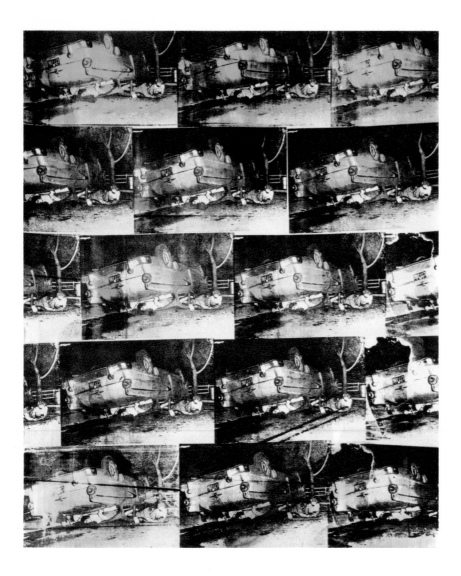

Fig. 9–3.   *ANDY WARHOL.*
Black and White Disaster No. 4.
1963. Silkscreen from photograph,
104×82″. Collection of the artist.
Courtesy of the Stable Gallery,
New York. Photo: John D. Schiff.

there is an enclosing fragment of night landscape and the partially evident
figures of four shocked and broken young people—two men and two women.
Each rectangular unit is realized in black and white and a rather limited
range of grays. That these units are fundamentally the same is obvious:
Warhol has derived them from a single news photograph. By a purely
mechanical process, a silk-screen stencil was made of this photograph. It
was from this single stencil, then, that he produced all the units and parts
of units which cover the more than 60 square feet of this canvas. It is this
insistent repetition that works a powerful unity over the entire surface.

That we respond to this multiple and recurring assault on our senses,
goes without saying—especially when we stand in front of this painting
which is almost 9 feet high and just short of 7 feet wide. It has the character
of a nightmare in which an immense image of catastrophe flickers incan-
descently right in front of our eyes. Escape from it seems impossible; we
continue to look hard at what we do not wish to see. The artist succeeds in

producing something of a hypnotic effect in us as we continue to stare at these separate but similar images of one of our domesticated nightmares—the deadly, deforming highway smash-up.

Here, then, in Andy Warhol's *Black and White Disaster* we have a clear case of unity achieved by repeating similar elements and qualities. The artist has varied his single black and white unit by making some prints of it darker than others, by painting over certain parts, by the addition of wide horizontal and slanting lines, and by including seven partial units along with nine whole units. Still, it is the repetitious rhythm of the violent black and white contrasts that holds this work together and which informs all the specific and tragic details.

In a painting much further removed than Warhol's from the actual physical world, Lyonel Feininger gives us clear evidence of a unity based on repetition. In *The Glorious Victory of the Sloop "Maria"* (Color Plate 16), he does not depend upon the simple repetition of an image; rather, he causes certain qualities of the visual elements to pervade the whole picture area and so unify it. In the case of the two strongest elements in this painting—shape and color—Feininger has emphasized angularity and bluishness. There is not a single rounded shape or curved line in this whole configuration. All of the controlling shapes are related to the rectangle, the triangle, the parallelogram, and the trapezoid. All lines are straight. All but one or two passages of color contain blue: the lavenders, violets, and mauves, the blue-greens and greens, and even the grays and browns. More than this, the entire surface of the painting is so handled that a more or less sandy texture is implied. It is by means of repeating these particular qualities of shape, line, color, and texture that Feininger has unified this watercolor painting.

LYONEL FEININGER. The Glorious Victory of the Sloop "Maria." *City Art Museum of St. Louis (Eliza McMillan Fund). See Plate 16.*

In a somewhat subtler way, Jacopo della Quercia's *Sin of Adam and Eve* (Fig. 9–4) exemplifies this same means for achieving unity. Because this relief was carved in stone of a rather uniform color, it is this color as it appears in light and shadow that provides one of the most pervasive visual qualities working to unify this sculpture. The fact that Jacopo brought the entire surface of this relief to approximately the same degree of smoothness means that this similarity of texture is working closely with the one-color scheme. Besides these similarities of color and texture, the sculpture is further unified by the repetition of shapes, or volumes, which exhibit strong similarities. Whether we look at the image of Adam or Eve, at the shapes of legs, arms or shoulders, or at the curiously pierced tree with its classical foliage and anthropomorphic serpent, we are impressed by a generally rounded, organic quality of shape. Whereas in the Feininger painting (Color Plate 16) there is not a single rounded shape or curved line, here in the Jacopo della Quercia relief we fail to find a single straight line or one strongly angular shape.

Fig. 9–4.
JACOPO DELLA QUERCIA. Sin of Adam and Eve. c. 1425–1438. Marble, c. 34 × 27". Main portal, S. Petronio, Bologna. Photo: Alinari.

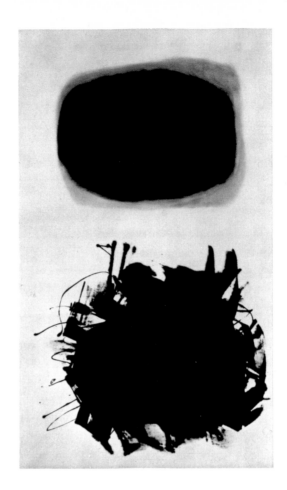

ADOLPH GOTTLIEB. Blast III. *Private collection. See Plate 17.*

Our second way to achieve unity, we have said, is by counterbalancing the influences of elements and qualities which are not alike. When we see a work of art, the unity of which depends on this sort of balance of dissimilarities, most of us respond to it with ease and directly. Few would say, for instance, that Adolph Gottlieb's painting *Blast III* (Color Plate 17) is not a unified work. Violently contrasting in some ways, this configuration of visual elements still does constitute a unity; but to say just how this unity is accomplished is not a simple task.

To begin with, let us take a careful look at the words of our definition; they have been chosen with an eye to precision of expression. The first key word is *counterbalancing*. By its use here we mean to indicate a type of action whereby the effect of one power or weight is neutralized by another. And our definition goes on to speak of counterbalancing the *influences* of elements and qualities which are not similar. Notice here that we are not speaking of the elements and their qualities *as such;* we are speaking about their *influences*. Now, what do we mean by the *influences* of the visual elements and their qualities? By the word *influences* in this context we mean the power to produce effects of one kind or another by visible or even invisible means.

It should be obvious by now that the phrase *counterbalancing the influences* signifies the key requirement for achievement of unity among elements and qualities which are dissimilar. Making a few substitutions in our first full definition, we could now have it read: the second way to unity is by neutralizing the power of different visual phenomena that produce dissimilar effects. In an almost diagrammatical way, Gottlieb's *Blast III* exemplifies this way of achieving unity. Just what is it that takes place, visually, in this work? What can we say, for instance, about the functions and influences of these two very unlike shapes? What makes them compatible? How is it that the parts of this painting can be so different in character and still contribute to a quality of coherence and a condition of unity?

To get at answers to these and other questions, it will help to look at the Gottlieb painting, one half at a time. Covering the top, let us look at the lower half which contains the stark, jagged-edged shape. This shape, appearing to be suspended in a deep space, is far from being passive or soft in its general character. It is an active, dynamic shape suggestive of an explosive charge immediately after detonation. It is, we could say. a visual counterpart of an auditory blast which rocks the entire lower half of the painting. The visual clues given to us by the size and color of this severe shape, which seems to expand violently into the surrounding space, produce in us a sense of shock waves. These waves are invisible; they are part of the *effect* created by the particular elements and qualities brought together here, in this precise way, by the artist. They are the strongest *influences* exerted by this visual configuration. No matter how long we look at this part of the painting, we continue to experience the exertion of this influence—as if the explosion was being forever sustained.

Now let us cover the lower part of Gottlieb's painting and look at the upper half. Here we find an exceedingly different kind of shape. It is rounded, of a different range of color, and with softened edges. Its compactness and its quality of self-containment suggest an inward rather than an outward movement. There is something about this shape, in this context, that makes us feel that it began as a squarish rectangle and now is in the process of becoming circular. The particular character of its "rounded corners" and indeterminate edges suggests a quality of transformation toward a more circular, more compact, and smaller shape. Far from suggesting a violent explosion which sends out shock waves, this shape suggests a muffled *implosion,* a muted inward collapse. The force of this quiet internal breakdown (or consolidation) and of the compression which seems to shrink and round out this shape are just as invisible as the shock waves of the first shape. They are the *effects* created by the particular elements and qualities presented here. They are the *influences* exerted by the particular qualities of the elements of this configuration, and they continue active no matter how long we look.

Now, having indicated the very different kinds of influences exerted by the upper and by the lower parts of Gottlieb's *Blast III,* let us look at both, at the whole painting. Seeing these two sets of dissimilar qualities simultaneously and in close proximity is an experience entirely different from

ADOLPH GOTTLIEB. Blast III. *Private collection. See Plate 17.*

seeing them separately at different times. Now the force of the shock waves being created by the lower explosion exists at the same time and in the same total configuration as the force of the upper implosion. These invisible and quite different effects continue to be exerted concurrently and very close to each other; they beat against each other. As they continue to beat—which is as long as we continue to look at the painting—a *third* effect or influence comes into existence. This third effect is a direct result of the other two and could not exist without them. It owes its existence to our perception of the *difference* between the upper and lower parts of this painting.

As an analogy of this, we can take the example of a twin-engine aircraft. Let us say that we are riding in such a plane and that we are seated midway between the two engines. With some effort we can hear first the starboard engine and then the portside one. Rarely, if ever, do both such engines sound exactly alike. Almost always the sound of one is pitched higher than the other, perhaps because no two engines can be identical, nor can they operate in exactly the same way at exactly the same time. The surrounding air is set in more rapid vibration by one engine than by the other. One engine is producing vibrations of a certain frequency per second while the other is producing vibrations at a greater or lesser frequency. These vibrations affect the organs of hearing differently, and so one engine sounds higher in pitch than the other. And besides being able to hear the particular sound of each of the engines, we can, if we listen closely, hear a *third* sound. This third sound is the result of the other two sounds as they beat against each other. It is what we call a *beat note:* a note or pitch whose frequency equals the *difference* in the frequencies of the sounds, in this particular case the sounds of the two aircraft engines.

And if you have ever sat between two aircraft engines hour after hour high above the ocean, as many of us have, you may have found yourself listening with more than casual interest to the subtle variations of these three sounds. For a variation in the sound of either engine causes the beat note to vary, and the running of even the finest engine must vary with the weight and the drift of the air. After a while we sense the intimate relationships of these three sounds; how at any given moment, and continuously, they are not only compatible, but united by an inexorable logic.

There is something of this logic, this kind of union, to be experienced with Gottlieb's *Blast III.* The specific qualities of the visual elements and how they are disposed in this painting create particular effects. They exert particular influences. The visual phenomenon of the upper half produces one sort of influence, the lower half another, quite different, sort. But these highly contrasting halves are such that their individual influences meet to form a third effect which serves to bridge the gap between them. This third effect shares the qualities of the opposing influences and provides a fulcrum or shaft upon which these opposing influences can turn. This is what happens in *Blast III.* This is why we can say that in this painting Adolph Gottlieb has achieved unity principally by counterbalancing the influences of elements and qualities which are not similar.

Because this way of achieving unity through the creation of invisible "beat effects" and by counterbalancing is by far the richer and more engaging, we must say more about it. The Gottlieb painting provided us a good beginning because of its stark simplicity of statement. We can now move on to a relatively more complex example of this kind of unity. Giotto's early fourteenth-century fresco panel titled *Inconstancy* (Fig. 9–5) should serve us very well.

This panel, painted entirely in grays, is one of a series of allegorical figures of the Virtues and Vices painted by Giotto in the Arena Chapel in Padua, Italy. Among the Virtues we find *Justice* and *Fortitude;* among the Vices, *Injustice* and our lady, *Inconstancy.* Tradition of Giotto's time would have him identify Inconstancy with such traits as fickleness, unhappy changeableness, irregular behavior, and a lack of steadfastness. In his own masterful way, Giotto did just that. He accomplished this on both levels of expression—the specific and the general. Specifically, we see the painted image of a woman in an awkward moment of losing her balance. This loss of balance is of a special variety since the balance our woman might like to keep has never really been hers, and, in fact, is for her a virtual impossibility. We see that she is attempting to ride, unassisted by anything or anyone, on the rim of a rolling disc. The slanted plane of the floor contributes to her unhappy

Plate 17.   *ADOLPH GOTTLIEB. Blast III. 1958. Water-color, 69×40″. The specific qualities of the visual elements and their disposition in this painting create particular effects. The visual phenomenon of the upper half produces one sort of effect, that of the lower half, a quite different sort. But these two highly contrasting effects are so matched that they create a third unifying force that pervades the entire work. (Private Collection.)*

Plate 18. HERCULES SEGHERS. Mountain Landscape. c. 1630–1635. Oil on canvas, 22×40". We feel this painted landscape to be weighted more heavily near the bottom. This may be partly because we think of the actual earth as heavier than the actual sky. But it is also because the darker and warmer colors employed to represent the earth appear heavier in themselves. (Uffizi Gallery, Florence. Photo: Art Reference Bureau.)

imbalance as she makes some last futile gestures toward a steadier fate. The specific details of these images indicate to us that this figure of a woman is not at all steadfast, that she is inconstant.

Turning now from descriptive detail, let us see what Giotto did to suggest the mood of changeableness by means of the visual elements themselves. First of all, the large, light, irregular area occupied by the image of the woman and the disc is constructed along two strong diagonal axes. The first of these runs from the lower left, through the image of the woman, to the upper right of the panel. The other crosses this one, not at right angles, about two-thirds of the way up, at the level of the woman's arms. This scissors-like combination of axes is so placed in the rectangular panel that it appears to be toppling to the right. (This is what makes the image of the woman appear to be falling.) Undoubtedly we would experience this feeling of falling even if the cross pattern made by these two diagonals was placed on a plain white or a plain black background. This is not what Giotto does, however. Around and seemingly behind the woman's image, he painted a

Fig. 9–5. *GIOTTO. Inconstancy. 1305–1306. Fresco, Arena Chapel, Padua. Photo: Alinari.*

replica of an extremely upright and stable stone doorway, or shallow niche.[2] In its clearly defined, exactly vertical and exactly horizontal construction, it contrasts strongly with the pattern of the toppling diagonals. The figure of Inconstancy is made to appear much more unbalanced and unreliable by silhouetting her against this icon of four-square stability. And, reciprocally, the niche is made to appear much more solidly stable by contrast with the irregularity and insecurity of the woman.

Now, this particular panel strikes us as a cohesive whole, as a unit. One of the means which contributes to this unity is the repetition of a single color—gray—over the total area. Still, it is difficult to feel that this image of Inconstancy succeeds as a unit simply because of that. In fact, the more significant means for achieving unity in this panel is that of counterbalancing the influences of the quite dissimilar visual qualities evident in the figure of the woman and of the niche. At a given moment we sense more strongly the toppling woman, at another moment, the stable niche. Our attention oscillates rapidly between these two, and in a much more restrained way than in *Blast III,* we are made aware of a third, intermediate effect. It is this intermediate effect, created in us by the other two, that provides the reference and the means for counterbalancing the other opposing influences.

Giotto's *Inconstancy* is a unified, balanced work of art. As an artist he must have known that *expressing* the quality of inconstancy is different from presenting works which, in themselves, are unsteady and unbalanced. Giotto expresses the wavering character of inconstancy in a painting which, while showing widely separated qualities, still comes through to us as a convincing unit.

Although in an entirely different mood from either Giotto's or Gottlieb's paintings, *The Wyndham Sisters* (Fig. 9–6), by John Singer Sargent, achieves its unity in largely the same way—by counterbalancing differences, rather than by repeating similarities.

This large vertical painting is divided almost in half along a diagonal that connects the shoulders of the sisters seated on the left and on the right. The half below this diagonal is given over to portraits of the three Wyndham sisters, and images of flowers, a divan, and a cushion. The area is painted to appear as soft and light as whipped meringue. The flesh and dresses of the young ladies are merged with the fabric of the billowy divan, all in a delicate confection of illusory light. A very special, airy quality pervades this lower half of the painting, in which we fail to find a single straight line. All lines, actual and implied, are either curved or diagonal, with a relatively strong upward movement implied from left to right. This combination of whitish color, elusive line, airy shapes, and silken texture produces its own unmistakable effect.

---

[2] The lowest parts of the frame of this doorway, or niche, do not appear in architecturally logical relation to the plane of the floor. This is most likely because of the loss of parts of the fresco in these areas, and faulty subsequent restoration.

How different Sargent has made the upper half of this painting! With

the same painting facility evident in his brushwork, he has created a dark shadowy mass in which we see, almost on dead center, a vertical rectangle. This is flanked by two much smaller ovals. All three of these shapes are indicative of picture frames hanging on a darkened wall, and together they suggest a huge, leering face. The formally balanced character of this upper half, the strong vertical sides of the central painted picture frame, and the heavy, dark tonality with its somber air of mystery—all these contrast radically with the general character of the lower half.

Still, *The Wyndham Sisters* strikes us as a brilliant, easy performance, as unified as the single instant in which they seem to have been painted. By using much the same means evident in the Gottlieb and Giotto paintings, Sargent has managed by his skill as an artist to equalize the very opposing influences of the two halves of this triple portrait. It is true that Sargent's bravura, especially evident in his brushwork throughout the painting, does

Fig. 9–6. *JOHN SINGER SARGENT.* The Wyndham Sisters. *1900. Oil on canvas, 115 × 84¼″. The Metropolitan Museum of Art, New York (Wolfe Fund, 1927).*

help to pull the halves together. This is part of his strategy, too. But far more determinative of unity here is Sargent's success in counterbalancing the strongly opposing effects of what otherwise would have been two separate visual configurations.

Let us turn now from these relatively uncomplicated paintings to the solution of a complex task which involved architecture and sculpture. Figure 9–7 shows us two walls of the Medici Chapel in the Church of San Lorenzo in Florence, Italy. The architecture as well as the sculpture of this room is the work of Michelangelo, who worked on it for 14 years. The original plans called for the accommodation of four tombs in this tall chapel, one against each wall. Michelangelo managed to complete only two—those for the less magnificent Lorenzo and for Giuliano de' Medici. In our angular view we see the tomb of Giuliano against the wall on our right. Although it is virtually impossible for most of us to experience architecture via drawings or photographs, some of the fundamental characteristics of this chapel do come through rather clearly here. For one thing, it is a surprisingly large room. Something of its scale can be sensed by knowing that the doors are

Fig. 9–7. *MICHELANGELO. Medici Chapel, New Sacristy (1524–1534), S. Lorenzo, Florence. Photo: Alinari.*

Fig. 9–8. *MICHELANGELO. Tomb of Giuliano de' Medici. Marble, height of central figure 71". Medici Chapel, New Sacristy (1524–1534), S. Lorenzo, Florence. Photo: Gabinetto Fotografico, Florence.*

about 7 feet tall, and that the seated figure of Giuliano is just 1 inch under 6 feet. Inordinately high for a room of this amount of floor area, we feel a kind of shrinkage of our own bodily height as soon as we step into it. Then we are all but assaulted by the powerful contrast of very dark and very light stone. The pattern of the dark stone which traces out the structural logic of the room in verticals, horizontals, and arcs seems to advance toward us. It holds our attention as if by command. A power, more mechanistic than vital, seems to charge the air and to challenge us no matter where we stand. This is not a room in which we walk freely. What we feel is tension and power, not grace or pleasure. And this does not say that all this is inappropriate for the tombs of the Medici.

Now, in this room Michelangelo had his sculptures of Lorenzo and Giuliano and four allegorical figures installed. The way we see them today is how he himself desired them or allowed them to be. And as we look at them, there can be no question that they strike a very different note from that of the rest of the room. Between the hard-edged ribs of the room's skeleton, Michelangelo developed two classicistic sets, in and before which he placed his sculpture. Figure 9–8 shows the tomb of Giuliano from somewhat above normal eye level. Giuliano sits above the allegorical figures of Night on the left and Day on the right. All three figures, but especially the nudes, contrast sharply with their architectural setting simply because of the organic quality of the human shape. But Michelangelo seems to have played up the rounded, rippling surfaces of these torsos, legs, and shoulders in counterpoint to the flat static surfaces which frame them. The figure of Giuliano, in a position of false ease, appears to suffer physically from being jammed into a cubicle which, even though considerably larger than those on either side, is much too small for this Grand Duke. The figures of Night and Day bear little specific relation to their setting. Were it not for the relation of the stone color to that of the wall, and the fact that the figures very obviously echo the bisymmetrical plan of the wall they might better be in a number of other places. This, however, is obvious, and no one today believes that these allegorical figures were cut for this specific place—and no one knows, though many guess, what Michelangelo might have meant to say by means of them.

But we are supposed to be speaking of unity; what can we say about that in regard to the Medici Chapel? What happens with the architecture and sculpture of this room?

For one thing, the architecture and the sculpture of this room may be one of the most *superficially* unmatched pairs in the history of art. The architectural scale is very large—larger, really, than the actual space in which it is expected to function; the scale of the sculpture is relatively small. The architecture is unusually powerful in its contrasts of dark and light stone, horizontal and vertical lines and directions; the sculpture is of one light color and has little relation to either the horizontal or the vertical. The sculpture feels entirely outside the rigid grid of the walls. The powerful contrasts within the architecture itself cause it to dominate our attention and make it seem to advance toward us; the sculpture, by comparison, appears weak—even in its struggling—and seems to recede from us. The walls, with all their niches, pilasters, pediments, and flutings, are still straightforwardly flat; the sculpture is richly rounded, so much so that we wish it were possible to walk around it. The architecture, so geometrically diagrammatical in its nature, impresses the viewer as being mechanistic; the sculpture, on the other hand, writhes and twists like a group of wounded or troubled organisms.

Still, with all these contrasting visual qualities, what is it that obliges us to continue to look and be impressed by this ensemble? It is an almost electric quality of tense, unresolved, monumental power that fills this room. It is developed largely by the architecture alone, but the sculpture of the two tomb walls makes a significant contribution. By its frankly non-architectural quality, the sculpture holds out against the architecture. The triangular shape into which the sculptured figures fall beats against the network of horizontals and verticals which form the classicistic decoration of the wall. The slowly writhing sculpture seeks survival against the enclosing weight and power of the architecture. And it is the *action of these forces against each other* which affects us more than either the sculpture or the architecture alone.

The "beat effect" in this case is not so much a counterbalancing agent acting between these very different visual qualities as it is an overwhelming phenomenon in itself. The character of this "beat effect" resembles that of a deadlock; we sense that the powerful and contradictory forces in this room achieve an exact but opposite intensity from which it is impossible for the forces to move in any direction. This may be why, as we actually stand in the Medici Chapel, it is so terribly difficult to *see* either the architecture or the sculpture. They have been unified not so much by a simple counterbalancing of superficial differences as by an exact matching of profoundly opposing forces. Our sensibilities are taken over by the invisible effect of this irresolution of power, and we are held by it. We stand as spectators at the finish line of a race that was run almost four and a half centuries ago and which still keeps ending in a dead heat here in the Medici Chapel.

Besides the two ways to unity of which we have been speaking, there are gross and subtle combinations of these. In fact, all the examples of unity by counterbalancing that we have cited have made some use of the strategies of unity by repetition and dominance. It matters little what devices, strategies, or ways are employed. The goal is that *sine qua non* of art—unity. Most of the drama and excitement of life, as well as of art, lies in an eternal quest for this oneness and coherence. In life, as well as in art, the real kick, the genuine reward, comes in creating order and unity out of disorder and chaos. And, lest we forget, the wise, aware person knows in his bones that it is man's fate on earth never to be satisfied for long with any one order or any one unity that he creates.

CHAPTER TEN

Balance:

SYMMETRY AND ASYMMETRY

All of us are familiar with the word *balance*. Its connotations, in no matter what context, are generally positive and good. We think well of a balanced diet, a balanced curriculum, a balance of power, and a balance of trade. We think rather differently about an unbalanced diet or a person accurately described as mentally unbalanced. It appears that on the whole we care for balance, and not for imbalance—very much as we care for harmony and unity and not for discord and chaos.

When we use the word *balance* in the context of the visual arts, we refer to such phenomena as *equilibrium* (equal balance between opposing forces), *equipoise* (equal distribution of weight), and *counterpoise* (counter-balancing of weights and positions). And it would appear that whatever our particular concept of balance, it is tied up with and directly related to how we as human beings are constructed and how we move.

Our bodies are constructed and grow in a symmetrical manner. Or, more precisely, our bodies are bisymmetrical from the front and the back, with the left side very much like the right side. Leonardo da Vinci's drawing (Fig. 10–1) makes a point of this, as well as of relations between arm and leg length, and the relation of all to a circle and a square. Internally, we are not so nicely paired off; our hearts and stomachs are off to the left, our liver and gall bladder more to the right, but they, along with our other organs, are wonderfully counterpoised. The sense of balance that we experience is our evidence of the interrelation of the nature and function of our bodies with a moving and energy-charged universe. The symmetrical character of our bodies is certainly related to our sense of balance. Even the semicircular canals associated with the maintenance of equilibrium are paired off—three

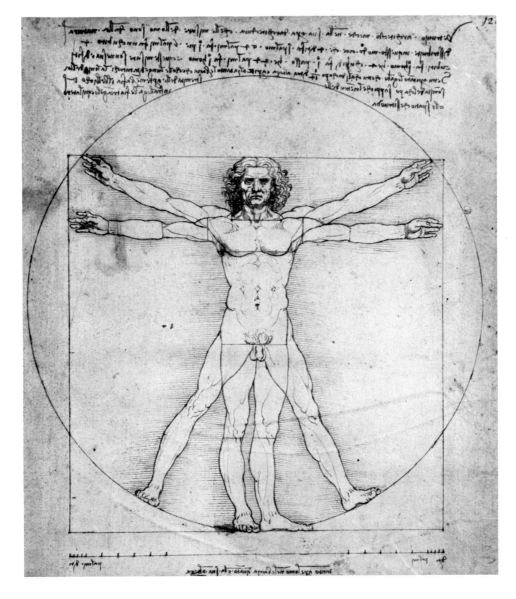

Fig. 10–1. *LEONARDO DA VINCI.* Proportions of the Human Figure, *after Vitruvius. c. 1485–1490. Pen and ink, 13¹/₂ × 9³/₄". Academy, Venice.*

in each of our inner ears. Whether we are standing, seated, walking, or running, or rolling in a supersonic jet, it is the radical form and location of our bodies in the universe that lend us a sense of balance. It would seem that whatever we do bears some relation to this particular sense of bodily environment—even the thoughts we think.

We are disturbed, or at least jarred, by situations which in one way or another are not in equipoise or not in a dynamic equilibrium such as we ourselves are in when we move. We feel uneasy in the presence of lopsided or unreciprocated leaning objects, although in some situations these may be very entertaining—all the way from comical to macabre. Coming for the

Fig. 10–2. *Campanile, Cathedral of Pisa. Begun 1173. Photo: Alinari.*

first time upon the finest example of this, the campanile of the Cathedral of Pisa (Fig. 10–2), we experience a deep feeling of something gone wrong. Seeing the tremendous size and sensing the great weight of the so-called "Leaning Tower" at this angle triggers a feeling of impending disaster. It looks as though it is falling down—as it will someday, unless it is supported. It frustrates some of our most fundamental expectations.

For all our lives, except if we are swimming or skydiving, we go with a sense of the recalcitrant earth below us. We feel and know the earth as a base which pulls us to it. And as men leave the earth for other planets or platforms, it will be this sense of the earth, of home, that they take with them. Until that future generation of men who will never have felt the peculiar pull of earth's gravity and the effects of its turning, men will sense the earth as this kind of base. It is this sense of the existence of the earth under us and of our relation to it that leads us, generally, to require that stationary objects be weighted toward the bottom. And if the objects are not stationary, we expect them to be balanced in some manner related to our own predilection for maintaining equilibrium while in motion. This may be too narrow a requirement; it may even limit our enjoyment of cer-

HERCULES SEGHERS. Mountain Landscape. *Uffizi Gallery, Florence. Photo: Alinari-Art Reference Bureau. See Plate 18.*

tain kinds of balance which we ourselves cannot readily experience. But that would not alter the fact that, routinely at least, we expect balance in things outside ourselves to relate to our experiences of balance.

In the case of a descriptive landscape such as Hercules Seghers' *Mountain Landscape* (Color Plate 18), we feel the painting to be weighted more heavily near the bottom. This may be partly because we think of the *actual* earth as heavier than the *actual* sky, but it is also because the darker and warmer colors employed to represent the earth seem heavier in themselves. There is no question that in this case the painting appears top-heavy when we look at it upside down.

Piet Mondrian, in his *Flowering Apple Tree* (Color Plate 19), uses the same kind of weighted balance as does Seghers, even though Mondrian's painting is rather unnaturalistic. It suffers less than the Seghers when inverted, however, and this may be primarily because it does not require us to look at upside-down trees.

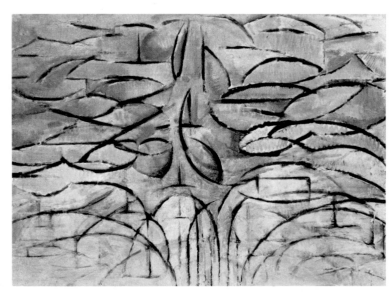

PIET MONDRIAN. Flowering Apple Tree. *Haags Gemeentemuseum, The Hague. See Plate 19.*

81

Fig. 10–3. Seated Scribe, *from Saqqara. c. 2500 B.C. Limestone, height 21". The Louvre, Paris. Photo: Giraudon, Paris.*

Fig. 10–4. *HENRY MOORE. Recumbent Figure. 1938. Green Horton stone, length c. 54". Tate Gallery, London.*

In the case of sculpture it may be even truer than in painting that we require stationary objects to be weighted toward the bottom or balanced in ways related to our own bodily experience of maintaining balance while in motion. The fact that sculpture is three-dimensional—that it occupies the same kind of actual space that our bodies occupy—may account for this closer identity. We feel at ease, for instance, in the company of the Egyptian *Seated Scribe* (Fig. 10-3) completed 2,400 years before the birth of Christ, as well as in the company of Henry Moore's *Recumbent Figure* (Fig. 10-4) of a few decades ago. In both cases the principal weights of the sculptured masses are low, and all weights are distributed in ways that bear close relationships to the human body. This is true, also, of the nonrepresentational sculpture *Ptolemy* of Hans Arp which we saw earlier (Fig. 7-1).

In the case of Giovanni da Bologna's *Mercury* (Fig. 10-5), our reaction is of a more active sort. We respond to this piece of sculpture as if it were a series of volumes in *dynamic* equilibrium. We know, however, that the

Fig. 10-5.
GIOVANNI DA BOLOGNA. Mercury.
1580. Bronze, height 69". National Museum, Florence. Photo: Alinari-Art Reference Bureau.

sculpture is hard, fixed, and immobile. Still, it communicates a sense of "living balance"—an equilibrium managed by the suggestion of animation in the figure—as if Mercury could shift his weight and turn as we actually can. For a living person to hold Mercury's position for more than a split second would require a great number of reciprocally related movements. These, of course, Mercury cannot make—nor is he expected to, for he is an *image* of a mythical being, cast in lifeless bronze. Nevertheless, this is clearly a case in which the balance of the work of art has taken its cue from the ordinary human experience of maintaining balance while in motion.

A much more subtle matter of relation between experiences of balance *in* our bodies and experiences of balance outside ourselves is based in our capacity to sense balance *vicariously.* By this we mean that all of us have the habit of "changing places" with other objects and situations, many of which balance in other ways than are actually possible for us. For example, we watch the hummingbird dart into view, hover in a mist of swiftly working wings, and then suddenly disappear. Now, although none of us can actually *do* what the hummingbird does, we can have the feeling of changing places with the bird and, to some degree, sense the forces at work in its acts. Likewise, we can project ourselves into a great variety of animate and inanimate situations and, as a result, experience qualities of balance outside the limitations of our own bodies.[1]

What we are saying, then, is simply that the balanced nature of our bodies and our sense of equilibrium while in motion contribute to our sensing and desiring some kind of balance in things outside ourselves. Balance in its broadest connotation is characteristic of works of art. It contributes to unity, while imbalance works to destroy unity. But, as we have begun to suggest, balance in art is not so simple a concept as balance in a system of avoirdupois weights. When we say that a work of art is in balance, or balanced, we mean that *its elements and their qualities have been poised against each other in such manner that they are equalized.* And the ways in which visual qualities can be counterpoised so that an equilibrium results far outnumber the ways in which actual weights can be manipulated to insure balance.

Even though it is the basis of the simplest and most obvious sort of balance, we must comment upon the phenomenon of symmetry. In talking about symmetry, let us think of the term in its stricter sense, in which it means *an equal distribution of elements and their qualities about a center line or a central point.* It should be understood that with this definition we mean that there is *an exact correspondence of size and position of opposing parts of the configuration.* Later, we will try to care for the broader and more slippery connotations of this word in other contexts.

---

[1] Psychologists use the word *empathy* as the name for this power of projecting one's personality or feeling into the object being contemplated.

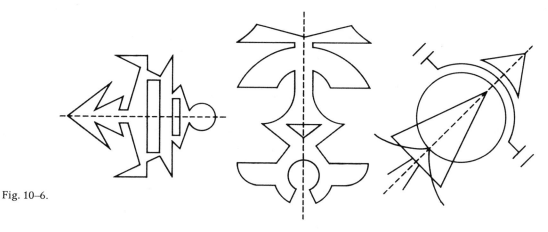

Fig. 10–6.

All of us are familiar with the type of symmetry that makes use of a center line as the division between two similar sides. Figure 10–6 gives some diagrams of this kind of symmetry, in which one half of the configuration appears as the "mirror image" of the other. Balance is achieved by pairing similar elements and qualities on either side of a line which divides the area into nearly exact, but reversed, patterns. This is referred to as either *bilateral symmetry* or, simply, as *bisymmetry*. Since the majority of works of art which rely upon this means of balance avoid exact correspondence of parts, we should introduce the term *relieved bisymmetry*. Figure 10–7, a ceramic candelabrum from Puebla, Mexico, provides an almost diagrammatic description of relieved bisymmetry. On first seeing this object, we sense an exact balance of the right and left sides. Our successive viewings of the object, however, reward us with disclosures of more or less subtle differences in positions, sizes, shapes, colors, and textures of the paired

Fig. 10–7. *Candelabra, from Izucar de Matamoros, Puebla. 20th century. Ceramic, height 30". Private collection.*

85

DUCCIO. Maestà, *or* Madonna in Majesty. *Photo: Alinari. See Plate 12.*

Fig. 10–8. Khafre (Chefran), *from Giza. c. 2600 B.C. Diorite, height 66". Egyptian Museum, Cairo. Photo: Hirmer, Munich.*

Fig. 10–9. Statue of a Youth of the "Apollo" Type. *c. 600 B.C. Marble, 73¹/₂". The Metropolitan Museum of Art, New York (Fletcher Fund, 1932).*

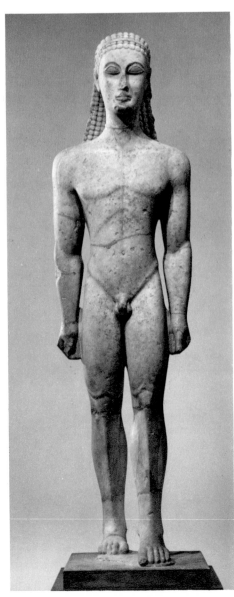

86

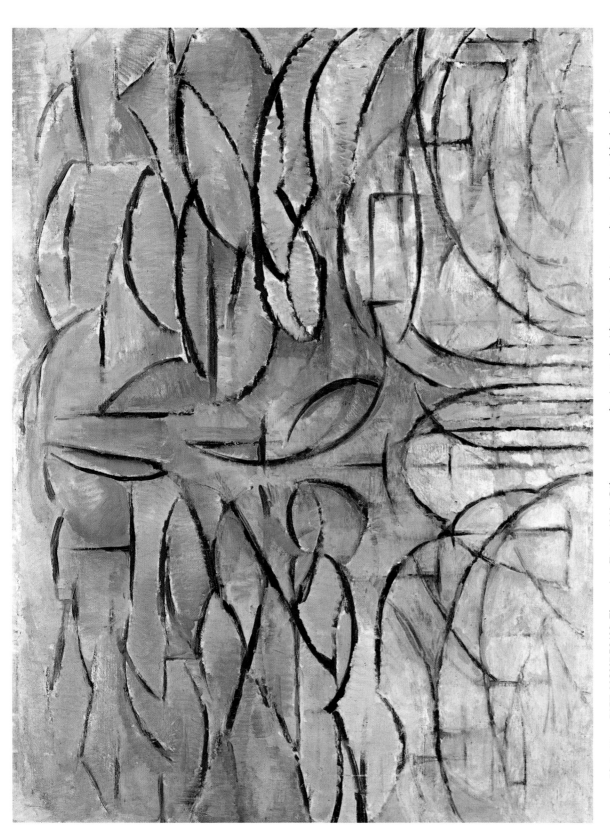

Plate 19. PIET MONDRIAN. Flowering Trees. 1912. Oil on canvas, 25¹/₂×29¹/₂". The unnaturalistic paintings of Mondrian depend on a weighted kind of balance similar to that required of the finest naturalistic paintings. And even though this painting could be inverted without our being made uncomfortable by the spectacle of upside-down, lifelike trees, it is obvious that it is shown here right-side-up. (Segaar Art Gallery, The Hague. Collection of G. J. Nieuwenhuizen.)

Plate 20.   *EDGAR DEGAS. Prima Ballerina. c. 1876. Pastel, 23×16¹/₂". What Degas has done here is to develop an informal balance of many unequal and dissimilar visual qualities. Without any system so rigid as those that determine symmetrical balance, he has, for instance, balanced intense color with rough texture, and large size with irregularity of shape. (The Louvre, Paris. Photo: Giraudon, Paris.)*

parts. And because our eyes are naturally given to making such comparisons and discovering differences, our interest is fed for a much longer time.

In painting, balance of a bisymmetric type is almost never nearly exact; the sides, or the upper and lower parts, are almost always kept noticeably different. Even in the highly symbolical works of a painter such as Duccio, we are engaged by the exceptions to a true bisymmetrical balance, even while we are responding to the insistence of such a system. His *Madonna in Majesty,* or *Maestà* (Color Plate 12), is clearly balanced by a system of relieved bisymmetry. Even in the outer thirds of this altarpiece, where at first there appears to be exact correspondence, we see differences of position in the paired figures, differences of gesture, type, color, and much more.

The avoidance of exact or nearly exact bisymmetrical balance is a characteristic of sculpture, as it is of painting. Even the most straightforward front views of figure sculpture tend to favor a relieved bisymmetry. In one of the most symbolical Egyptian figures, the statue *Khafre* from Giza (Fig. 10–8), we find that the positions of the hands and lower arms are at considerable variance. This is true, too, of archaic Greek sculpture. Figure 10–9, which shows a front view of the *Statue of a Youth of the "Apollo" Type,* documents the fact that even within this rigidly established schema of the human figure, the Greeks must still have considered it suitable to deviate from the strictly bisymmetrical system. By having the left leg and foot of this figure placed ahead of the right—even though this action is not reciprocated in any part of the rest of the figure—the constrictions of an exact bisymmetrical balance are overcome and movement is implied.

Now, besides bilateral or bisymmetrical balance, which is related to and dependent upon an actual or implied center line, there is what we call *radial symmetry.* It employs a point around which sets of visual elements are repeated in a corresponding manner. Figure 10–10 diagrams what is essential to all truly radially symmetric configurations: that the exactly repeated units be correspondingly disposed in relation to both a central point and the radii of an actual or implied circle.

If the units are of an even number, then the configuration also conforms to the description of bilateral symmetry, since one half of such a pattern is a mirror image of the other. If the units are of an uneven number, then only the term *radial symmetry* applies.

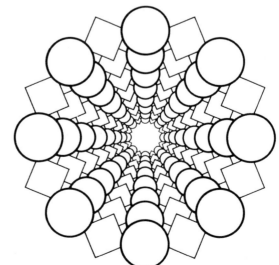

Fig. 10–10.

True radial symmetry almost never occurs in either painting or sculpture, although we do know of it in some symbolic medieval and Byzantine art, and recently in so-called "Pop Art" (Fig. 10–11). We find it most often in architecture and in the so-called minor arts. R. Buckminster Fuller's dome (Fig. 10–12) and the *Panamint Indian Gambling Tray* (Fig. 10–13) are good examples. A close look, however, will disclose that even in these there are noticeable variations from the system of common measure and exact correspondence of parts. Strictly speaking, we would have to say that both of these are examples of *relieved* radial symmetry. And Andrea Mantegna's fresco painting on one part of the ceiling in the Ducal Palace in Mantua (Fig. 10–14) is a most free employment of some of the characteristics of radial symmetry. Mantegna's concern, it is safe to say, was more with the phenomenon of perspective than it was with symmetry, as such.

Fig. 10–11. *JASPER JOHNS. Target with Four Faces. 1955. Encaustic on newspaper on canvas, 26×26″, surmounted by four plaster faces in a wooden frame, 3³/₄×26″. The Museum of Modern Art, New York (Gift of Mr. & Mrs. Robert C. Skull).*

Fig. 10–12. *R. BUCKMINSTER FULLER. Dome, Union Tank Car Company. Baton Rouge, 1958–1959. Courtesy: R. Buckminster Fuller.*

Fig. 10–13. Panamint Indian Gambling Tray, *from California. c. 1890–1910. The University Museum of the University of Pennsylvania.*

Fig. 10–14. *ANDREA MANTEGNA. Detail of ceiling, Camera degli Sposi. c. 1470. Fresco. Ducal Palace, Mantua. Photo: Alinari-Art Reference Bureau.*

Both bilateral and radial symmetry result in formal types of balance. A work of art is either more or less formal in quality depending upon the degree to which it deviates from exact correspondence of its parts. The greatest degree of informality is achieved by works which are balanced in ways that make next to no reference to either bilateral or radial symmetry. This kind of balance, by far more complex and interesting, is referred to as *asymmetrical* balance. It is related more to our experiences of balance while we ourselves are in motion, than it is to the symmetry of our bodies while standing at rest.

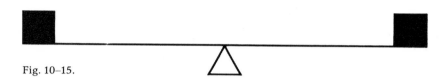

Fig. 10–15.

The word asymmetrical means *without symmetry,* just as amoral means *without* morals and ametallous means *without* metal, or nonmetallic. In an asymmetric configuration there is no common measure, nor are the parts arranged correspondingly. But there can still be balance. In the simplest terms, we can liken symmetrical balance to the effect achieved when we place two identical weights equidistant from a central pivot or fulcrum, as in Fig. 10–15. Diagrammatically, it exhibits exact and common measure in the equal weights, and a correspondence of parts by their equal distance from the central fulcrum. In a different way, we can represent asymmetrical balance with Fig. 10–16. Here we see diagrammed unequal weights at different distances from the fulcrum, but still in balance.

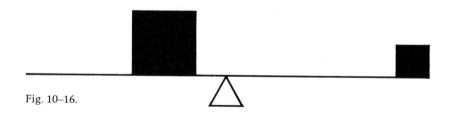

Fig. 10–16.

Turning to actual works of art that are organized and balanced asymmetrically, we find that we respond rather readily to them. However, to get a "feel" for just how the artist manages to accomplish this sort of balance may take a bit more time and effort. For instance, when we look at the pastel *Prima Ballerina* (Color Plate 20), by Edgar Degas, we are impressed by, and we accept, the off-center configuration. It communicates something of the quality of the high-speed photograph or the rapid glance. The obvious fact that it bears no relation to bilateral or radial symmetry offers no obstacle to our enjoyment of this work. We would agree that this pastel is balanced even though the ballerina is almost completely in the right half of the picture with no large figure or object to balance her on the left. We look in vain for evidences of a common measure; nothing in this work resembles anything like exact correspondence of parts. The visual elements and their qualities are not paired off. What Degas has done here is to develop an informal balance of many unequal and dissimilar visual qualities. Without any system so rigid as those which determine symmetrical balance, he has, for instance, balanced intense color with rough texture and large size with irregular shape.

In order to find our way to an understanding of how the artist achieves balance in asymmetrical ways, it will help if we sharpen our awareness of visual qualities as *forces*. It will help in seeing how it is that quite different visual qualities can balance each other because of the *degree of visual force* which they exert in a given configuration.

EDGAR DEGAS. Prima Ballerina. *The Louvre, Paris. Photo: Giraudon, Paris. See Plate 20.*

CHAPTER ELEVEN

Visual Forces
and
Balance

Instead of thinking of the work of art merely as a material mass or a decorated surface, it can be thought of as a *field of visual force.* It may even be of assistance to think of it as a field of force comparable to a magnetic field, or to any field of stresses and strains, pushes and pulls.

Now, to recapitulate: in a symmetrically balanced configuration—either bilateral or radial—we have balanced pairs or groups of similar visual forces. In the bilaterally symmetrical view from the center of the nave of the Church of San Lorenzo in Florence (Fig. 11–1), the left side exerts a visual force just about equal to that of the right side. With the exceptions created by the variance of light in the aisles, this field of visual force is balanced shape-to-shape, position-to-position, color-to-color, all the way through.

In an asymmetrically balanced configuration we respond to a field of visual force *balanced by an informal disposition of different and unequal forces* exerted by the visual elements and their qualities. In Color Plate 21, a bronze and steel sculpture titled *Sunrise,* by David Hare, we have an excellent example of asymmetrical balance. Here the artist had to measure the quality and power of different visual phenomena and play each of them against all of the others to produce this balanced field of force. The fact that his work is approximately 6 feet tall and intended to be viewed from all sides further complicated his task. But let us see what David Hare did to achieve the balanced field of force presented in this single photographic view. First of all, the total configuration implies motion. In this respect it has certain affinities with the bronze sculpture *Mercury,* by Giovanni da Bologna, which we were looking at earlier (Fig. 10–5). We respond to both of these sculptures in ways related to our bodily experience of balance

Fig. 11–1.
FILIPPO BRUNELLESCHI. Nave
of S. Lorenzo, Florence. c. 1420 to
1469. Photo: Alinari-Art Reference
Bureau.

GIOVANNI DA BOLOGNA.
Mercury. Photo: Alinari-Art
Reference Bureau. Figure 10–5
repeated.

DAVID HARE. Sunrise. Albright-
Knox Art Gallery, Buffalo, New
York (George Cary Fund). See
Plate 21.

Fig. 11–2.
LEONID BERMAN. Ma-
lamocco. *1948. Oil on
canvas, 36×28". The Mu-
seum of Modern Art, New
York (Purchase).*

while in motion. From our first split-second view of these configurations we are aware of a dynamic sort of equilibrium maintained by a complex inter-action of visual forces. Nothing in these works leads us to expect any sort of simple, static, regularly measured disposition of elements.

Although David Hare's *Sunrise* appears to spring upward from a solid base, this base is relatively small, and it rides above the floor on four thin steel rods. This, and the generally open character of the work, lends to the whole a quality of airiness and levitation easily associated with our expe-riences of the rising sun. To establish and maintain a kind of balance related to and expressive of this airiness and gravity-defying force, the artist has made generous use of openings through the sculpture. These "holes" and their particular shapes and positions in relation to each other play a crucial role in the balancing of this piece. The large triangle of open space on the

94

left is balanced partly by the irregular vertical opening on the right and partly by the darkly colored, curved shape which hangs suspended near center. Here, Hare is balancing large against small size, transparent against opaque density, curved against straight lines or contours, and bronze against steel. This is true also in how he has balanced the bright, shiny, crablike shape high and to the left against the long, dull, saberlike shape near the center, and the roughly textured rocklike shape at the base. Throughout this piece of brazed and welded sculpture the artist has balanced unlike elements and unlike qualities against each other. By a fine sense of the degree of relative force exerted by each of the elements in this unique configuration, he has managed to create the kind of balance we experience when we look at his *Sunrise.*

Before we attempt to make some more or less generally applicable observations concerning the relative strengths of various visual phenomena, let us look for a moment at a very simply constructed painting by Leonid Berman. In his *Malamocco* (Fig. 11–2), an informal, asymmetrical balance is achieved by playing combinations of unequal visual forces against each other. Just off center to the lower right we are attracted to a visually powerful concentration of curved and angular lines, strong light and dark contrasts, and a very irregular and complex contour. Together these form the image of a boat, its fittings and its reflections. Now, besides whatever interest this image may have for us simply because it is that of a *boat,* it commands even more of our interest because of its visual irregularities and strong contrasts. Its position near the center of the painting further heightens its visual force. It is, in an older terminology, the "center of attraction" of the painting.

Still, with such a commanding force generated in an area which is considerably off center, the painting does not appear unbalanced. Even though the visual character of the boat-complex is not repeated in any other area of the painting, an equalization of forces is maintained. How is this achieved? First of all, let us recognize that *certain* of the qualities of the boat-complex are echoed in the distant (small) light-colored boat above and left of center, and in the light triangular shape on the right just above center. These echoes do contribute something to the harmony of the painting, but they are not crucial in determining its balance. Rather, it is such visually powerful passages as the large, light-colored, gently curving shape that strikes from the bottom, up the left edge, to the center of the painting, and the largeness and lightness of the triangular shape on the right which work to equalize the force of the boat-complex. Different from each other as these separate passages are, they still combine to exert a force which almost equals that of the "center of attraction." The remaining spill-over of force generated by the boat-complex is equalized by the gentle forces created by the graduated color hazes that run to darker values at the top and bottom of the painting, and by the action of all the smaller remaining parts.

Leonid Berman's *Malamocco* is an informally balanced field of visual force; and even though any attempt at verbal explanation of just how this works will be inadequate, we have gotten at part of the story.

Some time ago we said that the visual elements have expressive potentials in themselves. Now we are saying that not only can they be expressive of general moods or feelings, but that they exert varying degrees of force and that these forces act upon each other in any visual configuration. And even though we know that in the final analysis it is the artist's own sensitivity to the degree and quality of the various visual forces that determines the kind of expressive balance he achieves, we can still say some rather definite things about all this. If we can come to some understanding of the relative amounts of visual force generally exerted by different visual qualities, we may be better able to recognize and enjoy their functions in works of art and in life in general. Our aim in doing this is not to develop any sort of formula, but to gain some better feeling for the operation of visual forces and how they are balanced.

Remembering that each work of art is unique and that the particular play of forces in any visual configuration must be experienced in its own terms, we still can cite certain facts which are generally applicable. Given an otherwise neutral field, we find, for example, that large size exerts more visual force than small size, and that intense color exerts more force than dull color. This kind of relationship of degrees of visual force may be paired off as follows:

MORE FORCE	LESS FORCE
Large size	Small size
Intense color	Dull color
Warm color	Cool color
White	Other values
Sharp, angular shape	Blunt, rounded shape
Sharp, angular diagonal line	Vertical, horizontal line
Rough texture	Smooth texture
Strong contrast	Weak contrast
Proximity	Distance
Motion (actual or implied)	Motionlessness

Besides these more strictly visual phenomena, there is, of course, the whole range of representational images—images derived from and referring to the life and objects of the physical world. For each of us, depending on our own personal experience, certain images exert more force than others. For someone, the image of a steam locomotive may exert more force than that of a wolf or a baby. For someone else the image of the baby may far surpass the others in force. For most of us, images which serve to recall rich or intense past experience are the ones that command our attention. And when we see such images, in whatever visual configurations, they exert considerable force. Because of this we can say that for the majority of us, images of familiar things are more powerful than images of the unfamiliar. At the same time we say this, however, we must not overlook the concomitant fact that in any complex of familiar images, the presence of unfamiliar or previously unknown images will be felt with great force because of their contrast or disparity. So much depends on *how* particular images are presented to us—their size, shape, and color, for instance—that in the last analysis we must consider each one in its own specific visual context. However, the history of art as well as the nature of our own experience are witnesses to the fact that of all images it is that of the human being which most commands our attention and generally exerts more force than any other.

Now, when we think of the work of art as a field of visual force, and consider balance the result of an equalization of those forces, we can become involved with extremely subtle matters. It is true that many of the greatest works of art achieve their equilibrium with utmost simplicity. This is true, as we have previously observed, of works balanced symmetrically or nearly so. It is true, also, of works that are balanced asymmetrically but which rely on the action of relatively few factors in a simple field. This is true of the brush and ink drawing *Six Persimmons,* by Mu-Ch'i (Fig. 11–3). In it we see six principal shapes ranging from nearly round through oval to two shapes which are about midway between circular and square. Five of these shapes form a broken horizontal row which lies at about one-third of the distance from the bottom to the top of the picture format. A sixth shape lies below this row and noticeably to the left of center. Around all of them there lies a mottled gray field, which supports and interacts with the positive shapes.

Fig. 11–3. *MU-CH'I.* Six Persimmons. *13th century. Ink on paper,* 14¹/₈ × 11¹/₄". *Dai-Tokuji, Kyoto.*

Without trying to describe in words the precise degree and exact functions of all the visual forces at work in this drawing, let us point to some of the factors which contribute to its asymmetrical balance. To begin with, let us notice that a very strong visual force is developed in the area of the darkest persimmon shape. This shape, the third in the row, gains its superior force by virtue of its large size and nearly central position. In fact, this shape occupies a good share of the central focal area of the drawing. Besides this, increased force is generated by the persimmon shape because of its comparatively "rectangular" quality and the strong value contrasts developed between its sharp left edge and the light gray plane against which it shows. Now this set of forceful characteristics which operates in the lower right quadrant of the drawing—largeness of size, comparative angularity of shape, sharpness of outline, strong contrasts of value and direction, and nearly central location—is equalized by a variety of other forces. Among the forces which work to keep this drawing from appearing unbalanced to the lower right we should be aware of those developed by the small separate persimmon shape. Its isolation from the row of shapes immediately above, and the fact that it is the only shape completely surrounded by the light gray field, increases its interest for us. A considerable force is developed by this and by the high degree of value contrast existing between the dark shape and its enveloping light field. Even though this shape is one of the smallest of the group, its position low in the format creates an illusion of its being closer to us. The visual force created by this apparent proximity overcomes the limiting characteristics of small size and roundness of shape. Adding further to the visual force of this small persimmon shape is the fact that it lies directly below and very close to the only gap in the row of shapes above. The shape, size, and value of this gap—as isolated and as contrasting as the shape, size, and value of the persimmon—joins its force, as it were, to that of the persimmon shape. Together these two visual phenomena create a force that pulls us to the left and downward. It is almost strong enough to cancel out, or balance, the pull to the right created by the largest and darkest persimmon shape. This left-to-right balance is finally assured by the force created far to the left by the lightest of all the persimmon shapes.

Still to be considered is the balance of the area which lies above the row of shapes with that which lies below. The upper area is roughly twice the size of the lower area, and by this fact of size alone the upper area should greatly overpower the lower. However, all the commanding shapes occur in the lower half of this drawing. And not only do we have their combined forces working against the very much larger upper area, we also have the force of the complex negative shape surrounding and defining the shapes of the positives—the persimmons. Together these forces equalize that of the upper area to give us the asymmetrically balanced field of visual force we experience when we look at this brush drawing. And whether or not the artist, working 700 years ago in China, was conscious of these visual forces in the way that we have been here is not of first importance. What is of importance is that they exist in his work and that they are there for us to respond to and be satisfied by.

Something of the complexity, variety, and subtlety of solutions possible in situations involving visual forces and balance can be suggested by looking at Piero della Francesca's fresco *The Discovery and Proving of the True Cross* (Fig. 11–4), and Joan Miró's oil *Dutch Interior* (Color Plate 22).

Fig. 11–4. *PIERO DELLA FRANCESCA.* The Discovery and Proving of the True Cross. *c. 1455. Fresco, height 11'8". S. Francesco, Arezzo. Photo: Alinari-Art Reference Bureau.*

Remembering the play of forces in Mu-Ch'i's simple black and white drawing limited to merely six primary shapes in a rather plain field, we can appreciate the much more complex interplay of visual forces in the Piero, which employs a full range of color. Not only does Piero balance the forces generated by sizes, colors, shapes, lines, textures, contrasts, and illusions of space and light over this tremendous area (the figures are nearly life size), he also balances the forces generated in us by images of human beings, landscape, architecture, and a variety of recognizable objects. To diagram or tell in words just how and to what degrees all of these forces work upon each other and together would take more time and patience than any of us could easily muster. But no matter the complexity of a work of art, it is still true that visual forces do function and that artists do bring them to equilibrium in any successful work. In the case of Piero's fresco, he has brought those forces into an equilibrium of a sort expressive of silent reserve and calm, heroic strength.

Likewise, Joan Miró has managed to create a compatible complex— often of violently opposed forces. With no traditional or collectively understood theme to hedge his own personal delight in working with the visual elements, he can be freer, perhaps, than Piero may have been to indulge his talents in concerns for the more general operations of visual phenomena. Even though we recognize certain images in Miró's painting—a catlike shape, a dog, a human foot—still it is clear that his painting deals more with his own responses to purely visual phenomena as they function in this particular configuration. From this standpoint, his painting is as richly rewarding to us as is Piero's, but whereas Piero achieves a highly specified classical sort of restraint in his work, Miró achieves a generalized dramatic flamboyance. Nevertheless, both paintings have been realized by means of balancing opposing visual forces in a way that brings all parts together in a network of equalized forces.

JOAN MIRÓ. Dutch Interior I. *The Museum of Modern Art, New York (Mrs. Simon Guggenheim Fund). See Plate 22.*

CHAPTER TWELVE

Cohesion, Tension, and Closure

In our discussion of visual forces and balance we have, in fact, been speaking of more than just achieving balance. Insofar as we exemplified what we said by reference to totally realized works of art, we were dealing with matters of unity almost as much as with matters of balance. For when a work achieves, as we said, "a network of equalized forces," and when this network, no matter how sparse or dense, functions throughout the entire configuration, the work then impresses us as a cohesive whole. No part of such a network of forces can be altered without throwing the whole out of equilibrium and into disunity. Changes in any part of a field of equalized forces require compensatory changes in another part or in several parts of that field. Indiscriminate altering of forces destroys the *cohesion* of an equalized field.

When we use the term *cohesion* in the context of the visual arts we mean to imply a condition of forces similar to that in nature which causes the molecules of a body to hold together. Once a field of visual forces has been brought into equilibrium, a condition of cohesion prevails. It is this condition, existing between and among the parts of any work, that lends to it whatever unity it may possess.

Earlier we spoke of relative degrees of force exterted by various visual phenomena. We said, for instance, that large size and intense color exert more force than their opposites. And we observed, especially in the Mu-Ch'i drawing, that the artist balances these variously forceful visual phenomena. Now we must focus our attention not only on the *location* of various centers of force in a work of art, but on what happens *between* those locations.

In dealing with what happens between, shall we say, the three circles (Fig. 12–1), it should be understood that we must become occupied with phe-

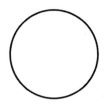

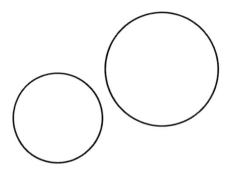

Fig. 12–1.

nomena which are *invisible*. It should strike us as contradictory that our concern for the visual arts leads us into this need for considering the invisible. Our acceptance of this contradiction will be less unsettling if we know in advance that what we are about to do is consider forces which are invisible because they are psychological. And it should help at this point if we can think of the work of art as a field of *magnetic* force, since the forces in such a field are also magnificently invisible.

The two forces with which we must deal are called *tension* and *closure*. By *tension* we will mean the action of stretching or the condition of being stretched. We will use the term to refer to a strained condition produced by two forces pulling in opposite directions. And in consonance with our analogy of the work of art as a magnetic field of force, we will think of tension as stress along lines of force in such an electric field.

By *closure* we will mean the act of closing up intervening spaces or gaps. To some extent our use of the word closure will connote *compression*, inasmuch as we sense a compression of space when a gap is closed, or when we sense that the gap is in the process of being closed. In this context, a force of closure, which compresses, is the opposite of tension, which stretches.

It appears psychologically sound to say that every shape—the circle, square, triangle, and every variant and combination—possesses its own inner structure.[1] This structure, although an inexorable consequence of the visually perceivable qualities of the particular shape, is not visible. In our acts of visual perception we *intuit* the presence and operation of these concealed networks of forces; we do not see them. When we look at an "empty" square, for instance, we are made aware of more than just its apparent emptiness. The length of the square's sides, their 90° relation to each other, the parallelism existing between opposite sides, and whatever else contributes to the "squareness" of the square—all these visible characteristics work to assert the presence and functioning of forces otherwise concealed in the square.

---

[1] See Rudolf Arnheim, *Art and Visual Perception* (Berkeley: University of California Press, 1954), pp. 1–5.

Plate 21. *DAVID HARE. Sunrise. 1954–1955. Bronze and steel, 71×42×27". Although this sculpture at first appears to spring upward from a solid base, this relatively small base rides above the floor on four thin steel rods. This, and the generally open character of the work, lends to the whole a quality of airiness and levitation. (Albright-Knox Art Gallery, Buffalo. George Cary Fund.)*

Plate 22.   *JOAN MIRO. Dutch Interior I. 1928. Oil on canvas, 36¹/₈ × 28³/₄". With no specific traditional or collectively-known theme to hedge his own personal delight in painting, Miró is free to deal with* *his own responses to purely visual phenomena as they function, for example, in this particular configuration. (The Museum of Modern Art, New York. Mrs. Simon Guggenheim Fund.)*

Plate 23. EDGAR DEGAS. The Nieces of the Artist. 1865. Oil on canvas, 23⁵/₈ × 28³/₄″. It is only after we have responded to the quiet elegance and unobtrusive monumentality of this double portrait that we become concerned with Degas's strategy in balancing the forces of the painting. It is then that we begin to respect the crucial function of the very small, wedge-shaped light area in the lower left. (Wadsworth Atheneum, Hartford.)

Plate 24. WILLIAM MERRITT CHASE. Hide and Seek. 1888. Oil on canvas, 27¹/₂×36″. With a keen sense of actual body-mind experiences inherent in playing this game of hide and seek, Chase presents equivalents of those experiences in terms of purely visual forces. (The Phillips Collection, Washington, D.C.)

Fig. 12–2.

The square in Fig. 12–2 is by all visible evidence "empty." But if we do not immediately dismiss the image, if we stare at it for several seconds, we can become consciously aware of lines of force within and, to a limited extent, beyond the square. In the simplest terms, these lines of force are those drawn in the figure below (Fig. 12–3). One set traces out the diagonals of the square. Their intersection marks the center of the figure and emphasizes the logic of the horizontal and vertical lines of force which bisect the sides at 90° angles. Besides the radiating pattern created by these directional forces, there are patterns created by the edges of the square itself. These are more like magnetic fields elongated in the direction of each side. In all cases there is a tendency for concealed forces to activate the field immediately surrounding the outer limits of the square. The diagonals push out a bit beyond the corners, the horizontal and vertical center lines push through the sides, and the forces in the edge of the square pulse to both sides of the strictly drawn contour of the figure. However, in no case is the authority of the square subdued or even challenged. One intuits the forces as being both the content and the enclosing shell of the figure. These concealed forces both fill and shape the "empty" square.

Fig. 12–3.

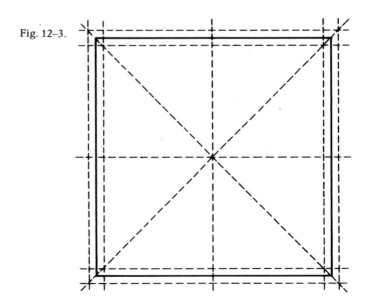

Now when any shape or mark is introduced into an otherwise unoccupied figure, the forces of the second figure mingle with those of the first. To understand precisely what takes place when, for instance, we place a small circular shape within a larger rectangle would require a complete intuitive grasp of the forces in both figures and a full awareness of the play of these forces against and with each other. Even if that were possible for us, we still might not be able to give a full report of the phenomenon. Our purpose here is to encourage interest in the operation of concealed forces at work in any figure as a basis for understanding how tension and closure work. And at this point in our discussion we are especially interested in what happens when visually perceivable elements are introduced into the field of a figure such as a square or rectangle.

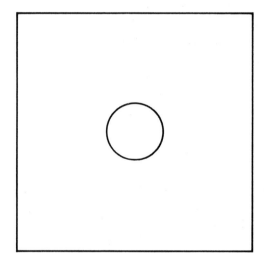

Fig. 12–4.

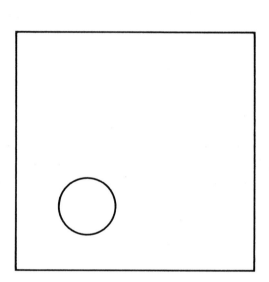

Fig. 12–5.

If we place a circle within a square as in Fig. 12-4, we sense that the combination of shapes is in balance. The circle is at rest in a field of equally reciprocal forces. In this case the circle is centered; its center coincides with the center of the square. The point in the circle at which all of the diametral lines intersect has been identified with the point of intersection of all centrally located lines of force in the square. Here we have congruence of forces, perfect equilibrium, symmetry.

Something quite different results if, instead of centering the circle, we place it off to one side and low in the square (Fig. 12–5). The result is quite clearly imbalance. The forces at the center of the square have been overtaxed, and the configuration falls to the lower left and appears unbalanced to us. In addition, we are made aware of the operation of forces acting between the circle and the edges of the square. An attractive force operating

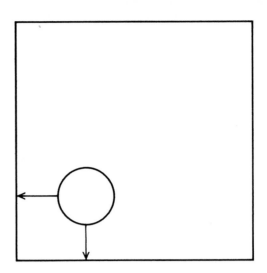

Fig. 12–6.

between the circle and the left and lower edges of the square (Fig. 12–6) increases the apparent weight of the lower left area of the configuration. This force, which acts to pull the circle still further to the left and downward, is the one we are calling *closure*. It is evidenced by our feeling that the circle is being pulled in those directions, that the gap between the circle and the lower left corner is being closed. Along with this feeling, there exists a concomitant sensation of compression of the space which lies in the gap. We can say this in another way: this particular situation induces in us a feeling of motion—as if the circle were, in fact, moving to the lower left. However, the circle does not "move" without that motion being affected by other forces at work in the square. For instance, the attractive forces of the *opposite* edges of the square—the top and right side—continue to operate also (Fig. 12–7). But the much greater distance lying between these sides and the circle acts to reduce the effectiveness of these pulls to the right and upward. We sense that this is a very unequal tug of war, and that the space between the circle and the top and right edges is being widened or stretched. This is what we are calling *tension*. In the two diagrams (Figs. 12–6 and 12–7), the directions of closure to the lower left and tension in the upper right have been indicated with straight lines running outward from the circle and at right angles to the respective sides of the square. This is, of course, an oversimplification.

Fig. 12–7.

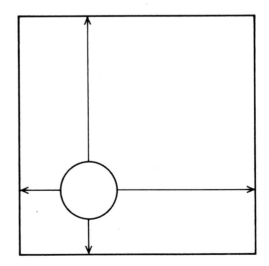

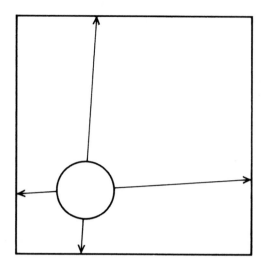

Fig. 12-8.

What we must consider in addition to everything we have said so far is that the forces concentrated at the center of the square—the forces that operate even in an "empty" square—continue to operate in this situation. The effect of this central attractive force is one which modulates the directions of closure and tension *toward the center* of the square (Fig. 12-8). The degree of this modulation depends on the position of the smaller shape or shapes in reference to the center of the larger enclosing format, in this case the square. Were we, for instance, to move our circle far to the right and upward, the same play of forces would result in a situation suggested by the diagram below (Fig. 12-9).

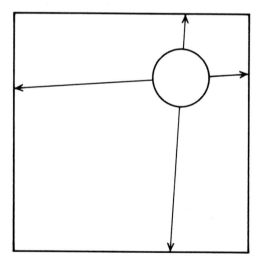

Fig. 12-9.

Let us see, now, what happens in somewhat more complicated visual configurations. In order to avoid excessive complexity at this point, we will continue to work with simple square and circular shapes. In Fig. 12-10 we

106

Fig. 12–10.

have two circles low in a square format. The circle at the left is the same distance from the left edge of the format as the circle at the right is from the right edge. Both are equidistant from the bottom. The closeness of these shapes to their respective sides of the square encourages equal but opposing forces of closure. The left circle would close to the left edge and downward, the right circle to the right edge and downward. This implied movement away from each other creates a tension between the circles. We feel that the space between is being pulled out or stretched. But this condition of being stretched is not of a character that can be properly diagrammed with a straight line. For along with pulls downward and to the right and left, there is the attractive force of the center of the square, which lies above the line of tension between the circles. In the simplest way, this has been indicated by raising the center of that line (Fig. 12–11). The attractive force of the center is also responsible for the fact that the lines of tension between the circles and the top of the square do not meet that edge at right angles. These lines, similar to the lines of closure already mentioned, are pulled away from the right angle by the action of the force at the center of the square.

Fig. 12–11.

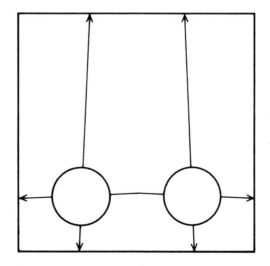

Applying what we have said about tension, closure, and the force at the center of the square, let us see what happens in a variety of somewhat more complicated situations. In the following figures, lines of tension and closure are marked with the letters *T* and *C*, respectively. In Fig. 12–12, a very strong tension is developed between the circles. Besides its purely directional character, this tension spreads out over a generous area because of the force exerted at the center of the square and because of the tensions existing between the circles and the sides furthest away from them. It should also be pointed out that the tensional force between the circles is further increased because both lie on a single diagonal of the square.

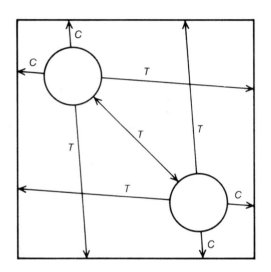

Fig. 12–12.

Moving to a situation involving three circles in a square (Fig. 12–13), we find that because of their positions they work to increase force in the central area of the square. The principal lines of tension—those between the circles —are of such strength that a *shape*, roughly triangular, is implied. Were

Fig. 12–13.

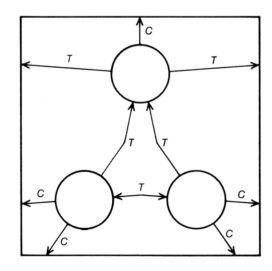

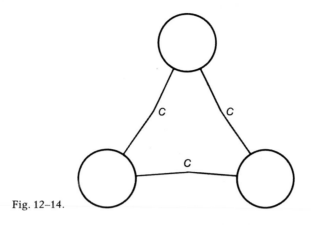

Fig. 12–14.

these three circles *not* in a square (Fig. 12–14), this triangular shape would still be implied by their positions and their proximity to each other. The triangle would be implied by lines of *closure*. However, when the circles, spaced as they are in Fig. 12–14, are inside a small square (Fig. 12–13), the triangular shape is implied by lines of *tension*, since the circles are being pulled away from each other by the attractive forces of the edges of the square. The function of the edges of any enclosing format is of great importance to the draftsman, the printmaker, and the painter who work on flat surfaces with clearly defined edges. In this regard the sculptor who creates sculpture intended to stand in free, unbounded space deals with tension and closure in somewhat different ways. He can count on the force of closure working only between parts of his sculpture and the pedestal or ground on which it actually stands. However, if his work is suspended or held in space by the action of electromagnetic forces (Fig. 12–15), he cannot count in the usual way on closure with the ground. In general, the sculptor is concerned with closure taking place between volumes and voids *within* the sculpture itself. He must of necessity be less concerned with the possibility of closure working between the outermost parts of his sculpture and anything beyond.

Fig. 12–15. *ALBERTO COLLIE. Dimensional Abstraction #2. Stainless steel with nylon. Dallas Museum of Fine Arts.*

The fact that not only lines but shapes can be implied by forces of tension and closure is of great value to the artist. He can organize his paintings, for example, in ways that will create lines of force that will direct the viewer's attention along paths he determines. And he can organize his works in such ways as will create implied shapes that tend meaningfully to lock together various elements of his subject matter. It should be understood that even though our responses to a work of art—to a cohesive field of purposively functioning visual forces—can be direct and almost immediate, the field itself may be of great intricacy. Ideally, as we said in our earlier discussion of total configuration, the viewer of a work of art is first impressed with the quality of the whole visual field. This often comes through to us as a simple unit possessing a specific character. It is only when we go beyond our first grasp of the total configuration that we become aware of the subtle and complex means used for effectively balancing the visual forces.

Before we consider the operations of these forces in the contexts of some actual works of art, it may be helpful to remind ourselves that so far we have emphasized two categories of visual force. The first category had to do with the relative strengths of visual elements and qualities: large size stronger than small size; warm color stronger than cool color, and so on. We focused our attention on the visible location of these various centers of force and how they worked to achieve balance in a visual field. Our second category, the one we have just been discussing, has to do with the operation of invisible forces that function between visibly located centers of force. Now, in responding to the work of art as a whole, we are made conscious of the *interworkings* of all these forces. Whatever degree of expressive power the balanced work of art may possess is made real and meaningful to us by virtue of, and in terms of, the particular character of the pattern created by the interworkings of these forces.

Starting with a comparatively simple painting, let us look at Edgar Degas's *Double Portrait: The Nieces of the Artist* (Color Plate 23). It is hoped that what we have to say about this painting will not detract from its own quiet elegance and its beguiling quality of deceptive monumentality.

Almost immediately upon seeing this painting for the first time, we are made aware of two yellowish-pink ovoid faces high in a dark, horizontally rectangular format. It is only a split second later that we become consciously aware of the complex and highly textured negative shape, which is darker and warmer than the face areas. And at about the same time, and in the same way, we become aware of the somewhat larger, dark, positive shape which covers most of the lower part of the format. This shape, which resembles the silhouette of overlapping beehives, describes the upper parts of the girls' bodies. It is only later, when we become concerned specifically with Degas's strategy in balancing the forces of this painting, that we respect the function of the very small, wedge-shaped light area in the lower left quadrant.

What, then, is happening in this simple double portrait? First of all, the highly placed, clear shapes of the girls' faces take our attention. Because of their humaneness and their positions close on either side of the vertical center line and on the diagonals of the rectangle, they exert great force. This, it would appear, is entirely appropriate for a work devoted to giving us an image of two people. Portraits, no matter if they show the whole body or only part of it as here, never omit the head. It would seem that the generally unclothed parts of the human body—the head or face, hands, and to a lesser extent the arms and legs—are the prime visual clues to the identity of human beings in our culture. If an artist would paint a portrait, he is committed to painting the head, or more specifically, the face. Degas does just that, and he concentrates all manner of visual force in the faces of these two girls. But he does more than merely make these faces the most commanding passages of the painting: he balances the forces which congregate in and about them—and in a very particular way. Against the high, small, light areas of the two faces he balances the low, large, darkly mysterious area of their clothed upper bodies. And into this large, textured mass he paints the very small, light wedge shape below center and to the left. Because of its sharp angular shape and its isolation in the comparatively huge, dark field, a very strong contrast is developed. The force generated in this small area is further enhanced by the fact that the light wedge shape lies on the diagonal that runs between the lower left and the upper right of the format. Here we have a case in which a very small shape, advantageously placed, goes far to balance two much larger areas in the shapes of human faces. Balance is further guaranteed by the visual force created at the exact center of the painting. At the point where the diagonals of this painting intersect, we find the contours of the inward-slanting shoulders of the girls. These contours, almost as straight as the diagonals they trace, contact each other at only a little less than a right angle. A strong force is generated at this point, and since it lies below the heads, it works, along with the small wedge shape below, to pull them down and closer to the "center of gravity" of the painting.

EDGAR DEGAS. The Nieces of the Artist. *Wadsworth Atheneum, Hartford (Ella Gallup Sumner and Mary Catlin Sumner Collection). See Plate 23.*

This downward pull of the heads is against the force of closure exerted between the heads and the top edge of the format. In equalizing these forces of tension and closure, the little wedge shape assumes an even more significant role: it works to pull both heads a little to the left. This tension is required by the fact that even though the heads are tightly locked laterally in forces that run through them and to both the right and left edges of the format, the girl on the right is *turned* to the right, and she *looks* in that direction. Now, one of those nicely documented phenomena is that we tend to look at what other people appear to be looking at. This means that if someone near us turns his head away, we are inclined to turn ours that way too. It is as if we wished to see what the other person is finding of interest off to the left or right, up or down. In paintings such as this one by Degas, our interest is carried to the right because the girl on the right is looking that way. And since there is so little space between her and the edge of the painting, we are inclined to look even *beyond* the limits of the format. The little wedge shape in the lower left could be compared to a sharp, short noise from that direction: it serves to divide our attention and so equalize it at a point somewhere in between. To realize this painting, Edgar Degas has enlisted all these visual forces, and more, to give us this image of two human beings, who, although very closely associated in time and space, as well as by blood, still retain their own unique identity.

Moving to another painting, let us look at the portrait *Robert Louis Stevenson,* by John Singer Sargent (Fig. 12–16). Here, in a highly asymmetrical configuration, Sargent has mustered the visual forces to create qualities of movement and transitoriness within a stabilized pattern. At almost the same time that we experience the first instantaneous impact of this total configuration, we fix our attention on the image of the man in the left of the format. Painted in an attitude of walking further to the left, and turning his head toward us as he goes, the image heightens our interest and hence the visual force of the figure. The suggested movement of the man is augmented by forces of closure at work pulling him to the left edge of the format. Reciprocally, this implied movement develops a tension in the remaining two-thirds of the painting, which lies to the right of the man. We feel that this space is being stretched, or rather that it has reached the limit of its capacity to expand any further, especially since it is securely bound at its right extremity by the already closed shapes descriptive of two framed pictures and a woman in a chair. The condition of high tension existing between the image of the man and the far right side of the format is modified by the interposition of the large, dark doorway. The shifting of our eyes to the left and then the right and back again between the images of the man, the doorway and the row of light shapes along the right edge induces a kind of stepped movement—as if the man were stepping to the left, stopping, and then taking that *very same step over again.* We experience motion within a stabilizing field of force.

The lightest areas in Sargent's painting set up a very active field of forces. They work in a series of directions that cross the center of the format

Fig. 12–16. *JOHN SINGER SARGENT*. Portrait of Robert Louis Stevenson. *1885. Oil on canvas, 20 × 24". Collection of Mr. & Mrs. John Hay Whitney, New York.*

in diagonals closer to horizontal than vertical. The powerful attractive forces of the head and hands of the walking figure are linked by lines of tension to the light areas on the far right. These lines of force cross the center of the painting, which lies between the man and the frame of the doorway. The attractive force of the center aids in holding the man in position, as do the forces of the diagonals of the format. The latter are enlisted in the angle of the bottom of the wall and the edge of the carpet in the lower left. The centralizing force of the diagonals is also made use of in the slant of the man's shoulder, his trailing leg, the angle of the woman and chair, and the top and bottom edges of the open door. The symmetrically attractive forces of the center and of the diagonals serve, in the main, to balance the asymmetrical pattern of shapes, colors, and gestures that imply movement in the painting. Balance and the required restraint of implied motion are finally achieved by the subdominant network of relatively static vertical and horizontal lines of force traced across the format.

The quite wonderful qualities of active reflection and measured security that Sargent has managed to bring to this image of his friend Robert Louis Stevenson depend on the operation of the forces we have mentioned. Just how we might "explain" the quiet air of domesticated mystery and the feeling of impendence that pervades this painting would be another matter.

WILLIAM MERRITT CHASE. Hide and Seek. *The Phillips Collection, Washington, D.C. See Plate 24.*

Another work sharing some of the artistic strategies evident in the Sargent painting is the oil *Hide and Seek,* by William Merritt Chase (Color Plate 24). Without discussing it in detail we still should observe that Chase, like Sargent, has employed visual forces to express the balanced kind of asymmetry we experience in our own bodies when we are in motion. And both of these artists specify such qualities in terms of experiences that, in themselves, are not extraordinary.

By far, most of the objects imaged in Chase's painting occur above the diagonal that runs from the lower left to the upper right. He manages to balance the visual force of the colors, shapes, and textures of two human figures, a curtain, chair, a picture on a wall, and a draped doorway mainly with one huge expanse of highly textured reddish floor, which lies to the right. He has made use of the force of the diagonal that thrusts from lower left to upper right to increase the tension between the figures of the two little girls. The highly charged space between these visually forceful shapes owes much of its strength to the fact that it includes the center of the format. We are convinced of the stability of the lower, seemingly nearer girl: no space exists between her and the edge of the painting. She is anchored there. And, equally, we are susceptible to being convinced that the smaller, seemingly more distant girl is moving away, under tension, toward the light behind the draped doorway. With a keen sense of actual body-mind experiences inherent in playing this phase of the game of hide and seek, Chase has found equivalents in terms of purely visual force.

How comparatively simple is the situation we find in such paintings as Piet Mondrian's *Composition 2* (Color Plate 25). Here the artist has purposely limited his concern to balancing relatively few, flat, colored rectangles in a format that is only a fraction of an inch from being a perfect square. Still, Mondrian, as well as any other painter, succeeds by virtue of his sensitivity to, and skill in, working with the visual forces. Mondrian, it should be clear, is not interested in having his equilibrated field refer in any way to specific human experiences. In a sense, he is concerned only with the techniques involved in creating balanced fields of visual forces. His paintings refer to themselves with the pristine simplicity of the most efficient diagram. They provide us with excellent examples of equalized fields of force, and they can assist us in the study of much richer and more complex works of art.

PIET MONDRIAN. Composition 2. *The Solomon R. Guggenheim Museum, New York.* See Plate 25.

Fig. 12–17.   *ANTONIO DEL POLLAIUOLO.*
Hercules and Antaeus. c. 1475. Bronze, height
18" (with base). National Museum, Florence.
Photo: Alinari-Art Reference Bureau.

Turning to sculpture, let us consider the visual forces, especially tension and closure, in one freestanding work, the *Hercules and Antaeus,* by Antonio del Pollaiuolo (Fig. 12–17). This small bronze is excellently suited to our purposes since both the subject—a wrestling match between a god and the son of a goddess—and the sculptor's evident interest in the opposition and balance of forces conspire to give us a genuine tour de force.

In order to see freestanding sculpture in the way it is intended to be seen requires that we view it from all points around the sculpture and at the proper distance or distances from it. Because this sculpture is only 18 inches high, including the base, it should be viewed from closer up than if it were, shall we say, life-size. It is ideal to view it from a distance of between 3 and 4 feet, either walking around it or having it turned and tilted before our eyes. Disposing ourselves in this manner would make it possible for us to experience the almost unlimited variety of silhouettes and combinations of interior solids and voids that together make up this piece of sculpture. This is not possible in our immediate case. Instead, we see this intricate work from a single point of view—the view of the camera that took this particular photograph. And, of course, we look at a flat image of a different size than the original, which exists in three-dimensional space. Nevertheless, it is possible to see the excellent view presented here, and much can be inferred from that.

Unlike the basic situation in painting or any of the two-dimensional arts, there is no confining format to describe the outer limits of forces generated by freestanding sculpture. This sculpture stands in the clear air. And even though we can modify the effect of such sculpture by the space in which we place it—a small, low room, a large, high-ceilinged one, an intimate garden, or a wasteland—it still must function without the benefits or restraints afforded by a closely circumscribing format.[1] This means that the forces of tension and closure must of necessity function within the sculpture itself and, to a limited degree, across and through the negative spaces, or air, surrounding the sculpture.

Seeing the *Hercules and Antaeus* as we see it in this commanding view, it is clear that the sculpture is organized around a center. This center lies at the midpoint of abdominal contact between the two figures. The upper legs of both figures, as well as the upper parts of their torsos, point to, or radiate from, this center. Because there is no enclosing format to act in support of, or in resistance to, the force of this center, we are free to experience these radial lines of force as acting either centrifugally or centripetally. By a shift of quality in the attention we give this sculpture, it is possible at one moment to feel that the radiating parts are tending to fly off into space, and at another moment to feel that those parts are being drawn inward toward the center. We sense both tension and closure, or compression, working about the center. This is, of course, a kind of general description of what, specifically, this sculpture is about: Hercules presses Antaeus against him, and Antaeus struggles to free himself from this pressure. And it is the meeting and intensification of these two violently opposing forces that finally breaks Antaeus' back.

Forces of tension and closure interact between a variety of points evident to us in this silhouette of the sculpture. The force existing between the two heads owes its extreme effect to the fact that visually it induces a strong force of closure. At the same time, we understand the gesture of Antaeus' left arm as *resisting* this movement toward complete closure. Here the genius of Pollaiuolo has dramatically wedded purely visual forces with forces we know about kinesthetically and intellectually. All these work powerfully to a common end.

Between the head of Antaeus and his out-swinging right leg and foot, we experience a closing force. The backward thrust of the head establishes a direction that is picked up in the angle of the foot. This direction is so clear that it affects us as a single line across the shortest distance between these extremities. Again, this visual force of closure is supported by the intellectually understandable physical force seemingly exerted by Hercules against Antaeus, and by Antaeus against Hercules. It should be remarked that the powerfully convincing illusion of a real wrestling match going on here makes it possible for us to imagine these figures in actual motion. This being true, we are inclined to sense this particular force of closure turning into one of tension with the next implied movement of the wrestlers.

---

[1] It is true that many freestanding sculptures generate a kind of "cocoon" about and outside themselves. However, this cocoon is developed by forces from *within* the sculpture, and its evanescent outer limits exert next to no force *back into* the sculpture. It is more like a "radiance" than a boundary.

ANTONIO DEL POLLAIUOLO. Hercules and
Antaeus. *Photo: Alinari-Art Reference Bureau.
Figure 12–17 repeated.*

Between the feet of Antaeus we sense a tensional force which acts reciprocally with the force of closure operating between the right foot and head.
This tension is increased by virtue of the force of closure operating between
Antaeus' left foot and the feet of Hercules. At the base of the sculpture,
where the three feet and drapery tend to cluster, we experience strong
forces of closure. A kind of knot of forces is formed here. This knot marks
the bottom terminus of the center line of the sculptural group. It courses
upward through the sculpture, passing through dead center and out through
the gasping mouth of Antaeus. It is the force of this central axis, which
closely adheres to absolute vertical, that establishes the stability of the
whole configuration. And by contrast with diagonal and curving directions
of force, it increases our awareness of stress and strain and the qualities of
movement they imply.

Were we to have the actual sculpture before us, we could respond to
the visual forces at work in all three dimensions of this piece. For instance, a
great force works between Antaeus' right elbow, which juts far out in our
direction, and Hercules' arm, which lies behind. The same is true in the
spaces between the knees of both figures, and between all interior voids of
the sculpture. Unless we have actually seen this object, we must take it on
faith that its forces tend to *oscillate* as we move around it. By our movement,
a process similar to mutation changes forces of closure to forces of tension
and back again; the relationships of solids, voids, directions, sizes, and
shapes are changed with our changing viewpoint. Through all such phases,
however, the *Hercules and Antaeus* remains one of the most deceptively
complex and completely balanced fields of expressive visual force in the
history of sculpture. And that is to say nothing specific about how Pollaiuolo
has managed to fuse the figures of these two super-beings by seeming to
graft the upper half of each onto the lower half of the other. This inter-
identification of participants when engaged in mortal combat is at once a
great artistic achievement and a deeply moving philosophical expression

118

CHAPTER THIRTEEN

Proportion

In several of our preceding discussions we alluded to, or spoke directly of, situations in which matters of *relation* and *relationships* are of key importance. We were directly concerned with relationships when we spoke of the graduated scales of visual qualities, and again when we discussed monotony, harmony, contrast, and discord. The matter of relationships existing between parts of visual configurations is of prime importance to what we said about unity and balance. And our last discussion, of reciprocal operations of visual forces, would have been meaningless against any conceptual background except one which was primarily concerned with relationships and their functions in the visual arts.

Now, it is true that without having used the word *proportion* up to this point, we have been dealing with it tacitly in all of our references to relationships of every kind. To deal directly with proportion may be to call up in many of our minds certain, not entirely happy, situations. For many, the mention of the word *proportion* starts up thoughts about the proportion of the human figure. And because some of us remember with little joy our guided or unguided attempts at drawing or modeling the human figure, the word proportion rings magically and often frighteningly in our minds. The words "out of proportion" and "correct proportion" have been used so often —almost always by people who never quite manage to say *how* a thing is *in proportion* and who never get around to telling what makes "correct" proportion "correct." In the ensuing discussion of proportion we mean to be much more inclusive than were, for instance, the half-stated concepts of proportion and the human figure we may remember from another time. We do not intend to become specifically concerned with proportions of the human figure, but since the subject has been broached, something more should be said.

Long ago when someone peered over our shoulder at the drawing of a

Fig. 13–1. Poseidon (Zeus?). *c. 460–450 B.C. Bronze, height 82". National Museum, Athens. Photo: Hirmer, Munich.*

man we were making and advised us that the man's legs were "too short," what did he mean? And when he told us that the nose was "too long," what did he mean? If what we were doing at the time was drawing directly from a live model and our intention was to make our drawing look as much as possible like that model, then we knew what he meant. He simply meant that our drawing did not accurately reproduce the proportions of the model; we had not copied it well. This is easy to understand; there need be no argument over this. And to remedy the situation—to get our drawn image to repeat the proportions of the model—all we need is a calipers or other measuring device, time, and patience. But if a friend looks at a drawing of an *imaginary* figure we have made, and if he says it is "out of proportion," what does he mean then? Or what does he mean when he says the proportions are "wrong" in a drawing we have made *without* using a live model or any other model? In both of these cases it usually means that he is comparing our work with some *ideal* or *preconceived* set of proportions for the human figure. For, as we know, nothing can be out of proportion or wrong except in comparison to something which is in proportion, and hence correct.

Now, even though we may not be interested in making use of our friend's unstated canons of proportion, it should be of interest to us (since we are interested in our friends even when we are not ready to act on what they say) to know what he thinks the ideally correct proportions are. Usually, it is impossible to discover for certain just what system our friend is using as the basis for measuring our work. Most often he does not even know, or cannot say, by what ideal standard his criticism is motivated. But if we grant that our friend is not under the influence of some current fad such as those that show up in commercial fashion drawings, "girlie" magazines, or mail-order physical fitness advertisements, it is safe to assume that his unstated ideal is Greek in origin. It appears true that in most cases the stated or unstated ideal proportions of the human figure are closely related to those developed by artists living in Greece five centuries before the birth of Christ. Not only did the Greeks of that time establish ideal proportions for the figure, but in a real sense they also invented the nude as an art form.[1] And it appears true that the figures created out of the imaginative experience of those Greeks still haunt and beguile us as "correct" and perfect models of human proportions.

These proportions are evident in the over life-size bronze *Poseidon* (Fig. 13–1). The order of articulated relationships between the parts of this figure—their sizes and shapes as well as their apparent weight and functions—was first established by the Greeks. The Romans copied and varied this order, and it was principally the artists of the Italian Renaissance who brought it into modern times. There is no doubt that for the Greeks of 450 B.C., the proportions of the *Poseidon* represented the ideal. But what

---

[1] See: Kenneth Clark, *The Nude: A Study in Ideal Form* (New York: Pantheon Books, 1956), especially Chap. I.

Fig. 13–2. *Jamb statues, West Portal, Chartres Cathedral. c. 1145–1170. Photo: Giraudon, Paris.*

about such figures as those from the jambs of the west portal of Chartres Cathedral (Fig. 13–2)? Are they less than ideal or unideal, incorrect because they are at variance with the Greek? Is the head of the *Virgin* (Fig. 13–3) from the twelfth-century church of San Clemente de Tahul in Spain out of proportion because it does not follow the proportions of the *Athena Lemnia* (Fig. 13–4), which repeats those of the ancient Greek? Categorically, none of these is incorrect—not the Greek, the French Gothic figures, or the Spanish Romanesque *Virgin*. Each of these orders of proportion is correct within the context of the particular work and its intended function. Proportion, as we shall see, is an artistic matter; and in the case of the human figure, men create images of it in whatever proportions best embody and express their particular concept of the human figure or of man's condition in general.

122

Fig. 13–3. Head of the Virgin, *from S. Clemente de Tahul. 1123. Fresco. Museum of the Art of Catalonia, Barcelona.*

Fig. 13–4. Athena Lemnia *(head). Roman copy after an original of 450 B.C. by Phidias. Marble. Museo Civico, Bologna. Photo: Alinari-Art Reference Bureau.*

Taking it from the beginning, proportion means simply a portion or part in its relation to the whole. It has to do with the relations existing between things or magnitudes, as to size, quantity, number, and so on. For our purposes we can reduce such definitions to a simple sentence: *proportion refers to relationships of size, amount, and degree.* And when we speak of size, amount, and degree, we are referring to the visual elements and to qualities that are either attributes of those elements or are generated by them. In all cases, our focus is on relationships.

The simplest of all proportional relationships are those of size. In Fig. 13–5, shape *a* is smaller than shape *b*. Conversely, shape *b* is larger than shape *a*. More precisely, shape *b* is three times as large as *a*, and conversely, *a* is one-third as large as *b*. The proportion existing between these sizes is 1 to 3 or 3 to 1.

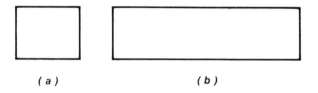

(a)   (b)   Fig. 13–5.

In the next diagram (Fig. 13–6), shapes *a* and *b* are of the same size. The proportion existing between them is 1 to 1. But there are more dots in *a* than in *b*. An unequal *proportion of amount* of dots exists between these equal-size shapes. By actual count this proportion turns out to be 4 to 1: there are 80 dots in *a* and 20 in *b*. This is a proportion of *amount*.

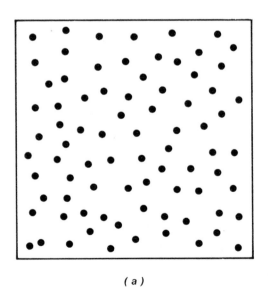 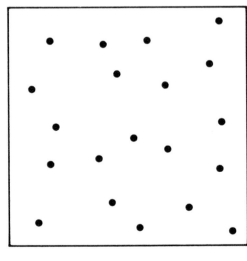

(a)   (b)

Fig. 13–6.

In the next diagram (Fig. 13–7), lines *AY* and *BX* are the same length; we can say that they enjoy the same *amount* of length or, roughly, that they are the same size. In this category they are in a 1 to 1 proportion. However, the lines exhibit more than just length. We see that they are both curved, but that line *BX* curves more than *AY*. Between these lines there exists a proportional relation of curvature. This is a proportion of *degree*.

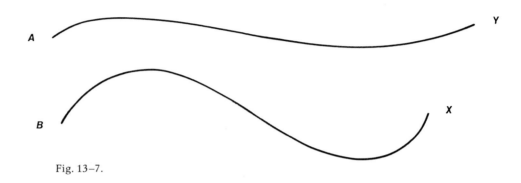

Fig. 13–7.

Likewise, a proportion of degree exists between the *values* of the two circles (Fig. 13–8)—*a* is lighter than *b*. On a scale running from white to black, we could determine that *a* is about twice as light as *b*; the proportion of degree of lightness is about 2 to 1.

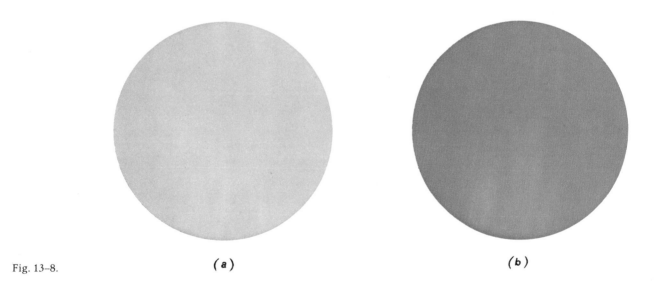

Fig. 13–8.   *(a)*   *(b)*

Proportions of degree also exist within ranges of intensity: one color can be as intense as another, or more intense, or less intense. The same is true for texture, density, and even for the invisible forces of tension and closure.

Now, proportion is one of the expressive means available to the artist. Different proportional relationships of size, amount, and degree affect us in

GEORGE INNESS. The Coming Storm. *Albright-Knox Art Gallery, Buffalo, New York. See Plate 26.*

different ways. And even though it may be true that no two people can respond in exactly the same way to any given proportional relationship, there is still a wide area in which our responses overlap and are akin to each other. When, for example, we look at *The Coming Storm* (Color Plate 26), by George Inness, perhaps not one of us escapes the drama produced by the visual elements and their qualities as they work to give us this image of a particular place and event in nature. With a nearly equal division of the painting—an almost 1 to 1 proportion between its large upper and lower areas—something of an unresolved drama of forces is communicated to us. Within this all-encompassing drama, our eyes soon find the figure of a man in the lower left. By comparison to the total area of the painting, this figure is exceedingly small—in a proportion of about 1 to 3,000. Were it not for the fact that this very small area is in the recognizable shape of a man, it would have no more interest for us than the rock shapes in the lower right. But it *is* in the shape of a man, and we cannot help but think of it as a man in a huge, surrounding natural environment. Nor can we help but feel how this man is overpowered by the forces of nature all around him. In this deep and dynamic romantic landscape, man figures as an ineffectual or lost entity; this is part of what Inness expresses by means of this painting.

Plate 25. *PIET MONDRIAN*. Composition 2. *1922. Oil on canvas, 21³/₄×21". Mondrian is not interested in having such paintings as this refer in any way to specific human experiences. He is concerned with the techniques involved in creating equilibrated fields of visual force. His paintings refer to themselves with the pristine simplicity of the most efficient diagram. (The Solomon R. Guggenheim Museum, New York.)*

Plate 26. GEORGE INNESS. The Coming Storm. 1878. Oil on canvas, 26×39″. In this deep and dynamic romantic land- scape, man figures as an ineffectual, or lost, entity. This is part of what Inness expresses by means of this painting. It is achieved primarily by proportion—by the great discrepancy of size that exists between the man in the lower left and his surrounding environment. (Albright-Knox Art Gallery, Buffalo. Albert Tracy Fund.)

Plate 27. AUGUSTE RENOIR. The Moulin de la Galette. 1876. Oil on canvas, 51¹/₂×69″. In this painting, Renoir found it suitable to closely intermingle images of men and women with their environment. The closely related proportions of size, amount, and degree contribute to an expression of compatibility among human beings, the things they have made, and the lighted place in which they congregate. (The Louvre, Paris. Photo: Art Reference Bureau.)

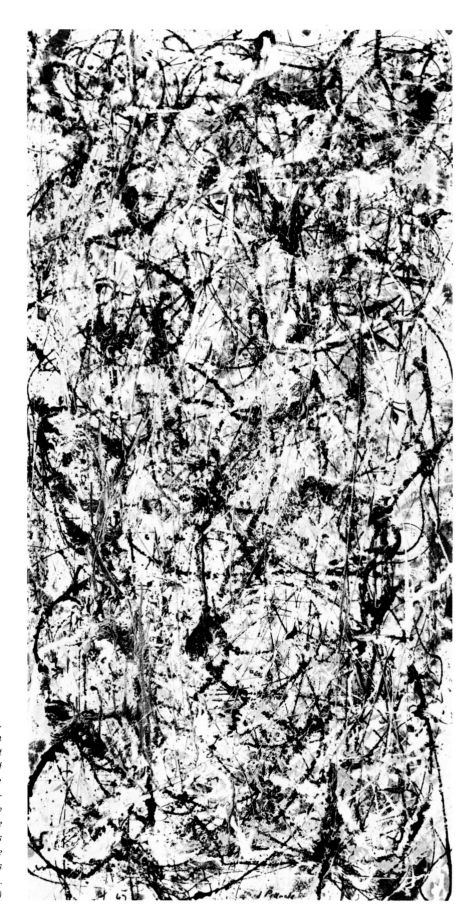

Plate 28.   *JACKSON POLLOCK.*
Cathedral. *1947. Mixed media on
canvas, 71½×35¹/₁₆″. In no part
of this painting's entire area of
18 square feet are we made aware
of gaps created by disparate proportions. As a result we follow
the lead of a lost and found line
that takes us on a more or less
continuous course through the
painting and back again. (Dallas
Museum of Fine Arts. Gift of Mr.
& Mrs. Bernard J. Reis, New York.)*

It is achieved primarily by proportion—by the discrepancy of size that exists between the man and his environment.

How different is our response to Millet's *The Sower* (Fig. 13–9), in which the figure of the man occupies so much of the area of the painting. Instead of a 1 to 3,000 proportion as in the Inness, we have a proportion of about 1 to 3 in the Millet. The figure of the sower, we can say, is a thousand times bigger than the figure in the painting by Inness. The difference of effect, because of this difference of size relation between figure and landscape, is enormous. If in the Inness we feel man to be insignificant and lost within the tremendous expanses and force of nature, in the Millet we feel him to be a dominating hero as he stands in, yet strongly against, nature.

Speaking in more general terms, we can say that when a work of art depends for its effect upon proportions created by great differences of size, amount, and degree, then the smallness of the small and the largeness of the large are accentuated. We experience strong contrasts. And more than that, we are made aware of *gaps* existing between elements or qualities. By extension, we are also made aware of gaps existing between things and concepts—gaps in our own experience. It may not be necessary to add that none of this is extraordinary.

Fig. 13–9. *FRANÇOIS MILLET. The Sower. c. 1850. Oil on canvas, 40×32¹/₂". Museum of Fine Arts, Boston.*

Fig. 13–10. *FRANCISCO GOYA.* The Giant. *Before 1818. Aquatint, $11^5/_{32} \times 8^1/_8''$. The Metropolitan Museum of Art, New York (Harris Brisbane Dick Fund, 1935).*

We are made conscious of such gaps when we look at Francisco Goya's *The Giant* (Fig. 13–10). Our very first impression—that this hulking nude figure is seated on a log—is quickly dispelled; he is sitting just over the horizon. The "log" is a great stretch of Spanish countryside. We can see houses immediately below him, and they are no larger than his eyes. By means of proportion, by means of relating immensity with the miniature, Goya has made us conscious of "gapness," a great discrepancy. In this case his artistic aim was quite specific: to move us to something close to terror by a vision of tremendous brutishness on the intimate land. But an artist's aim need not be specific, in the way Goya's was, in order to express qualities of hiatus in experience. José Clemente Orozco does it in a much more general way in his *Metaphysical Landscape* (Fig. 13–11). It is true that we see this at first as a landscape with the earth occupying about one-eighth and the sky about seven-eighths of the format; but this easy recognition is quickly thrown into question by the huge, dark, four-sided figure high in the painting. We are left with a powerful feeling of ambiguity which petitions us for something that remains unnamed. This painting transports us to an area of our experience which lies between the real and the unreal. And some of its capacity to do this for us lies in the character of its proportions: very large to very small, as in the relation of the sky area to the ground, and the relation of degrees of sharpness, as in the geometric figure in the sky and the very ungeometric, cloudlike shapes around it.

There is, of course, another kind of proportion at work in this painting —that of degrees of objective reality. The upper area looks like a cloudy sky—all except for the large dark shape that looks like a hole sawed in the sky, a trapdoor. This shape, besides being very different in visual quality from the textured area around it, is decidedly nonobjective in character: it looks like nothing we have ever seen in any sky. This contrast of the ordinary and the impossible, or miraculous, in such close spatial proximity contributes in great degree to the mysterious quality of the work. And, again,

Fig. 13–11. *JOSÉ CLEMENTE OROZCO.* Metaphysical Landscape. *1948. Pyroxlin on masonite, 87×49". Museo "José Clemente Orozco," Mexico City.*

it is the proportion created between such widely divergent modes as the ordinary and the miraculous that heightens our awareness of a noncontinuous quality in experience.

On the other hand, proportions created by little differences of size, amount, or degree emphasize qualities of harmony and sympathy. By their easy compatibility they encourage and support our predilections for affinity and continuity. This is often accomplished in works of art by providing many intervals between the greater and smaller measures. Instead of revealing large gaps, this strategy provides many closely related proportions across which the viewer can move in easy steps. Gaps are closed or obliterated in this way, and we are left with a feeling of community and uninterrupted duration. It is this quality of sentience that pervades the painting *Le Moulin de la Galette* by Auguste Renoir (Color Plate 27). At the same time that we see large areas of dark blue and violet and small areas of pink, orange, and off-white, we are aware of a great variety of in-between sizes and colors. We are given so many intermediate proportions that the effect of the most contrasting ones is compromised. And in this configuration, which has the character of a tapestry woven of common threads, Renoir has found it suitable to closely intermingle images of men and women with their environment. Proportionately, we sense a continuity existing among human beings, the things they have made, and the lighted place in which they congregate. Little wonder that Impressionist paintings such as this have been described as visions of an earthly paradise, the miraculousness of which lies only in their utterly believable naturalness.

AUGUSTE RENOIR. The Moulin de la Galette. *The Louvre, Paris. Photo: Agraci-Art Reference Bureau. See Plate 27.*

In quite another mode, Jackson Pollock achieves the same quality of harmonious continuity in his painting *Cathedral* (Color Plate 28) by means of close relationships of size, amount, and degree. In no part of its entire area of 18 square feet are we aware of disparate proportions. As a result, we follow the lead of a lost and found line that takes us on a continuous course through the painting and back again.

Now, it perhaps goes without saying that every proportion is the result of at least a two-term situation: in order to have a proportion of any kind there must be a basis for comparison. In the case of a single sheet of paper we have a relation of length and width. In the case of two sheets of paper we have relations of areas, but we cannot relate or compare the area of a single sheet of paper to itself. All of this is almost ridiculously obvious, but what is not so obvious is that in a very special way proportions are *three-term* situations.

JACKSON POLLOCK. Cathedral. *Dallas Museum of Fine Arts (Gift of Mr. & Mrs. Bernard J. Reis, New York). See Plate 28.*

Fig. 13–12. *Left:* Woman with Child. *Black ceramic figure from Coyotepec, Oaxaca. 1957. Height 30¹/₂″. Private collection. Right:* Male Deity. *Ceramic figure from Jacotepec, Jalisco. Height 9¹/₂″. Private collection.*

132

When we look at the two ceramic figures from Mexico (Fig. 13–12), we are immediately conscious of the fact that one is taller than the other. Since the figure on the left is about 30 inches tall and the one on the right about 10 inches, we sense this 3 to 1 proportion. But more than just this relation between the two sculptures, we sense *our own* body height in relation to both. The taller of these two figures is less than half as tall as we are, and the other proportionately less. And whether or not we are thinking about ourselves as we look at these figures, we still do sense that both of them are smaller than we are; our own physical size functions as one of the unseen terms in this situation. More than this, our awareness of *how* we are in many ways—our weight, how we are jointed, the texture and color of our skin, the generally resilient quality of our colloidal bodies—all these matters of self-awareness function as terms in proportions that seem to lie entirely outside of us. We ourselves are bigger than some things, smaller than others. We can climb up the sides of some objects; others we can hold in one of our hands; and some are so small we must bring our eyes down upon them to see them at all. The object before us is so much harder or softer than we are; it is colder or warmer, redder or darker than we are. And when we really look at things, and feel and think our way into them, we cannot help but become involved with them. We cannot deny our role in the perception of things outside of us without some loss to both the object and ourselves.

So what we have been saying is that in looking at things—in our case, works of art—we are made aware of our own size and of the amounts and degrees of whatever comparable phenomena exist in us. All matters of proportion involve our person. And the artist is sensitive to this as he works. Proportion is an expressive means; we respond to it in terms of the special conditions that accompany and establish our human scale, whether we know it or not.

At the beginning of this discussion we spoke of proportion and what determines its "correctness." We said that proportion is correct within the context of the particular work and its intended function. Now, and in light of what has been said in between, we can be somewhat more specific. First, proportion is correct when the specific size, amount, and degree relationships are *engaging in themselves*. By this we mean that any proportion that engages our interest in a winning way is by that fact correct. Such relations of size, amount, and degree attract our attention, win our continuing interest, and reward us in some obliging way. In another context, all of us have met people who were—right from the first moment we saw and talked to them—engaging in themselves. Expecting nothing specific of them, we merely opened ourselves to whatever they wished to be in our presence, and we found them to be engaging. They charmed us; they engaged us in a winning way. Some proportions do the same for us. This is true, for example, of the construction in wood, glass, wire, and string by Alberto Giacometti which he calls *The Palace at 4 A.M.* (Fig. 13–13). The proportional relationships existing between the sticklike solids and the blocky voids engage us

Fig. 13–13.
ALBERTO GIACOMETTI. The Palace at 4 A.M. *1932–1933. Construction in wood, glass, wire, and string, 35 × 28¹/₄″. The Museum of Modern Art, New York (Purchase).*

for their own sake and in terms of themselves. The range of straight-sided shapes—rectangles, trapezoids, and triangles—gives us harmony with engaging and often unexpected contrasts. It is a distinct pleasure for our eyes. And even if we can never know exactly what Giacometti had in mind when he called this *The Palace at 4 A.M.,* we are charmed by its appearance. Its proportions, as well as its other distinguishing qualities, are engaging in themselves.

In the second instance, proportion is correct when it has been developed for purposes of a *specific expression.* We are free to make whatever judgments we wish concerning the proportions of the women in Georges Rouault's watercolor painting *Two Prostitutes* (Fig. 13–14), but we cannot avoid being affected by them in ways that were certainly part of Rouault's purpose. If this image of hideousness, brutality, and depravity brings us to pain and causes an experience of fearful shame, then Rouault has succeeded. The proportions of these swollen lumps are expressive of imperfection, of everything contrary to healthy structure, and Rouault would have us know this by the image he has created. By the particular variety of relationships of size, amount, and degree evident in all the visual qualities of these painted women, he makes us feel the absence of their opposites. His vision of physical degeneracy serves to recall images expressive of human perfectibility. In fact, the *Two Prostitutes* "re-minds" us of such visions of perfection as Botticelli's Venus (Fig. 13–15), from *The Birth of Venus,* and the *Aphrodite of the Cnidians* (Fig. 13–16).

134

Fig. 13–14. GEORGES ROUAULT. Two Prostitutes. *1906. Watercolor and pastel, 26¹/₂×22¹/₄"* *Collection of Dr. & Mrs. Harry Bakwin, New York.*

Fig. 13–15. *SANDRO BOTTICELLI.* The Birth of Venus. *c.1480. Oil on canvas, 79×110".*
Uffizi Gallery, Florence. Photo: Alinari-Art Reference Bureau.

Fig. 13–16. Aphrodite of the Cnidians. *Roman copy after an original of c. 330 B.C. by Praxiteles. Marble, height 80". Vatican Museums, Rome. Photo: Alinari.*

In a less awesome, but nonetheless expressive way, Luis Eades works with proportions that serve his artistic purposes. In his *Salute to Dawn, the Rosy-fingered* (Color Plate 29), we see an image of a man whose bodily proportions vary so greatly from the norm that we are apt to think of him as a dwarf. The stumpy limbs, with their indications of limited articulation, cause us to feel this little man's inadequacy in making his desired salute to the dawn—a kind of insufficiency all of us have felt. Still, against this, the little man has an immense head, and his face registers a simple but powerful expression of happy reception of the dynamic dawning all around him. Eades' power as an artist is not limited to his strategic use of proportion, but without that this painting could never have been accomplished.

Our broadly inclusive definitions of correct proportion—when proportions are engaging in themselves, and when they serve the purposes of a specific expression—are not meant to be mutually exclusive. Proportions that serve to accomplish a specific expression can also be, and most often are, engaging in themselves. The converse of this is equally true. And as for "ideal" proportions, what can we say? Ideal proportions, like any other ideal conditions, are those that best serve the best in us; and there is always the possibility that when our most genuine requirements are fully and most graciously met we are then in situations that satisfy many others besides ourselves. It appears that each age or epoch, certainly each culture, develops its own range of ideal proportions. The ancient Greeks developed theirs, and so did the early Christians and the Renaissance Italians, even as we of the twentieth century work at ours. Some of these ideal proportions stay with us longer than others, perhaps because of some absolute appeal. That is why, we presume, the proportions 2 to 3 and 3 to 5, rather than 1 to 1 or 11 to 12, are generally considered "more beautiful." But however this is, matters of proportion in art involve us as we sense ourselves as the module by which we become humanly aware of proportions outside ourselves. And proportion, far from being a name for some special system, is one of the artist's means of expressing his experience, as well as a means of our experiencing his expression.

CHAPTER FOURTEEN

Space
and the Illusion
of Space

The visual arts are often called the *spatial* arts because they exist in space. They are, as we said in Chapter 2, presented to us totally and immediately in space. Without space there could be no visual art. And when we remember that there can be no space without time, and no time without space, we know that to talk of either is also to talk of the other. Under the word *space* in the Oxford Dictionary, the first words of definition are these: "denoting time or duration." Under the word *time* the dictionary gives this first definition: "a space." So when we say that the visual arts exist in space, we mean that they exist in *space-time* or in *time-space*. This is hardly unique or even a special thing to be able to say of the visual arts, since it can be said with equal truth about any thing or any condition. Space-time is not a *special* requirement; it is *the* requirement, the *sine qua non*. In this respect it is comparable to the requirement of life for human personality. Our interest in talking about space, then, is not to prove that it is the sphere in which the visual arts exist, but rather to explore *how* they exist there.

Space is all-pervasive and everlasting. It is present before the work of art is created, and it functions during the act of creation and in the finished work. It remains after the work has vanished. How we ourselves, as living, moving bodies, perceive and react to our perceptions of space crucially determines what we call our orientation to the world. And since it is in works of art that we can visually experience how others have oriented themselves to their worlds, it is of prime significance that we consider at length this matter of space.

For our purposes, we can think of space as *extension in one, in many, or in all directions.* Simply, space is what lies between us and the person next to us. It fills the intervals between our fingers, as well as those between the stars. It flows among and through the houses of the town, into the foxhole, and around the wings of the butterfly. We occupy it, and it occupies us.

Because our interests lie primarily with the visual arts of painting, drawing, the graphics, and sculpture, we can consider space under the related categories of two-dimensional space and three-dimensional space. Drawing, painting, and the graphics are almost exclusively two-dimensional; with them we are concerned with spatial conditions that obtain within the two-dimensional plane of the support—the canvas, panel, or paper. Their dimensions, directions, and areas actually exist only in a plane; their extensions do not, in fact, pierce or violate the plane; they do not, in fact, include extension in back of or in front of the plane of the support. Whatever of "depth" or three-dimensional qualities may appear to be present in a painting or drawing is a matter of *illusion,* not a matter of objective conditions. Of this we will speak later. It is in sculpture and, of course, in architecture that we become involved with space which actually does exist in three dimensions. Their spatial extensions are not bound to any single plane; they can operate in any and all directions. And just as with two-dimensional space, illusions of various sorts can also exist in three dimensions. For instance, illusions of more or less depth or more or less spatial curvature than actually exist in a specific sculpture or building can be created by artifice. We will come back to this when we discuss illusions of space.

Let us grant from the beginning that in a metaphorical sense at least, everything of our existence may be illusory. And having made that expression of an overriding possibility, let us settle down to the kinds of situations that are based upon what we like to call stubborn fact. And since most of us may be more at home in the three-dimensional world in which we walk and breathe, let us begin with some observations concerning sculpture.

Sculpture occupies three-dimensional space just as our own bodies do. Its volumes and voids, its convexities and concavities are subject to the same spatial conditions that we are subject to. Like any other object in the three-dimensional world, it can be as large or as small, as close to us or as far away, as any other object. Our sharing of the actual volumetric space in which sculpture exists contributes to a special kind of sympathy for it. It may be easier for many of us to identify our experiences of space with what we observe taking place in and around sculpture than it is to do the same with works limited to an actual world of only two dimensions, as in painting. Sculpture makes a more direct or primitive appeal to us. We are inclined to believe in its substance. In our visual transactions with sculpture we can permit a kind of bartering operation, an exchange of real goods: little or no intermediate agent—such as money, to continue the metaphor—seems necessary. All we are saying here is that this *seems* to be true in the case of sculpture; it is not necessarily true. And it does not mean that our experiencing of sculpture is simple, nor that it is poorer or richer than experiences of two-dimensional forms of art.

When we look at the life-size sculpture *Assia,* by Charles Despiau (Fig. 14–1), and especially if we approach it from a distance and then walk around it, we accept it in the direct way that we accept other objects in the physical world. There it is, in full round, before us. When we move around

Fig. 14–1. *CHARLES DESPIAU.* Assia. *1938. Bronze, height 72³/₄". The Museum of Modern Art, New York (Gift of Mrs. Simon Guggenheim).*

this bronze object, its volumes, voids, and surfaces fall into different relationships by the inexorable logic of human vision. When we stand at the figure's left, we cannot see the right arm; it is visually blocked out by the intervening mass of opaque bronze. The left arm disappears when we stand at the right. In order to see the face, we must stand so that it is not blocked out by one of the shoulders or the back of the head. If, while looking at this sculpture, we take a series of steps backward, it appears to get smaller in the same way that the railroad station seems to get smaller as we watch it from the departing train. Moving closer and closer to the figure, it appears to grow

Fig. 14–2. *ARISTIDE MAILLOL. The River. c. 1939–1943. Lead, 53³/₄×90". The Museum of Modern Art, New York (Mrs. Simon Guggenheim Fund).*

in size until it extends outside our field of vision and we can see only a small part of it. And from no matter what position we view this, or any, sculpture. the phenomenon we call *foreshortening* is operative. By that term we allude to the fact that any part of a three-dimensional object that does not lie in a plane perpendicular to our line of sight appears to be shortened. Our photograph of Despiau's *Assia* shows the figure as it would appear were we looking at it with one eye from a position several feet directly in front of a point lying midway between the breasts. Our plane of sight lies perpendicular to that line of sight. The parts of the figure lying in that plane do not appear foreshortened; all other parts do. This is why we see the figure's left lower leg and left upper arm as short as they are shown here. The angles at which those volumes lie are not perpendicular to our line of sight. A more dramatic example of this can be seen in the photograph of Aristide Maillol's allegorical figure *The River* (Fig. 14–2). In this case, the plane of our sight is roughly parallel to the front face of the rectangular base upon which the figure is poised. This plane lies perpendicular to our line of sight, which strikes the figure a little left of center. Because the right upper arm (high in the photograph) and left lower arm (low in the photograph) lie in planes almost opposite to our plane of sight, they appear very short. In effect, these volumes have been telescoped because we are looking along their longer axes. We are seeing them more from an end than from a side. This appearance of foreshortening would be much more convincing to us, were we looking at the actual, three-dimensional sculpture, since our vision is binocular and the camera is monocular. With two eyes, we see in "stereo." This being true, we would see further around these volumes than the single lens camera that took this picture, and the phenomenon of foreshortening would be more completely revealed to us.

What we are saying through all this is that the sculptor deals with actual three-dimensional space as perceived by our stereoscopic vision. His refined sensitivity to the material in which he works and how his shaped material functions expressively in space is what gives us experiences that are at once celebrations of art and of vision. The unknown sculptor of the bronze figure *Shiva Nataraja* (Fig. 14–3) moves us both by the image of this cosmic dance performed by a supreme deity within the orb of the sun and by the sheer visual excitement its forms engender in us. The artist's easy

Fig. 14–3. Shiva Nataraja. *11th century. Bronze, 43⁷/₈ × 40". The Cleveland Museum of Art (Purchase from the J. H. Wade Fund).*

Fig. 14–4. *GASTON LACHAISE.* Standing Woman. *1932. Bronze, height 88″. The Museum of Modern Art, New York (Mrs. Simon Guggenheim Fund).*

dependence upon the function of ordinary vision to reveal this extraordinary vision of a deity is evident at every point. Shiva Nataraja "dances" because he is given a form in actual space which is clearly evident of movement. He balances on one leg, which, as we see, is behind the other because his raised leg *overlaps* the one that supports him. One of his arms moves out toward us at an angle. We know this is true because it overlaps and blocks out part of his chest, because it catches the light from above as his chest cannot, and because it appears foreshortened in space. We sense the twisting of his body because its axes are turned in a variety of directions that intersect the plane of our sight. This implied movement is made the more convincing because of the insistent plane of the disc through which he pokes his elbows, knee and shoulder, buttocks, hands, and one foot. We see and feel, even as we do in our own bodies, how convex volumes push out into the air or space around them. We can see how the space surrounding the deity is punctured and how it pushes against the firm bronze shapes. All this goes on in actual, volumetric space. There are no spatial illusions here; only the natural functioning of our stereoscopic vision and the play of tensions between closed and open spaces, between the solids and voids of this sculpture.

The form the sculptor gives his work acts upon the space it stands in, and the enveloping space acts upon the sculpture. The nature of this interaction is responsible for whatever generally expressive power the sculpture may possess. Consideration of certain kinds of spatial interaction should help us see further how the sculptor works with actual three-dimensional space. In reference to the *Shiva Nataraja,* we touched upon the function of convex solids in space. More should be said of that next.

In a most unmistakable way, Gaston Lachaise has depended for expression on the function of rounded volumes in his over-life-size bronze *Standing Woman* (Fig. 14–4). It is the rich structuring of these convex shapes that gives to this image its almost overpowering command. Standing in the presence of this seven-foot figure, we cannot escape its power of self-assertion. It appears to swell muscularly against any imprisonment in the surrounding space. Even with the negative space pushing inward at every point on the surface of this very positive figure, there still appears no chance for it to invade the continually expanding body of material. The negative spaces trapped between the figure's arms and torso, and between the legs and base are, of course, the exact complements of the solid volumes that enclose and define them. The shape of these voids is concave. They appear to give way or collapse inward to accommodate the expanding convex volumes. It is this particular interplay of solids and voids that produces a visual phenomenon similar to breathing or a heaving and collapsing of actual three-dimensional space. The standing position of this figure, its size and attitude are certainly compelling. By simple identification of our own bodies with this image, we are caused to feel its overwhelming authority. But more than this, it is the quality of collapsing space around the figure that gives it its unquestionable power.

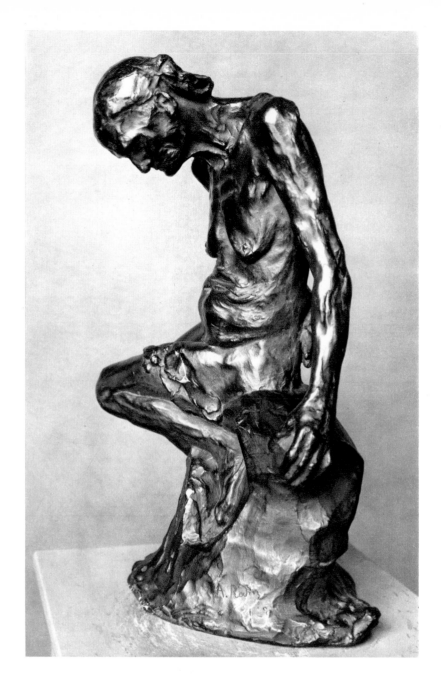

Fig. 14–5. *AUGUSTE RODIN*. La Belle Heaulmière. *1885. Bronze. Rodin Museum, Paris.*

How different is the effect upon us of Auguste Rodin's bronze *La Belle Heaulmière* (Fig. 14–5). Here we respond to a monumental *lack* of authority, power, and command. The shrinking passivity of this figure owes much to the fact that it is seated, not standing, that it is in a self-reflective attitude, and that we recognize the image as that of an old decrepit woman. But, again, the kind of relation existing between solids and voids, between the substance of the sculpture and the enveloping space, is decisive. And just what sort of relation is this? In short, it is almost the direct opposite of what we saw in Lachaise's *Standing Woman.* In the Lachaise, the substance of the sculpture bulges outward to compress and collapse the surrounding space; in the Rodin, the "substance" of the sculpture appears to collapse under the pressures of its spatial envelope. The greater amount of the surface of *La Belle Heaulmière* is made up of dished-out forms. Arms and legs, breasts and thighs—as well as the base of the sculpture—are composed of volumes that are predominantly concave in character. These concavities appear as evidences of invasion. The figure of the old woman appears to be losing a battle, to be losing her bodily substance to a process of forced diminishment. This effect could not have been achieved without a predominance of scooped-out and furrowed volumes. And this is the effect Rodin desired—the end image of exhaustion and decay of a once aggressive court prostitute.

For Rodin, the interplaying forces of convex negative space and concave positive space are enlisted in the service of a very specific expressive goal. This same kind of interplay can, of course, work to a quite general expressive end. We see this in David Smith's welded steel sculpture *Animal Weights* (Fig. 14–6). Here the very pronounced concavity of the positive space describes the convex negative with such force that we feel the sculpture is in danger of being compressed out of existence. The stark concave silhouette of the sculpture appears to be what is left of a material out of which was cut the more aggressive convex shape of the surrounding space. In a context left unspecified by the sculptor, we respond to a drama of forces in which welded steel is apparently being squeezed to nothingness by the pressure of the air around it. By virtue of this drama, we are caused to know the negative space, the air, as the material substance it is—dense enough to feel like stone against our falling bodies, and strong enough to carry cargo planes loaded with heavily armored tanks.

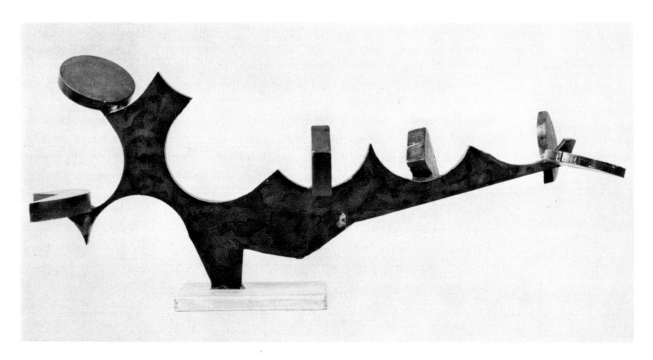

Fig. 14–6. *DAVID SMITH*. Animal Weights. *1957. Steel, 21¹/₄×49". Collection of Joseph H. Hirshhorn, New York.*

HENRY MOORE. Reclining
Figure. *Figure 5–5 repeated.*

The conscious exploitation of spatial forces in sculpture, a preoccupation of many of our contemporary artists, is clearly apparent in Henry Moore's *Reclining Figure* (Fig. 5–5). In this, as in many of Moore's works, he gives us a figure that includes both convexities and concavities of considerable strength, but the controlling form of the total configuration is concave. As a whole, his *Reclining Figure* assumes the shape of an irregularly elongated, shallow bowl. This lends to the figure an overall receptive quality—as if it could take other substantial and convex shapes into itself. In fact, it appears to be asking for its complement in material that is at least as substantial as its own solids. It is appropriately suggestive of a female figure. But Henry Moore does more than exploit the form possibilities of concave space; he goes the full measure and has the concavities penetrate the material of the sculpture. Moore's interplay of spatial forces includes what we cannot help but see as *holes*. In this particular piece two holes pierce the figure in positions comparable to those occupied by breasts in a live woman. The spatial reversing of these distinguishing forms—even in this highly nonobjective work—comes as a mild shock only *after* we have visually accepted these holes as breasts in the same way we accept the attenuated shapes on either side as arms. How can this be explained? What appears to take place in our first look at this sculpture is an instantaneous event in which these holes, even though they are "empty," exert a visual force *stronger* than the surrounding positive volumes. By unexpected contrast, they assume a force at least as strong as solid protruding volumes would generate. Here is a strategic employment of forces in three-dimensional space never before our age brought to bear with such willfulness and such success. It asserts the power of unfilled negative space and, by our easy response to it, does credit to the artist and to our own still only lightly-taxed perceptual capacities.

The function of the holes in Henry Moore's sculpture is not the same as the function of openings in older sculpture. Even though all sculptors worthy of the name have composed with negative space as well as with the space occupied by the material of their sculpture, Moore and others like him emphasize the substantive quality of unfilled space. This is partly due to a present-day concern for the work of art as a self-sufficient *object,* not as an *image* of something specific derived from the world around us. This concern leads to the creation of objects that refer to themselves and that exist primarily for what they reveal of the quality and functions of space, per se.

All visual evidence supports the surmise that Michelangelo, for instance, was not concerned with emphasizing the material quality of the openings in his monumental figure *David* (Fig. 14–7). It is true that the three large

Fig. 14–7. *MICHELANGELO.* David. *1501–1504. Marble, 18′. Academy, Florence. Photo: Alinari-Art Reference Bureau.*

enclosed negatives—between the legs and between both arms and the upper part of the body—do function powerfully to express the expanding positive volumes of the figure. But it appears clear from looking at and moving around this figure that these openings are not intended to function in any competitive way with the form of David. They exist to support the positive, not to assert themselves. These openings remain the necessary complements of the positive volumes; we experience no spatial reversal as we do with the holes in Moore's sculpture. Michelangelo employed his gifts as a sculptor to give us a unique and expressive image of the David who killed Goliath; Moore employs his gifts to give us functioning models of the interplay of spatial forces and qualities. And when Moore creates an object which is both a functioning model and a highly expressive image related to specific human experience, as he does with his *Helmet Head No. 2* (Fig. 14–8), we are moved by it in an especially powerful way. In such an image-model, impersonal spatial forces are brought to sympathetic interaction with our own equivocal human experience of solid men and hollow armor, and solid armor and hollow men.

Fig. 14–8. *HENRY MOORE.* Helmet Head No. 2. *1950. Bronze, height 13". Collection of Mr. & Mrs. Ted Weiner, Fort Worth.*

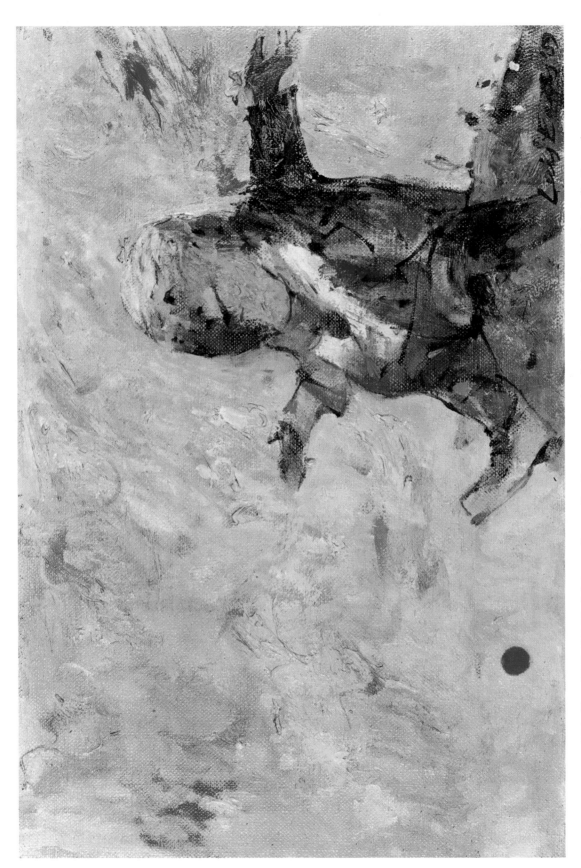

Plate 29. *LUIS EADES. Salute to Dawn, the Rosy-Fingered. 1959. Oil on canvas, 8×12″. Here we are given the image of a man whose bodily proportions vary so greatly from the norm that we are apt to think of him as a dwarf. The stumpy limbs, with their indications of limited articulation, cause us to feel this little man's inadequacy in making his desired salute to the dawn. (Private Collection.)*

Plate 30.

Henry Moore's preoccupation with the interplay of spatial forces in sculpture is certainly indicative of our recently accelerated interest in space in general and outer space in particular. At a time when we are concerned with new orientations in a space free of the force of gravity as we have long felt and known it, it is easy to understand the increased interest in sculptural works that tend to defy weight and solid substance. Ibram Lassaw, by turning three-dimensional sculpture into a kind of "drawing in the air," focuses our attention on negative space, the unoccupied passages of his sculpture. In his *Kwannon* (Fig. 14–9), it is the space between and around the wiry bronze and silver tracings that most engages our vision. We are won over by the measure and modulations of open space. The same is true of Richard Lip-

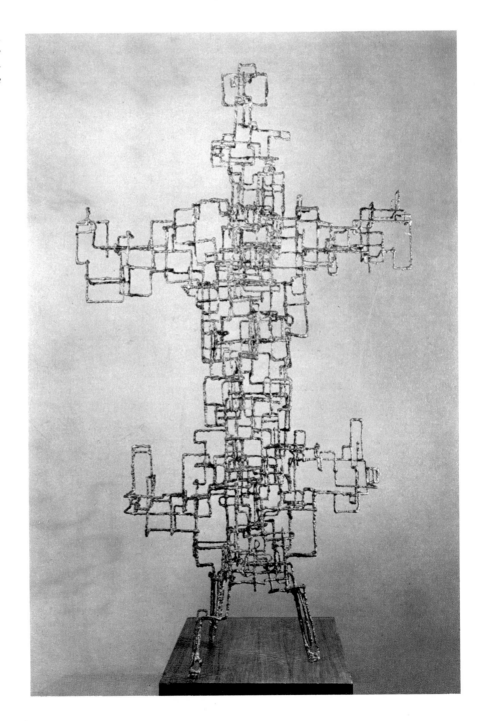

Fig. 14–9. *IBRAM LASSAW.* Kwannon. *1952. Welded bronze and silver, height 6'. The Museum of Modern Art, New York (Katharine Cornell Fund).*

Fig. 14–10. *RICHARD LIPPOLD. Aerial Act. 1950. Brass and copper wire, 31¹/₂×21″. Wadsworth Atheneum, Hartford.*

152

pold's *Aerial Act* (Fig. 14–10), the weightless quality of which is enhanced by the fact that this object is suspended and that it can turn and sway. The whole array of mobile sculpture, with which our age is familiar, is part of this same overriding interest in space as fluid and continuous throughout all time. Alexander Calder, the father of mobile sculpture, has given a lifetime to increasing our awareness of his sense of fluid and continuous space with such mobiles as his *Red Gongs* (Fig. 14–11). Constructed of sheet aluminum, sheet brass, steel rods and wires, and painted, this jointed and swivelled sculpture hangs suspended in free space. The least movement of air sets it in motion to provide our eyes with an almost infinite variety of modulations of positive and negative space.

The bases of our reactions to such works as the *Red Gongs* are different but integrally related to our reactions to all sculpture. Sculpture, as we said at the beginning of this discussion, functions in three-dimensional space. This is true of the *Red Gongs* and Michelangelo's *David* as well as of the unprepossessing statue in the square of the county courthouse. Even when

Fig. 14–11. *ALEXANDER CALDER. Red Gongs. c. 1950. Sheet aluminum, sheet brass, steel rod and wire, painted, length c. 12'. The Metropolitan Museum of Art, New York (Fletcher Fund, 1955).*

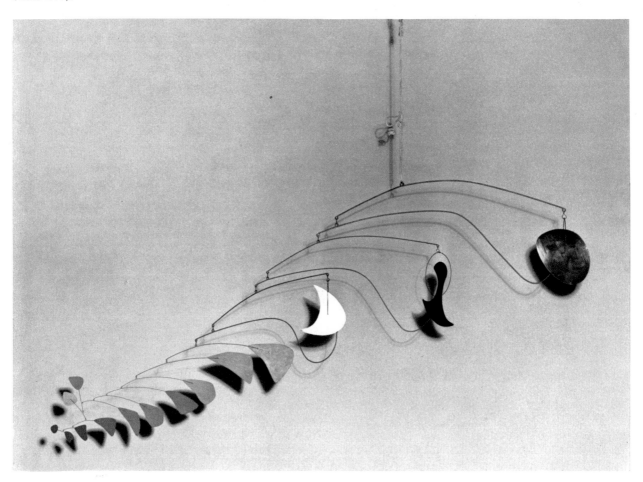

ALBERTO COLLIE. Dimensional Abstraction # 2.
Figure 12–15 repeated.

we are surprised or momentarily mystified by a work such as *Dimensional Abstraction # 2,* by Alberto Collie (Fig. 12–15), we can still be certain that no matter how this particular sculpture maintains itself in space[1], it is, for sure, being accomplished in actual three-dimensional space. And that is what we have been concerned with throughout this discussion of sculpture: actual three-dimensional space. Now, what we have been saying about positive and negative space, how sculptural volumes can actually overlap, how sculptural forms appear foreshortened because of the actual size and direction of volumes in relation to the plane of our sight, and how our stereoscopic vision sees and measures actual depth—all this will help us better understand what we mean by *illusions* of three-dimensional space created on a flat, two-dimensional surface. But before we go into that, let us try to get clear just what a two-dimensional space actually is.

When we use the term two-dimensional space in the visual arts, we refer to the simplest kind of geometrical surface, the flat plane, and to whatever can actually take place in that plane. By definition, a plane is a surface such that every straight line joining any two points in it lies wholly in that surface, or such that the intersection of two such surfaces is always a straight line. When we speak of the *picture plane* we refer to the flat surface of the support—the canvas, panel, or paper—upon which drawings or paintings are made. The picture plane, then, is a flat surface which actually exists in space only at the position in three-dimensional space where we happen to come upon it, or where it is placed. In other words, when we walk into the

---

[1] In this case electromagnets in the discus-like volume and in the drum-shaped base repel each other. The three thin lines between these volumes are not rigid supports, but rather flexible nylon threads that *moor* the disc in position above and free of the base.

art gallery and look across the room to a painting, that painting, because it is part of a flat surface, actually exists *only* in that plane and *only* at that position in three-dimensional space. The reason we wish to make this simple fact eminently clear is to avoid a confusion between the two-dimensional spatial characteristics of the picture plane itself and the varieties of three-dimensional space *illusion* that can be created in or upon that plane.

Ordinarily, we think of the picture plane as neutral in all ways except for the assertion of its own inherent characteristics—its flatness, its size or extent, and its shape. Strictly speaking, this is all we can say about two-dimensional space: it is the single plane. To do anything in or upon this surface is to set up visual tensions between the plane and whatever is marked or colored upon it. And by the still mysterious proclivities of human vision, *every trace we make upon the plane creates illusions of three-dimensional space.* So, having said this, it is time to speak about illusions of space.

Because of the nature of our visual circuitry and its functions, and because of our own experiencing of actual three-dimensional space in our day-to-day lives, we are prone to see the simplest of phenomena as implications of that three-dimensional space. Even when we locate nothing more than a dot in the plane in Fig. 14–12 (*a*), a depth is implied: the dot appears to lie above the plane. Strictly speaking, this appearance is physically correct since the ink of the dot does lie *on* the plane of the paper, not *in* it. However, in looking at our figure a considerable distance is implied between the level of the dot and the level of the plane behind it. This is an illusion of three-dimensional space, as is the case in Fig. 14–12 (*b*) in which the line appears to float well above the plane. The best explanation of this phenomenon is that our vision seeks the "simplest pattern obtainable under the circumstances."[2] It is simpler to interpret what we see as a continuous plane lying under the dot or line than it is to see the plane interrupted by a hole or an open incision. For were the latter the case, we would have to postulate the existence of another, darker plane lying behind the openings and showing through.

[2] See Rudolf Arnheim, *Art and Visual Perception* (Berkeley, Calif.: University of California Press, 1954), pp. 177 ff.

Fig. 14–12.

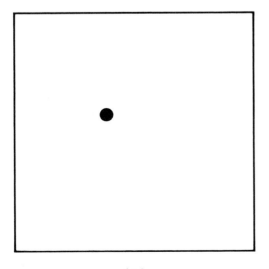

(a)

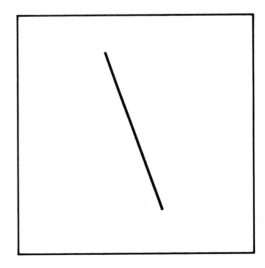

(b)

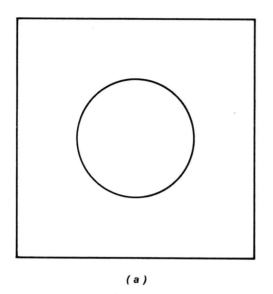
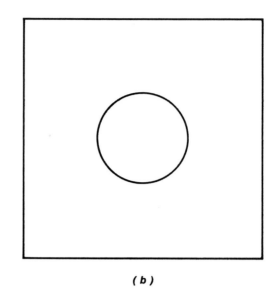

Fig. 14–13.

(a)   (b)

Three-dimensional space is also implied by *size* and by *gradation of size*. In Fig. 14–13 (*a*), the circle appears to lie above the plane of the rectangle. The plane appears to continue uninterrupted underneath the circle. But unlike the single dot or line, here there seems to be greater distance existing between the circle and the plane. This is a simple function of size: large size things appear close to us, small size things appear further away. This is made clearer by comparing Fig. 14–13 (*a*) with Fig. 14–13 (*b*). The larger circle in Square *a* appears closer to us than the smaller circle in Square *b*, but the plane in both cases appears to remain at the same distance from us. We can say this in another way: a thicker layer of three-dimensional space seems to exist in Fig. 14–13 (*a*). This is illusory, of course.

The illusion of three-dimensional space can be strengthened by introducing shapes of graduated size, as in Fig. 14–14. Here we interpret the gradation of size as if the largest shape were closest to us, the next smaller further away, and so on down to the smallest. We tend to see this arrangement of flat squares of unequal size as we would, in actuality, see a series of square panels, all equal in size, hanging above our eye level and at various distances from us. If we were, in fact, standing in a supermarket and looking ahead and up at a series of identical placards hanging vertically from the front to the back of the store, they would look very much like our figure. In that actual three-dimensional situation the placards would *seem* to diminish in size due to the normal distortion of vision. So, when we look at Fig. 14–14, we choose to interpret it as if it were a situation in three-dimensional space because that is a simple way to bring a perceptual unity to this pattern of otherwise illogically scattered squares. Our point is quite simple: gradation of size on a flat surface increases the illusion of three-dimensional space.

In speaking about space in relation to sculpture, we mentioned how one volume can overlap or block out another, just as our hand when placed

156

between our eyes and this page blocks out part of the page. Our stereoscopic vision, coupled with past experiences of such situations, lets us know that the hidden part of the page continues behind our hand. Now, this phenomenon, which actually exists only in three-dimensional space, is the basis for the *illusion* of overlapping that is possible on a flat surface. And, as we shall see, illusions of overlapping produce strong effects of depth on a flat surface.

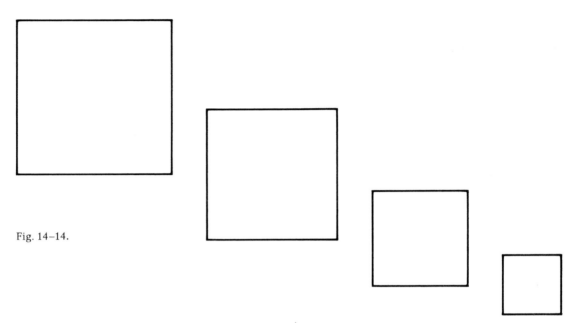

Fig. 14–14.

In Fig. 14–15 we have two shapes, one a rectangle, the other a thick L-shape. The only illusion of three-dimensional space here is of the kind we first mentioned: the shapes appear to lie at some distance above the plane, which continues underneath. But if we now rearrange these same two

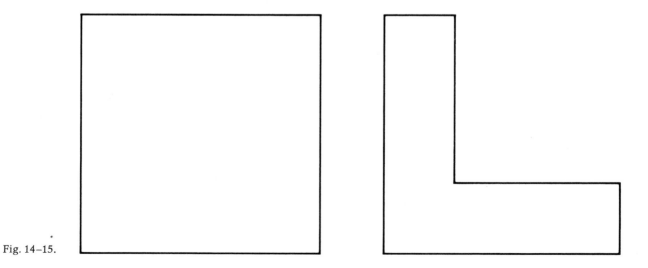

Fig. 14–15.

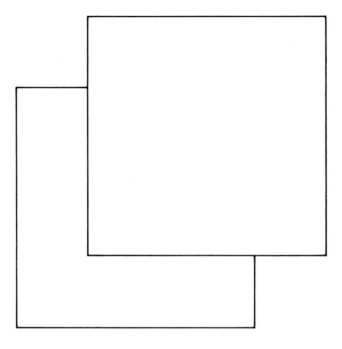

Fig. 14–16.

shapes in a certain way on that same plane, we noticeably increase the illusion of depth (Fig. 14–16). All we have done is turn the L-shape upside down and place its inner sides against a corner of the rectangle. The shapes are still the same flat ones of Fig. 14–15, but in this position we interpret the L-shape as a rectangle with part of its surface hidden behind the fully showing rectangle. As a result, the apparent depth of the configuration is increased since now there is the illusion of two levels of space—one between these two shapes and another between the upside-down L-shape and the background plane. Layers of apparent space can be piled up—or stacked backwards—by having many shapes appear as overlapping and being overlapped (Fig. 14–17). And the apparent depth created by this illusion of overlapping can be heightened by gradually diminishing the size of the shapes (Fig. 14–18).

It should be mentioned that in the illusion of overlapping, the shape whose outline appears interrupted is the shape that will appear to be overlapped. That is why our L-shape in Fig. 14–16 appeared to be behind the rectangle. The character of the rectangular shape is simple and direct: it appears "more complete" to us than the L-shape. Our eyes would have us preserve the quality of completeness, so we see the rectangle as if it were in front of the L. And the preference of our vision for simplicity has us pretend that even the L-shape is a rectangle—but in this case with just a part of it hidden from view.

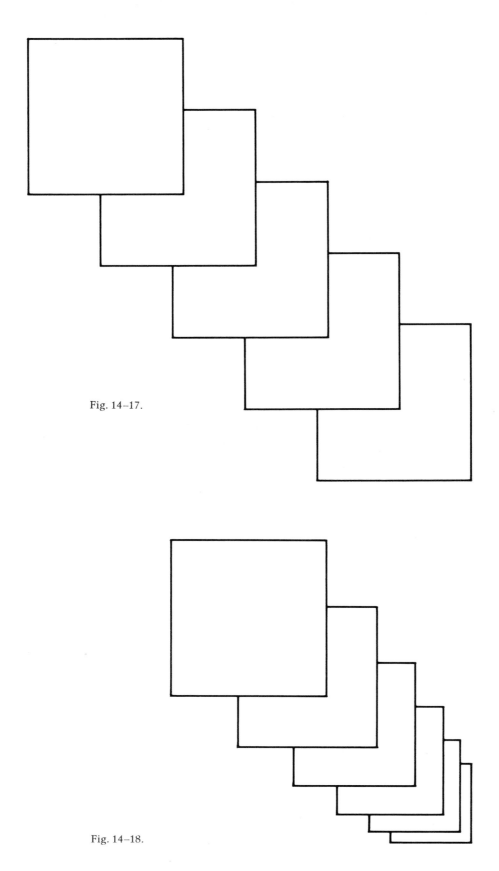

Fig. 14–17.

Fig. 14–18.

Fig. 14–19.

In situations where apparent overlapping does not occur, and even where sizes of shapes are equal, illusions of depth are increased by the relative positions of those shapes on the picture plane. In Fig. 14–19, the rectangles do not overlap and they do not diminish in size. Still, a depth is implied by the fact that some of the shapes are low in the format and some are high. The lower placed rectangles appear closer to us than the higher ones. In fact, we tend to interpret this as a row of blocks or cards standing at increasingly distant intervals from us. This situation is somewhat comparable to the one we discussed in relation to Fig. 14–14. In that earlier situation, however, we were working with shapes whose sizes were graded from large to small. Principally, it was that gradation of size that worked the illusion in

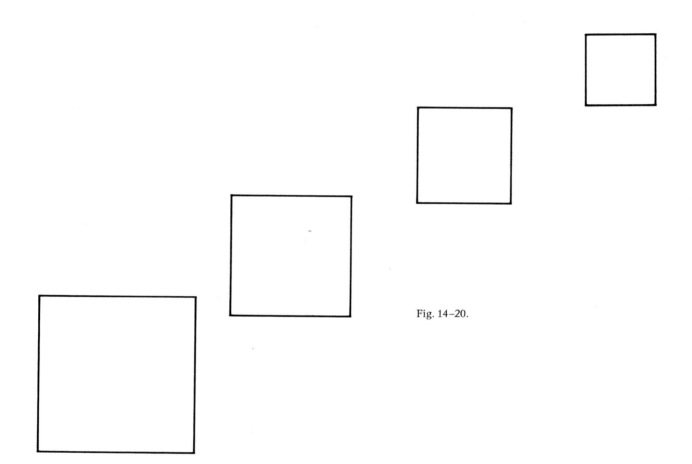

Fig. 14–20.

that case. In Fig. 14–19, however, it is only the relative positions of these rectangles that are the bases for the illusion of recession into space. This illusion is accomplished by the fact that we assume the existence of a tilted ground plane, which, like the floor of any room in which we have stood, appears to slant upwards from our feet to the base of the distant wall. Now we can say all this quite generally and doctrinally: the lower part of any plane lying perpendicular to our line of sight appears closer to us. This being the case, whatever elements lie in the lower parts of such a format appear closer to us than those which lie higher up. This illusion can be greatly intensified by diminishing the size of objects, the higher they lie in the format, and by arranging the shapes along a diagonal axis, as in Fig. 14–20.

(a)

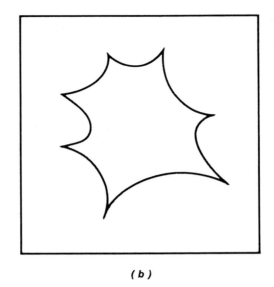

(b)

Fig. 14–21.

In our discussion of three-dimensional sculptural space, we observed that convex volumes appear to push out into space, and that concave volumes appear to shrink or to be compressed by surrounding convexities. This phenomenon is also observable in two-dimensional space. Figure 14–21 gives us two square planes of equal size, with *a* containing a convex shape and *b* containing a concave shape. In looking at *a* we sense a force of expansion operating in the convex shape. The opposite is true in *b* where the shape appears to shrink—as if the background plane, even though it is possible to see it as continuous below the figure, is compressing the concave shape. These phenomena vary considerably with variations in the proportions of figure to ground plane. However, it appears generally true that flat convex shapes appear to expand and that flat concave shapes appear to contract. Our main point here is an additional one, however. It is this: generally speaking, convex shapes appear closer to us than concave shapes. Looking back to our figure, shape *a* very definitely appears to be floating well above the background plane. The illusion of three-dimensional space existing between the convex shape and its ground plane is quite real—and constant. With shape *b*, on the other hand, it is easy for us to see it as a *hole* in the plane—as if we were looking *through* the concave shape to another plane *behind* the opening. Now this situation also produces an illusion of depth—depth *through the hole*. But this illusion is not as deep as the one created by *a*, perhaps because the focus of our attention oscillates between the concave shape and the plane. At one moment we interpret the shape as a hole; the next moment we see the plane as if it continued uninterrupted below the concave shape. The illusion is not constant. What is most important to us in this discussion of illusory space is that convex shapes appear to advance toward us, while concave shapes appear to recede—and that convexity of shape produces the illusion of greater space.

Another factor which functions in illusions of three-dimensional space is the quality of the edges of shapes. Still thinking in terms of shapes on a plane at right angles to our line of sight, those shapes with sharp edges will appear as if at a greater distance above the plane than those with fuzzy or unclear edges. In other words, shapes that are set off clearly from a background will appear closer to us than those that tend to fuse with the background (Fig. 14–22). The sharply defined rectangle on the left appears further above the surface than the hazily defined one on the right.

Fig. 14–22.

Likewise, rough textures produce an illusion of greater depth than do smooth textures. Granted, of course, that neither of the shapes in Fig. 14–23 possess any actual texture except that of the paper on which they are printed, still, the apparently rougher texture on the left appears closer than the one on the right. This may be due to the fact that rough texture can be interpreted as a function of size: the larger the granules or units of the texture, the rougher the texture—and hence the closer to the observer.

Fig. 14–23.

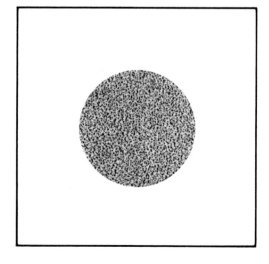

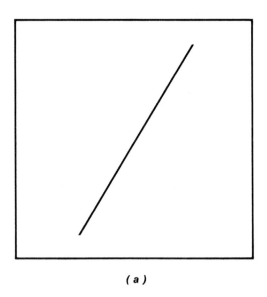
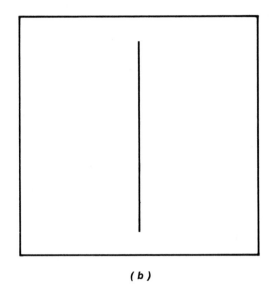

Fig. 14–24.

(a)   (b)

Although we have already touched upon it, we should specifically emphasize the fact that diagonal lines or directions tend to increase the illusion of deep space. Earlier we noted that when we arranged the squares of equal size along a diagonal from lower left to upper right, we increased the apparent space. This is true even with simple single lines (Fig. 14–24). Although the lines in both *a* and *b* appear above the surface of the plane, the line in *a* implies a greater depth. We interpret its diagonal direction as if it were part of a tilted recessive plane, a floor, that runs from close to us at the lower left to further away and higher up at the right. And something closely akin to this happens when we see a serpentine line or direction (Fig. 14–25). In this case, the meandering character of the line is interpreted as if it were a wire lying on the same tilted floor.

Fig. 14–25.

164

In an earlier discussion, we cited *value* and *intensity* as two attributes of color. We also mentioned that different colors are suggestive of different *temperatures,* and that because of this we speak of "warm" and "cool" colors. Now, all three of these characteristics of color function in illusions of space. These functions are both subtle and complex when we observe them operating in configurations that are rich in combinations of the visual elements and their qualities. However, some of these functions are constant enough to warrant our saying certain definite things about them.

In the case of value—the degree of lightness or darkness of a color—it is the lighter value that usually implies the deeper space. White, and the values that lie high on the value scale, as we have already said, exert more visual force. They take our attention more forcefully and appear closer to us. They appear separated from their background planes by thicker sandwiches of space. In Fig. 14–26, the rectangles are of equal size. One is white, the other black, and they actually lie in the same geometric plane as the middle gray background. The white shape, however, appears to rise higher from the background than does the black shape; it insists on prevailing. This becomes more noticeable when we reduce the amount of light coming into our eyes by squinting at the figure: the black rectangle drops away, as it were, at a greater rate than the white.

Fig. 14–26.

In the case of intensity, it is the more intense color that usually prevails, and as a result it appears to be further ahead of the background plane than the less intense color. In Color Plate 30, the rectangles are of equal size and the colors are of the same value. But the green on the left is more intense—more highly saturated with "greenness"—than the one on the right. Against the comparatively neutral gray background plane, it is the more intense green that prevails and appears closer to us. We say there is more space between it and the background.

The phenomenon of color to which we refer when we speak of "warm" and "cool" colors is not at all well understood by either artists or scientists

—or even by artistic scientists or scientific artists. What we do know is that colors show conditions that we interpret as "temperature." Red and yellow appear warmer than blue, and any addition of a warm color to a cool color will increase its temperature, just as the addition of a cool color to a warm one will reduce it. In all cases, the value and intensity of any color has much to do with its apparent temperature, and this richly complicates discussion of illusions of depth. Choosing to be quite simple about this, we can merely state what all the best evidence indicates to be true for the overwhelming majority of observers: warm colors appear closer to us than cool colors. Red and yellow, whether pure or as the controlling colors in mixtures of color, appear to come forth from neutral background planes. The color blue, pure and in mixture, appears to stay closer to such a plane—to recede from our vision. We know that red and yellow shapes seem to expand and that blue shapes appear to shrink. Looking again at Color Plate 30, we can see that both of the discs are equal in size, yet the yellow disc appears larger than the blue one. This illusion alone may account for the fact that the yellow disc appears closer to us, since large size appears closer than small size. But this is not all there is to it. The direct effect of the light energy, it appears, has something to do with it. But exactly how the different wavelengths—long in the case of yellow and red, short in the case of blue—affect us, is not known. Nor do we know why these different frequencies of vibration work in us as they do. For the time being we are content to experience light energy at work in us, and to respond to close warm colors and distant cool ones as if we were still primitives, which, of course, we are in many respects.

Fig. 14–27. *Columns of nave and aisle, St. Philibert, Tournus. c. 950–1120. Photo: J. Roubier.*

Plate 31.   THE LAST JUDGMENT. *12th century, recon-*
structed in 19th. Mosaic. The configuration of this mural
is based upon the tenets of the Creed, *which holds that*
after his crucifixion, Christ was buried, rose into Heaven,
and that "He shall come again to judge both the quick
and the dead." It is this metaphysical concept that deter-
mines the positions of images in the mural. (Cathedral,
Torcello. Photo: Art Reference Bureau.)

Plate 32.   *PIET MONDRIAN*. Composition London. *1940–1942. Oil on canvas, 32¹/₂×28". Much of the painting of our own century is not concerned with creating illusions of deep space, as we can see here in Mondrian's painting.*   *Mondrian's concern is for asserting the validity of the picture plane in an interesting way—and he is successful in doing this. (Albright-Knox Art Gallery, Buffalo. Room of Contemporary Art Fund.)*

Fig. 14–28. *PIER LUIGI NERVI. Stadium, Florence. 1932.*
Photo: Ferdinando Barsotti.

No adequate consideration of space illusion can be made without reference to the role that light plays in our sensory perception of depth. It is true, of course, that nothing we have said about space illusion could work in complete darkness. All along we have been presuming that we are experiencing these phenomena in light. There is, however, a special function that our past experiences of seeing actual three-dimensional objects plays when we look at figures or patterns on a flat plane.

In the photograph of the interior of the church of St. Philibert in Tournus (Fig. 14–27), we see what we readily interpret as cylindrical columns. Although the curved directions of the bricks and mortar help our perception of this roundness, it is the play of light on these volumes that most strongly defines their three-dimensionality. Standing in St. Philibert, we see the strongest light coming from our left. This light is obstructed by surfaces that lie in the path of that light and which face it. As a result, those surfaces catch the light and turn it back to our eyes. The surfaces turned away from the direction of the light are seen in relative darkness; they are the shadowed parts of the surfaces. And we know that these columns are round in section and not some other shape because of the *gradual* change from light to dark across their surfaces. If these columns were square in section there would be a sharp division between the sides facing the light and the sides turned away. By the same logic we understand which volumes are rounded, which are spiral in form, and which are cubical in complex organizations such as we see in Fig. 14–28.

It is this logic of light and shadow on three-dimensional objects that can be imitated in two dimensions—on the picture plane. All of us are familiar enough with this convention to be able to correctly interpret the flat patterns in Fig. 14–29, and to know the kind of three-dimensional form that each stands for. Not only can we interpret these flat patterns as solids,

Fig. 14–29.

but we are, in fact, given visual experiences of the third dimension through them. Because we can see these drawings as a cube, a cylinder, and a sphere, illusions of volumetric space are created on the flat surface. For our purposes we can refer to this phenomenon as the illusion of lighted volumes. And for the time being it will be the last phenomenon or device for creating illusions of depth on a flat surface that we will mention.

Now, since we will be concerned with all of these devices in reference to drawings, paintings, and the graphics, it may help to set them out in terms of their potentials for appearing close to us or farther away. A tabular arrangement of much of what we have said about space illusion would appear as follows:

APPEARS CLOSE TO US	APPEARS FARTHER AWAY
Large size	Small size
Overlapping	Overlapped
Low in format	High in format
Convex shape	Concave shape
Clear edge	Unclear edge
Rough texture	Smooth texture
Light value	Dark value
Intense color	Dull color
Warm color	Cool color

Besides these characteristics, which can be listed in tabular form, we considered the functions of diagonal and serpentine lines or directions and what we called illusions of lighted volumes.

Even if we were to limit ourselves to considerations of space and space illusion as phenomena in themselves, it could be a rewarding enough undertaking. But we have taken our time with these matters because space and the illusion of space are part of the artist's expressive means. How an artist works with actual space in sculpture and architecture, and how the painter and draftsman employ or do not employ illusions of deep space on the flat plane of their support are expressive of their orientation to the world in general.

It is time now that we look at a number of works of art and see the variety of attitudes that men have held toward space. We will start with two-dimensional works that are spatially "shallow" and move on to three-dimensional works that are fundamentally "closed," or non-exploitive of the continuous quality of space.

168

CHAPTER FIFTEEN

Illusions
of
Shallow Space

In using the term *shallow space* we mean to refer to two-dimensional works accomplished on a flat surface, works that show only a very limited regard for any of the devices for creating illusions of three-dimensional space or depth. Sometimes works such as these are alluded to as works accomplished in "flat space." However, we have already made a point of the fact that nothing but the *plane* or the support of paintings or drawings can be truly flat to our eyes. Every mark or trace made upon a plane immediately creates visual tensions between it and the plane, and we interpret this as three-dimensional space.

EGYPTIAN

Let us see what goes on, spatially, in a typically shallow illusion of space. In the detail of an Egyptian tomb wall painting called *Harvest Scenes* (Fig. 15–1), we should be struck first by the overall organization, or pattern, of the work. Should we interpret this organization as one in which shapes and figures low in the format are closer to us? If so, then the lowest row of figures and plants are nearest to us; the middle row stands in the middle distance; and the top row is farthest away, or deepest in depth. This obviously was not intended. This painting is evidently not based upon, or dependent upon, the implications of vertical placement for three-dimensional space. In that case, we can assume that each band or *register* should be interpreted separately, like rows of cartoons in a comic strip. To an extent this is true: both the wall painting and the comic strip are meant to be viewed in a series of lateral, side-to-side fixations of our eyes. That is why when we move our eyes vertically through either the mural or the comic strip pattern we miss what obviously was intended to be of first importance: a zoned, horizontally structured set of images suggestive of activity. Now what about the separate zones? Is the method of size diminution used to create an illusion of depth? Looking at the upper zone, we see a row of eleven standing figures. Eight of these are approximately the same height; the remaining three are only half the height of the others even though all appear to be adult figures. In a way, these smaller figures do appear to be farther back in space, but all eleven figures stand on a common base line, and the fourth tall one from the right places his hand on the head of the small figure immediately to his right. We know from what we have said about space illusion on a flat surface that this situation is spatially contradictory: the small figures appear farther back in space because of their relative size, but they are not higher up in the format and they are shown as if performing *alongside* the larger figures. All other evidences such as the color, texture, and quality of the edges of these shapes support our interpretation that these figures lie in the same plane. And if we are familiar with the conventions of Egyptian drawing, we know why some figures are shown so small and some so tall: the small figures are meant to be interpreted as personages of minor status *in Egyptian life*. They are not small in size because they are intended to be seen as if in the distance of this wall painting, but because they are of small importance in the structure of Egyptian society. The small figures are *factotums*—servants to the more important larger figures. This is a controlling convention in Egyptian drawing. It is as strong as the convention that requires that personages of high station, especially, be shown in the most commanding positions, even though those positions require combinations of front and side views. We are speaking, of course, of the Egyptian method of showing the shoulders and chest as if seen from the front, while the head, legs, and feet are shown from the side, simultaneously and in the same figure. Here, then, is a situation in which size is employed for *symbolic* reasons, granting in passing that the small plants in the upper parts of the top and bottom zones appear to contradict this.

With all the evidence that this is a symbolic rather than a naturalistic kind of art, we still do respond to implications of three-dimensional space. This is most clear in the artist's use of apparently overlapping shapes. The figures in the upper zone do appear to overlap the mass of grain which runs the full length of the panel, for instance. However, the function of overlapping is most effective in the drawing of groups of figures in the middle and lower zones. In the center of the middle zone an illusion of four figures is created by repeating the contours of a single standing figure. This creates an illusion of there being three figures behind the fully drawn figure "in front." Since the outline of only one of these figures is uninterrupted, we interpret that figure as overlapping the others. The other figures appear behind because their contours are interrupted or hidden from our view. And more than that, the existence of thin sandwiches of space between these overlapping figures is implied. We can see the same phenomenon at work in the left side of the middle zone and in most of the lower zone, especially where the arms of one figure are drawn to look as if they overlap and block out parts of another figure. This is also true in the majority of single figures where we see an arm or leg or both drawn across another part of the body as if overlapping it.

What, now, would be appropriate to say about this sort of "inconsistently" constructed shallow space of Egyptian drawing and painting? Should we feel sorry for these ancients who really wanted to make photographically "realistic" paintings of activities taking place in a spacious world and who were unfortunately ignorant of the means for doing so? It would seem not. Three thousand years before the birth of Christ, the Egyptians developed a logical system for symbolizing and presenting the subject matter and concepts they wished to present in their art. They settled early on presenting these symbols in horizontal bands, as in the *Harvest Scenes*. Principal figures and accouterments of the scene were assigned positions on a base line symbolizing the ground. These were presented in their most telling views—front or side, sometimes from the top, but rarely from oblique angles. The Egyptian was most interested in being *clear* in his presentation. He was not interested in the intricacies of optical illusion. He was interested in being clear about *concepts* held by the ruling group of the society, not in giving pictorial equivalents of visual phenomena. To the Egyptian, the picture plane is just that—a surface upon which to draw and paint the schema of his beliefs, not images of the natural world about him. Tomb paintings such as *Harvest Scenes* stand as symbols of a life which the Pharaoh would

Fig. 15–1. Harvest Scenes *(wall painting), from a tomb at Thebes. c. 1400 B.C. Distemper. The Metropolitan Museum of Art, New York (Egyptian Expedition, Rogers Fund, 1930).*

Fig. 15–2. A Pool in a Garden *(fragment of a wall painting), from a tomb at Thebes. c. 1400 B.C. Distemper. British Museum, London.*

take with him into an afterlife—amulets against death. Egyptian art celebrates what was held to be true and significant as idea and concept in a life which emphasized the spirit more than it did the passing phenomena of everyday life. From this standpoint, the Egyptian's drawing and painting is eminently consistent and entirely successful. The shallow space of his murals, with its emphasis on symbolic clarity, is perfectly expressive of his intentions. What more could anyone ask?

In a beautifully simple way, the painting of a pool from the garden of Amenemheb at Thebes (Fig. 15–2) exemplifies the Egyptian bias for clarity of concept rather than for virtuosity in creating illusions of three-dimensional space. What the Egyptian painter sought, it would appear, was to present a most revealing schema of a rectangular fish pool surrounded by plants and trees. *Knowing* that pools of this sort were, in fact, rectangular, the artist shows this one as such, even though it may have been impossible for him to have seen the pool from directly above. Nor was it necessary for him to see *any* actual fish pool from *any* point of view in order to draw one; for his role was to employ clear symbols, not to represent what he saw in nature. The symbol is clear: it stands for a rectangular pool, the four sides of which are at a 90 degree angle to each other—and so it is. And the fish and plants in the pool must be equally clear as symbols. Should they then be shown from the top? No, because top views of fish and plants are not as commanding, not as clear, as side views. So, they are shown in side views, as are the geese. And it is of no importance to the Egyptian that a "contradiction" exists in combinations of side-view fish and top-view pools. For him this "contradiction" cannot exist; he is concerned with something other than optical correctness.

This same preoccupation with simplicity and directness of symbolizations is evident in the trees and plants around the pool. At the top edge the trees are shown as growing upward from the rim of the pool. At the left side they appear as growing along that edge. The fact that we may see those on the left as lying on their sides does not change the other fact that they are in positions congruous with the fact that their trunks are at the edge of the pool—where they belong. At the bottom edge of the pool, something else happens that may not be so easy to explain. There it is the *tops* of the trees that are at the edge. The trunks of these trees are further down in the format, away from the pool. We are apt to interpret this situation as implying an area of ground lying between the bottoms of these trees and the edge of the pool. But from all Egyptian pictographic logic this was not the intention. The intention still was to symbolize trees standing along the bottom edge of the pool. Now if the artist had gone ahead as he had along the top and left edges of the pool, then the trees at the bottom would have had to be drawn upside down. It is reasonable to assume that the Egyptian artist was uncomfortable with upside-down trees, and also that such a symbol would not have been as clear as the one he chose to use. And, after all, the trees in their present manner of drawing *do* stand at the edge of the pool; their tops, that is, not their bottoms.

The implied space of Egyptian painting, then, is of a simple, shallow variety. Only for purposes of making visual symbols of intellectual notions clearer will the Egyptian resort to such devices as overlapping. Size, color, and position in the format are employed symbolically for purposes of expressing what was held to be true as matters of belief. This kind of shallow space illusion, its denial of the perceived depth and movement of the natural world, is expressive of concerns that are not primarily of the ordinary day-to-day life. Long preoccupied with the spirit, or *ka*, the Egyptian worked to insure its continued existence in a life after death. This is why they built the great pyramids (Fig. 15–3) and the rock-cut tombs (Fig. 15–4):

to preserve the body in which the *ka* dwelt until it went out of the body and into the next life. And even though much of Egyptian art is concerned with the activities of the times, images of these activities are flat, as if they were colored shadows on a wall—shadows cast into this life from images of the life to come.

Fig. 15–4. *Inner chamber of the rock-cut tomb at Beni Hasan. Photo: The Egyptian Expedition. The Metropolitan Museum of Art, New York.*

Fig. 15–3. *The pyramids of Menkure (c. 2575 B.C.), Khafre (c. 2600 B.C.), and Khufu (c. 2650 B.C.), Giza.*

Just as Egyptian painting exists in an apparently shallow and self-sufficient space, Egyptian sculpture, with some notable exceptions, exists in what we call "closed" space. It does not exploit the surrounding air. Much Egyptian sculpture is block-like in character and intended to be seen in conjunction with temple or tomb architecture. The over-life-size diorite figure of Chefran (Fig. 15–5) is a good example of the best in Egyptian sculpture. In looking at it, no matter from either side or from the front (Fig. 10–8), we sense the controlling force of the block of stone from which it was cut. The axes and planes of the block still function in the completed figure. It is the persistent quality of these planes that turns our eyes suddenly back from the sculpture; we are not invited in. The figure in no way reaches out into the surrounding negative space which we, as spectators, share with the sculpture. No openings pierce the stone between arms and chest or between the backs of the lower legs and the base of the throne. In fact, these areas are kept closed not by conceiving the arms as in contact with the chest, and the legs as if in contact with the throne, but by refusing to cut through the stone in those areas. Our photographs clearly show how the stone was purposely left engaged in those places. The air that would "naturally" have flowed between is kept out by the sculptor's refusing to pierce the stone.

Khafre (Chefran), *from Giza. Egyptian Museum, Cairo. Photo: Hirmer, Munich. Figure 10–8 repeated.*

Fig. 15–5. Khafre (Chefran), *from Giza (side view). c. 2600 B.C. Diorite, height 66". Egyptian Museum, Cairo. Photo: Hirmer, Munich.*

Even in that style of Egyptian sculpture that to our eyes appears more naturalistic, potential openings are kept closed, as in the *Seated Scribe* (Fig. 10–3). And even though this is a much less rigidly conceived figure than the Chefran, we still feel its relation to the vertical and horizontal planes of a stone block. The same is true for the slate figure group *Menkure and His Queen* (Fig. 15–6), in which potential openings are kept dramatically shut.

The sculpture of Egypt is no less symbolic than its painting. Almost no attempt is made to cause the sculptured figures to look as if they could move about or act as human beings. Their eyes appear either closed or fixed upon infinity; they do not ask for our attention. It is enough for the Egyptian that these more than human figures exist as symbols, permanently fixed and waiting for the life to come. For the Egyptian there is no need for the figures to appear as interacting with the space around them. They are closed and sufficient unto themselves. They just *are*—clearly, timelessly, forever as they are. This is what they express of Pharaonic Egypt. This is what we respond to in their presence. And how these figures function in space is a most essential element of their expressive power. Their closed three-dimensional quality functions to much the same expressive end as the shallow space of Egyptian painting.

Seated Scribe, *from Saqqara. The Louvre, Paris. Photo: Giraudon, Paris. Figure 10–3 repeated.*

Fig. 15–6. Menkure and his Queen, *from Giza. c. 2525 B.C. Slate, height 56". Museum of Fine Arts, Boston.*

BYZANTINE

Turning again to illusions of shallow space on flat surfaces, a word should be said about another long tradition of its use—the Byzantine. When we speak of Byzantine art we refer especially to works done during the existence of the far-flung Byzantine Empire from the fourth to the middle of the fifteenth century. Its headquarters were in Byzantium, the city we know today as Istanbul, in Turkey. Byzantine art is a Christian art and as such is concerned with whatever of that religion lends itself to visual presentation. This is of importance to us since we wish to make a point of the fact that Byzantine works often employ the flat surface more for creating visual diagrams of religious beliefs or hierarchies, than for creating illusions of deep space.

The Last Judgment. *Cathedral, Torcello. Photo: Art Reference Bureau. See Plate 31.*

One example may suffice to make our point—the immense depiction of the *Last Judgment* from the cathedral of Torcello, Italy, near Venice (Color Plate 31).

It is clear from our first look at this mosaic mural that it differs considerably from the Egyptian *Harvest Scenes*. It is considerably less shallow in its spatial illusion. This is due mainly to the illusion of lighted volumes that this Byzantine work creates, especially in the figures of the two upper tiers of the mural. The Egyptian, we remember, kept all his images in flat, undifferentiated color. However, the mosaic at Torcello, even with the illusion of light and shade and the generous use of the illusion of overlapping, is still a work that exists in an apparently shallow space. The space-creating effects of light and shadow and overlapping are compromised by the symbolic use of size and color and by the employment of a pictorial structure based on more or less regular bands or zones. The relative sizes of figures and objects are not intended to imply distance or depth. The figure of Christ in the center at the very top is larger not because he is meant to appear close to us, but because of his crucial role in the concept of the Last Judgment. The colors of his robe, like the colors used throughout this work, are not meant to create intervals in an illusory three-dimensional space. They are employed in ways consistent with an accepted system of color symbolism. And the horizontally zoned construction of the whole mural is a key strategy in expressing what this work is about.

Different from Egyptian painting arranged in bands, this Byzantine work is intended as one compact whole. It is meant to be seen and interpreted both horizontally and vertically. But this does not mean that the lowest zone is supposed to be closest to us, and that the upper zones are conceived as being gradually farther away. Here is a case in which high and low position in the format does have important significance— but this significance is not related to deepness into and beyond the picture plane, but rather to a vertical stratification upon that flat surface. This highly didactic work is concerned with Christ in Limbo (top zone), the Second Coming and Last Judgment (next lower zone), the weighing of souls (next lower zone), and the consignment to Heaven (left lower zones) and to Hell (right lower zones). This pictorial arrangement is based upon the tenets of the Nicene Creed of A.D. 381, which holds that after his crucifixion, Christ was buried, rose into Heaven, and that "he shall come again to judge both the quick and the dead." It is this metaphysical concept that determines the positions of images in the mural. This is why, for instance, the break appears between the second and third zones from the top, to indicate the relation between Christ's Second Coming and his judgment of souls. Here, then, is a clear example of employment of the picture plane *as a plane,* but this use still intends a definite kind of interpretation to be made from the location of images on that plane. In this Byzantine work, position in the format is expressive as symbol, not representative of visual clues supporting illusions of three-dimensional space.

Now, we should like to make sure that one thing is understood: because men or whole cultures produce paintings that give little illusion of three-dimensional space, this does *not* mean that such works are inferior to others that produce illusions of deep space. In ignorance, we often believe that the height of artistic achievement on a flat surface is characterized by the evidences of depth and volumed shapes. This is not demonstrably true. We said that space and space illusion are employed and articulated as *expressive means*. And if an artist or an age is not concerned with observed, perceptual three-dimensional space as such, then they ignore it in favor of something else. As we have seen, they may give us symbols that exist powerfully as flat images not necessarily subject to the physics of stereo-optics, which operates in our direct perception of the natural world. Much of the painting of our own century, for instance, is not concerned with creating illusions of deep space, as we can see in Piet Mondrian's *Composition London* (Color Plate 32). Mondrian's concern appears to be to assert the validity of the picture plane in an interesting way—and he succeeds. The same is true of Kenzo Okada's *No. 2* (Color Plate 33) and Henri Matisse's *Lady in Blue* (Color Plate 34). Both of these artists make their expressions in space illusions that are as shallow as those of Byzantine painting.

PIET MONDRIAN. Composition London. *Albright-Knox Art Gallery, Buffalo, New York (Room of Contemporary Art Fund). See Plate 32.*

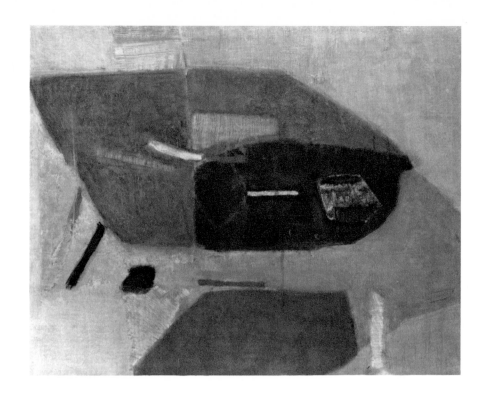

KENZO OKADA. No. 2. The Phillips Collection, Washington, D.C. See Plate 33.

HENRY MATISSE. Lady in Blue. Philadelphia Museum of Art (Collection of Mrs. John Wintersteen). See Plate 34.

CHAPTER SIXTEEN

Illusions of Cubical Space

Let us now turn to another variety of space illusion which exhibits specific enough characteristics to be called "cubical." We will call it by that name simply because this type of space illusion depends in large part on the reference it makes to rectilinear solids. In shallow space illusion, the visual elements are patterned over the flat surface with a strong feeling of their being parallel to the picture plane. With cubical space illusion we respond as if we were looking into a hollow cube or rectilinear box, and the visual elements often appear as if they were *not* parallel to the picture plane, but rather as if they existed within the *oblique interior space of the cube*.

THE JAPANESE CORNER ILLUSION

We find this kind of space illusion in the painting and graphics of a number of cultures, but let us consider it in the color woodblock prints of the Japanese. We choose the Japanese because one of their powerful illusions of cubical space emphasizes the *corner* of a cube as if seen from inside the cube. Also, we can speak of this Japanese corner illusion without reference to what we call "central perspective," of which we will speak later.

In Kiyonobu's print *Lovers* (Fig. 16–1), we may at first be struck with the flat, clearly defined color areas, which remind us of those characteristics of Egyptian painting. These areas, even though broken by decorative detail, appear for the most part to be parallel to the picture plane. However, the drawing of two of the faces and of the container low in the format are drawn as if seen from an oblique angle. And when we look a little more closely, we see that the entire picture has been spatially unified by a series of oblique and vertical lines. One set of oblique lines begins near the middle of the left side, rises toward the upper parts of the two lovers and is apparently lost

Fig. 16–1. *TORII KIYONOBU*. Lovers. *17th century. Woodcut. Private Collection.*

behind them. Another set of lines slants in an opposing direction from near the center of the right side, is interrupted by the shape of the single figure, and then continues in the direction of the set of three vertical lines. Although we cannot see it, we assume that these sets of lines have a common rendezvous behind the head of the male figure. The positions and directions of these two sets of oblique lines and of the set of vertical lines imply the existence of three planes, as indicated in Fig. 16–2. Together, these planes suggest the corner of a room with plane number *1* functioning as the floor, and planes *2* and *3* functioning as walls. This happens even though we see that a "raised" area occurs just in front of the pictorial scroll high in the upper right corner of the format. The illusion created by these implied planes is one in which we, as the observers, seem to be looking into the corner of a room in which three figures are resting on the floor. Because of

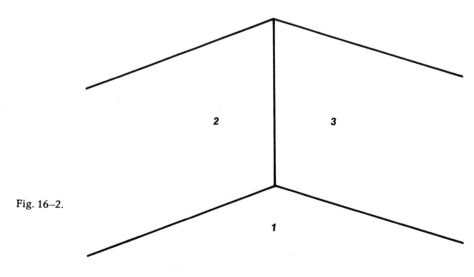

Fig. 16–2.

the organizing force of this illusion, we interpret the floor plane as rising toward the back, much as an actual floor appears to rise in three-dimensional space. It follows, then, that the container which is lowest in the format appears closest to us. This is obviously what the artist wished to make apparent to us. The lovers, because their lowest parts are located above the container, appear further back in space. And the single figure, because it is overlapped by one of the other figures, because it is diminished in size and rests higher in the format, appears behind the lovers.

The Japanese corner illusion is based on what we call *angular-isometric perspective*. It is angular because it is based on an oblique view into a cube; not one of its principal planes appears to stand at right angles to our line of sight. It is isometric because any plane lying between oblique lines is of equal and constant measure no matter if part of that plane appears closer to us or farther away. This is because the oblique lines indicating the sides of the cube, or the walls of a room, let us say, run parallel to each other. This should be made clear by looking at Harunobu's print *Woman on a Veranda* (Fig. 16–3). The large oblique plane behind the figure is actually a parallelo-

Fig. 16–3.
SUZUKI HARUNOBU. Woman on a Veranda. *19th century. Color woodcut.* © *Kodan-sha, Tokyo (Mitsui Collection).*

TOSHUSAI SHARAKU. The Actor Otani Oniji III, in a Role of October 14, 1794. *The Art Institute of Chicago. See Plate 35.*

gram. Its upper and lower sides are parallel, as are its vertical sides. Because of these parallelisms, this plane does not diminish in height as it seems to recede into the depth of the corner to the left of the figure. This is emphasized by the fact that every one of the light pane-like divisions in this plane are not only the same shape, they are also identical in size. This, as we shall see later, is different from *central* perspective in which vertical lines may be parallel, but not the top and bottom edges of oblique planes. In central perspective these are drawn in directions that would converge at the horizon, or in infinity.

What we are taking principal notice of in these Japanese woodblock prints is another kind of pictorial organization upon which the spatial unity of the picture depends. Besides a systematic use of the corner as descriptive of three-dimensional space, the Japanese artist also employs gradients of size, but only in the images of objects and figures that he presents as resting in this prism of illusory space. This, of course, increases the illusion of depth, as does his use of apparently overlapping shapes, positions high and low in the format, and diagonal and serpentine or curving lines. Still, these prints do not aim to represent the natural world of three-dimensional space as does the color camera or the more naturalistic of paintings. These prints are in many ways symbolic. This is especially true of the color, which bears little or no relation to the way we see colors of objects in the world around us. The Japanese artist keeps his colors flat. He reveals no interest in creating illusions of lighted volumes. His color describes only flat surfaces, as is clear in Sharaku's *The Actor Otani Oniji III* (Color Plate 35). The color does not change with the changes of shape that the lines and contours of the figure suggest—it is as constant as a divine radiance; it is symbolic in intent. And the drawing of the figures does not suggest that these Japanese artists wished to reproduce the outward appearance of nature. The proportions, attitudes, and gestures of these figures are "right" only in this secluded world of the print itself. And the unifying spatial illusion—this quiet, intimate prism of space into which we steal glances more as inexperienced outsiders than as welcome initiates—provides the basic reference to an orientation to life quite unlike what we have seen in the case of Egypt and Byzantium.

Fig. 16–4. Shah Jahan *(Mughal). 17th century. Painting on paper, 15×20". The Metropolitan Museum of Art, New York (Gift of Alexander Smith Cochran, 1913).*

But let us now look at the cube from another angle. With the eighteenth-century Japanese woodblock prints, we looked into a corner of a cube; with a seventeenth-century Indian manuscript painting of the Shah Jahan (Mughal), Fig. 16–4, we look directly into a cube from an open side. And although this cube is not completely delineated, it functions as the visual reference that unifies the space illusion of the painting. We see the underside of the top plane of this cube as a decorated canopy, the longest or front edge of which joins the top edge of the format. The shape of this canopy—a trapezoid with sides that slant inwards toward the center of the painting—implies a diminishment of size from the edge of the format to the back corners of the canopy. It reminds us of how the ceiling of a small room looks to us as we stand on the floor looking straight ahead: the ceiling appears to grow narrower as it nears the far edge where it joins the back wall. In our painting this ceiling plane appears to be supported in the front by the top edge of the format and in the back by two thin poles, the lower ends of which appear to rest on the fence line in the background. The areas between these two poles and between the poles and the right and left edges of the format suggest the side planes of a cube seen from the inside, as indicated by numbers *1* and *2* in Fig. 16–5. Number *3* indicates the underside of the top plane of the cube—the canopy of which we have spoken. The floor plane of this hollow cube is not specified by any lines as evident as those suggesting the other three planes. However, our eyes, responding to the force of the diagonals of the rectangular format, supply the missing edges of the floor plane (indicated by dotted lines in our figure) and so establish it as plane number *4*.

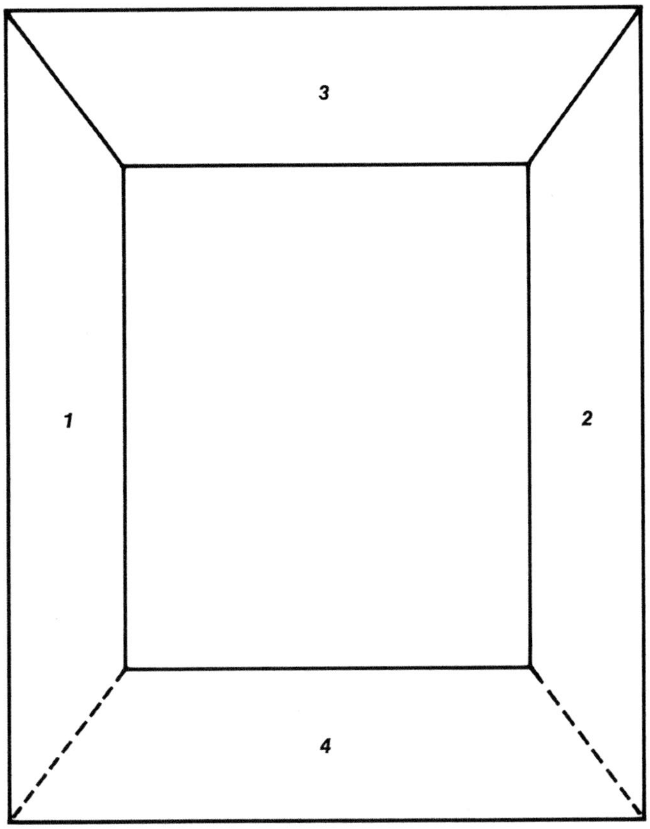

Fig. 16–5.

Now, within this illusion of cubical space, the artist has drawn and painted the image of a gazebo, in which the Shah appears. This gazebo is also suggestive of a cubical volume that is roofed with a truncated pyramid. The four transparent sides of this cube are implied by posts supporting the roof. The upper and lower planes are respectively indicated by the level line of the ceiling and by the floor on which the Shah kneels. This cube rides on four elaborately turned legs, the drawing of which reinforces the character of the cube above.

What we have here, then, is the illusion of a smaller cube within a larger cube. It is this double and mutually reenforcing phenomenon that most determines the illusion of volumetric space in this painting. It lends to the work a unifying persuasion, a spatial order strong enough to incorporate all the flat floral patterns in the foreground, the canopy and the roof of the gazebo. Within this spatial order, use is made of diminishing size, as in the supports of the gazebo, to imply depth. Likewise, overlapping and position in the format function to increase the illusion of three-dimensionality. As in the Japanese prints, color functions either symbolically or decoratively or both, but does not create the illusion of depth. The aim of this kind of painting is not to simulate nature through spatial illusion, but to give form to feelings of the sensuous order of a particular way of life. Its spatial order is another kind of logical system developed over time to satisfy the requirements for a persuasive expression of that life. It induces in the observer an awareness of a bounded, enclosed space that is scaled to lend support and give significance to the image of man and what he is about. This type of space illusion, similar to that of the Japanese, communicates qualities of a highly ordered kind of life. It is expressive of man's desire to see the world of blooming, buzzing confusion as an ordered place in which his own human qualities are of real grace and consequence.

THE MEDIEVAL CUBE ILLUSION
AND SPECULATIVE PERSPECTIVE

Moving from the Far East to the Western world, let us now consider a series of paintings in which we can observe a continuous and directed effort to bring the world of three-dimensional space to the flat surface of the picture plane. Our examples will be drawn from about two hundred years of Italian painting—from the beginning of the fourteenth century well into the sixteenth century. These years fall into the periods we know as the late Medieval, the Renaissance, and the High Renaissance. It is in these years that the "Middle Age" comes to its end, that the poet Petrarch hails secular studies—the humanities—above the study of Scripture, and that a renewal of interest in the classical worlds of Greece and Rome is witnessed in the works of living men. These are the years in which a whole new outlook on life and man's role in the world is born out of the fire of battle in the city of Florence and given its first monumental form in the works of its own citizens. These are the years made graceful by the lives and works of some of the greatest

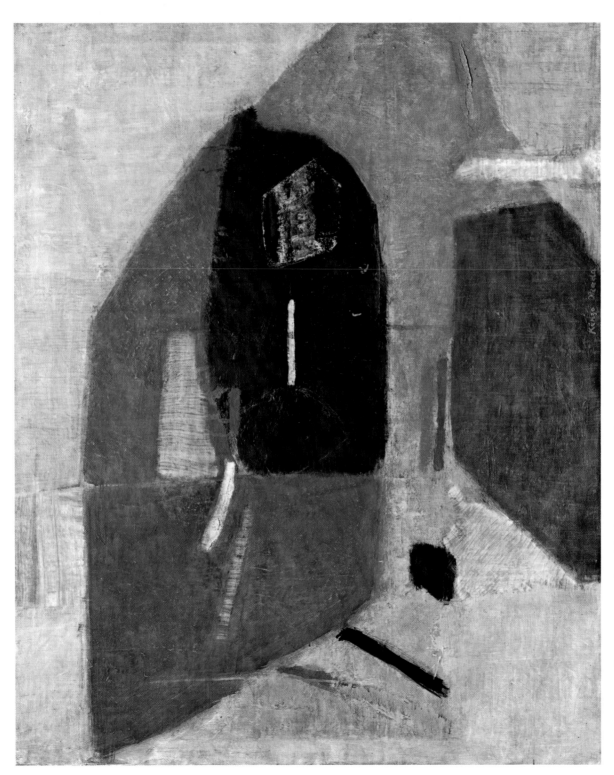

Plate 33. KENZO OKADA. No. 2. 1954. Oil on canvas, 31×39″. Okada is one of a great many contemporary painters who concerns himself with creating visual configurations that exist powerfully as flat images. These images are not necessarily subject to the physics of stereoptics that operates in our direct perception of the natural world. (The Phillips, Washington, D. C.)

Plate 34.   *HENRI MATISSE. Lady in Blue. 1937. Oil on canvas, 36¹/₂×29". Space and space illusion are employed and articulated as expressive means. And if an artist or an age is not concerned with observed, perceptual three-dimen-* *sional space as such, then they ignore it in favor of something else. For Matisse that "something else" concerns a flat array of visual qualities. (Philadelphia Museum of Art. Collection of Mrs. John Wintersteen.)*

Plate 35.   *TOSHUSAI SHARAKU*. The Actor
Otani Oniji III, in a Role of October 14, 1794.
*1794. Color woodcut, height 14³/₄". Sharaku
reveals no interest in creating illusions of
lighted volumes. His color describes only flat
surfaces. It does not change with the changes
of shape suggested by the lines and contours
of the figure. The color is as constant as a
divine radiance; it is symbolic in intent.
(The Art Institute of Chicago.)*

Plate 36. *MASACCIO*. The Holy Trinity with the Virgin and St. John. *c. 1425. Fresco, c. 16′×10′ 5″. With this painting Masaccio, for the first time, created the illusion of optically correct three-dimensional space on a flat surface.* *He accomplished this not only by linear perspective, but also by light and shade in both the architectural setting and the figures in his painting. (S. Maria Novella, Florence. Photo: Scala, New York and Florence.)*

artists of the Western world: Brunelleschi, Alberti, and Bramante in architecture; Donatello, Pollaiuolo, and Verrocchio in sculpture; Giotto, Masaccio,
Piero della Francesca, the Bellinis, Raphael, and Titian in painting—and
Michelangelo and Leonardo da Vinci in all three. It is a period in which a
conquest of the visible world is achieved with results which still inform our
best knowledge; and it is the period in which our modern scientific world
is born.

There may be no more direct way to confront the determinative character and convictions of this period than by an understanding of how its
artists unified pictorial space through a series of intuitive and rational
adventures. During the years 1303–1306 a young Florentine by the name of
Giotto painted a series of frescoes on the walls of the Arena Chapel in
Padua. They are among his most characteristic works and will serve best to
exemplify the highest achievement of cubical space illusion of late Medieval
times. Let us look first at Giotto's *The Washing of the Feet* (Fig. 16–6).

Fig. 16–6. *GIOTTO*. Washing of the Feet. *1304–1306. Fresco. Arena Chapel, Padua. Photo:
Alinari.*

Immediately upon looking at it, we sense the presence of a world quite outside those of Japan, India, and Byzantium, even though we may hear echoes from them. For one thing, we feel that this painting puts us in the presence of solid, well-articulated bodies that could function in the world we live in. They hold to firmly established positions in a pictorial space that appears more continuous with the actual space we stand in than anything we have seen from the Orient. These figures of Christ and the Apostles are drawn with live, fourteenth-century Italians in mind. They are painted in a way designed to create illusions of lighted volumes: the bodies are made to appear bulky and rounded by the use of light and dark colors. The drapery of robes is painted to create illusions of volume and to help describe the three-dimensional character of the bodies underneath. We are convinced that live men could be grouped as these images are grouped. Some seem close to us, others more distant; and it seems there is space enough for them to stand in the places they are assigned. We experience no difficulty in interpreting the illusion of overlapping, and the convex shapes of the figures stand out from a plane we readily interpret as tilted upwards as it recedes—a floor. These are all evidences of the fact that Giotto has unified the pictorial space of this painting in terms of our actual volumetric world. That is why we so readily accept this painting in part and in whole.

How has Giotto accomplished all this? In a word, first and foremost, by organizing his painting in reference to the cubical structure of the canopy and its supports.[1] In this respect there is a similarity to the Indian painting of the Shah Jahan (Mughal), Fig. 16–4, which we recently discussed. Unlike the Indian artist, however, Giotto is only negligibly concerned with the symbolic or decorative character of the canopy construction. For him, this device sets the stage; everything else in his pictorial structure should relate to this particular perspective, which is a hybrid between an angular-isometric kind and an incipient central perspective. Giotto is concerned with the optical consequences of this perspective throughout the painting. For instance, when we look at the canopy structure we seem to see up under the roof as if our eyes were at a level below its front edge. When we look at the plane on which the supports of the canopy rest,[2] that plane appears below the level of our eyes. Now, if the roof of the canopy structure is above our eyes and the floor upon which it stands is below our eyes, then our eyes must be at a level somewhere in between. Giotto has been cognizant of this, and for the most part the figures have been conceived as being seen from a level about midway between the top and the bottom of the painting.

---

[1] The obvious inconsistency of the length of the right front support, which stops short of the floor plane at the shoulder of the Apostle, and the complete absence of the left rear support is best explained not in terms of Giotto's probable intention but by the state of restoration of the painting when this photograph was made.

[2] Here our best visual references are the supports farthest to the right and left of the format. The one at the far right is a *rear* support; the one farthest to the left is a *front* support. From where these supports appear to contact the floor (where they end), we can estimate where the other two supports would contact the same plane.

Fig. 16–7. GIOTTO. *The Death of St. Francis. c. 1318–1325. Fresco, c. 9' 2¹/₅" × 14' 9¹/₁₀". Bardi Chapel, S. Croce, Florence. Photo: Alinari-Art Reference Bureau.*

This concern for a spatial unity based on the mode of visual perception that we experience in our actual three-dimensional world is what is new and significant in Giotto's painting. Giotto would like his painting to give us the illusion of seeing this scene as if we had come upon it in actuality and were viewing it from a position at the level of the Apostle who is in the middle and off center to the right. His means for accomplishing this had not been fully formulated and, as a result, several inconsistencies could be pointed out. But what is most important for us here is that Giotto is working intuitively toward an integration of pictorial space based upon the natural capacity of human vision for accomplishing this integration. His use of a cubical reference and of most of the devices for creating illusions of three-dimensional space on a flat surface are all evidence of this.

About twenty years after completing the frescoes in Padua, Giotto painted another series, this one in the Bardi Chapel of the Church of Santa Croce in Florence. *The Death of St. Francis* (Fig. 16–7) is from this later series and it reveals a still more visually convincing use of the cube as the basis for spatial unity. Here it is eminently clear that Giotto has quite consciously composed this scene as if it were being enacted on a stage. At both ends of a panelled back wall, which is shown at right angles to our sight, he paints two configurations that stand for walls with roofed doorways. These function as the sides of the stage, or cube, and we interpret them as standing at right angles to the back wall. Apparently running under these is the recessive plane of the floor, the tilt of which is reenforced by

193

Fig. 16–8. *GIOTTO*. Ascension of St. John the Evangelist. *Before 1329. Fresco, c. 9′ 2¹/₅″ × 14′ 9¹/₁₀″. Peruzzi Chapel, S. Croce, Florence. Photo: Alinari.*

appearances of shadows cast from figures and objects standing in the foreground. Although these side and back planes are not roofed over, we can sense the logic of that possibility. This, then, is an early example of what has often been called the "picture box"—a two-dimensional configuration made to look like a box with the front side removed. Instead of a flimsy canopy and supports thrown over and around the scene as in *The Washing of the Feet,* in *The Death of St. Francis* we have a situation in which the very sizes and positions of the figures are determined by the illusion of a specific shape and volume of space in which human action appears to be taking place.

As we stand on the floor of the Bardi Chapel, Giotto's *The Death of St. Francis* is above our actual eye level. We have to look up to see it. Nevertheless, the organization of the painting is spatially coherent enough that we assume the eye level predicated by the painting—a level just above the body of St. Francis. We are also encouraged to sense our position as being directly in front of the dead saint. This kind of spatial organization, which, by illusion, creates what amounts to a continuation of the natural world into the artificial world of painting, is characteristic of what we call *naturalistic* or *realistic* art. The work of Giotto stands as perhaps the most complete realization of this kind of art-illusion since the days of Pompeian painting, about thirteen hundred years before. Still, Giotto's magnificent realizations comprise only the first full step toward a genuinely naturalistic art based on illusions of space that are both compatible with and expressive of a scientific humanism. Giotto's cubical space illusion is still a speculative one, not a mathematical or scientific one. It is based as much on intuition as on reason. It is the great pioneering accomplishment of a single man which had to wait until more than a hundred years after his death to be formulated in the canons of central perspective. In Giotto's work we are made aware of the past out of which it comes—primarily the Byzantine—and the future to which it points, the High Renaissance in Italy. Giotto's concern for pictorial unity based on illusions of three-dimensional space, and his preoccupation with verisimilitude in the shape, bulk, and expressions of his figures—as if they were living, feeling persons—are indicative of humane interests that will later culminate in the destruction of the medieval world of Divine Law and metaphysical conviction. The impending clash of the old and the new is evident in Giotto's fresco *Ascension of St. John the Evangelist* (Fig. 16–8). In convincing, but still theoretical, cubical space illusion, Giotto has a bulky-bodied image of a man, St. John, drawn and painted in mid air between the floor of this cubical stage set and its upper storey. On the one hand we are convinced that St. John is a quite "real" man: his proportions are well within the human range, his head and arms look as if they could move as ours do, and he looks solid in the light that appears to be shining down on him. On the other hand, we see that this 200 pound natural man is intended to be rising in thin air. Our uneasiness with this situation is indicative of Giotto's own dilemma, the horns of which are the demands of the supernatural story of St. John's levitation and Giotto's personal concern for natural man in the environment of the surrounding physical world.

THE RENAISSANCE CUBE ILLUSION AND SCIENTIFIC ONE-POINT PERSPECTIVE

Giotto's dilemma is encountered, faced, and resolved in such a pointed manner by another Florentine painter that one is inclined to believe that he meant the resolution to be a lesson in itself. That painter is Masaccio; the work is his astounding fresco *The Holy Trinity with the Virgin and St. John* (Color Plate 36) in the Church of Santa Maria Novella in Florence. Let us examine it in detail since this work, completed when the artist was in his early twenties, is the first work in the history of art which is completely organized according to the principles of scientific *central* or *one-point perspective*. About the resolved dilemma we will speak a little later.

Completed in about 1425, this is a work of the Renaissance. Its structure relies almost unremittingly on the unifying effect of cubical space illusion. The fact that the apparent opening into deep space is rounded at

MASACCIO. The Holy Trinity with the Virgin and St. John. *Photo: Alinari. See Plate 36.*

the top should cause us no problem, since everything we see here is painted: what appears to be an architectural enframement and base is all the creation of Masaccio's brush. So, we have a work that is, by and large, a vertical rectangle. We seem to look through this close-up vertical enframement, through the arch, and into the depth of the vault. Highest in the vaulted area is an image of God the Father. Immediately below his head we find the Holy Ghost and then the crucified Christ with the Virgin Mary on the left and St. John on the right. On the level below this, and apparently outside the vaulted area, are portraits of the donors. Below the donors is a painted sarcophagus with a skeleton lying on top. As far as the representation of the Trinity is concerned, Masaccio kept within the existing rigid tradition. No real innovation is made there, but the means by which the space of this entire ensemble is unified is, for its time, unique.

Here in all probability is what Masaccio did: Assuming a position, his own bodily position, out from the wall of the church, he established the eye level for the painting about five feet above the floor. On this eye-level line he established a single point, the one point at which his line of sight met the wall at an exact right angle. This would be the side-to-side center of his painting. Having established this point, he thought of it as a point on a distant horizon far out and beyond the wall of the church. This horizon and

Fig. 16–9. *(Background photo: Grant Heilman.)*

the eye-level line were, quite naturally, thought of as one and the same. Figure 16–9 suggests the position Masaccio assumed in relation to his painting —out in front of it with his line of sight striking it at right angles precisely at the circled point low and in the center of our figure. It also indicates the relation of the painting to this eye level conceived as the distant horizon, shown here as if the wall of the church were transparent or nonexistent. Seeing this painting as it is presented in our figure makes it appear as if it were, in fact, a cubical construction standing on the earth in the open space

197

of the world and lighted from a diffused source in front and high above it. This is not unlike how we respond to it when we stand alone where Masaccio stood in the quiet of Santa Maria Novella. The quality of this illusion must not have been strange to him over five hundred years ago.

Now how did Masaccio create this extremely convincing illusion of three-dimensionality? First of all, by a consistent use of the single point that he established on the eye-level line. For a long time this point has been called the *vanishing point* because if any set of lines perpendicular to the plane of sight were extended to the horizon of a great plain they would appear to converge and vanish at that point. In this regard we are all familiar with the old diagram of the railroad track as seen from the back platform of the caboose of a train as it crosses very flat terrain, like that in west Texas (Fig. 16–10). Where the rails appear to converge is the vanishing point.

Fig. 16–10.

Because of the control exerted by this point in paintings such as Masaccio's *Holy Trinity*, we call the system based on its use *one-point perspective*. And, especially when the vanishing point is located in the lateral center of the work, it is called *central perspective*. We will refer to it by only one name: *one-point perspective*. Using this perspective, Masaccio knew that all lines drawn to the vanishing point would appear as if they lay at right angles to the picture plane. His lines did this, as indicated by the lines overdrawn in Fig. 16–11. They describe the longitudinal ridges between the coffers in the vault, the inner faces of all the capitals of the columns, the ends of the lid of the sarcophagus and the sides of the base on which it stands, and every other edge and plane, no matter how short or small, which we interpret as slanting away into depth. And this illusion works, as we can see, for edges and planes below, above, and on eye level. On the other hand, edges and surfaces that Masaccio intended to appear as *parallel* to our plane of sight

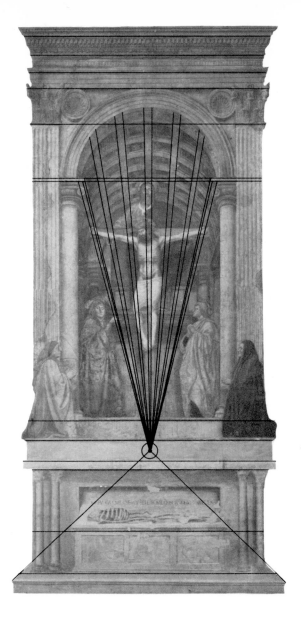

Fig. 16–11.

he drew parallel to the picture plane. That is why such details as the cornice at the top and the various levels of the structure on which the figures appear to rest are drawn straight across the picture.

It appears reasonable to assume, then, that at an early point in laying out this painting Masaccio had a network of intersecting lines composed of those radiating from the vanishing point and those drawn horizontally across them. His principal spatial problem then was to establish the optically correct degree of diminishment of size from the front to the back of his illusory cube of space. For instance, having established what he felt was the right size for the coffers in the front row of the vault, he had then to determine how much smaller the next row of coffers would appear if one were, in fact, looking at such a situation. This is possible mathematically, or more directly by a series of linear or geometric constructions. Without going into the complexities of this particular situation, but only to give a

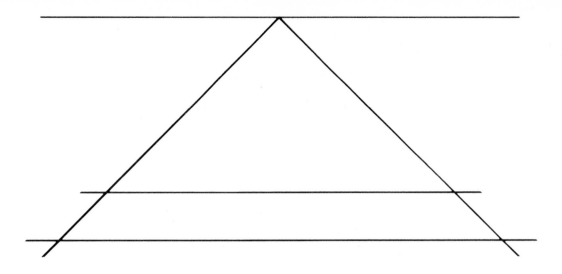

Fig. 16-12.

simple example of how such constructions can render consistent gradients of size, let us look back to our old railroad track situation. The question is: how can the crossties be systematically spaced to give an illusion of regular diminishment of the distance between them? This is done by first establishing a vanishing point on an eye-level line and then drawing the rails from that point. Next, the desired space is established between the first and second crossties as in Fig. 16–12. For simplicity we will draw each crosstie as a single line. Next, a diagonal, the dotted line, *AB*, in Fig. 16–13, is drawn across

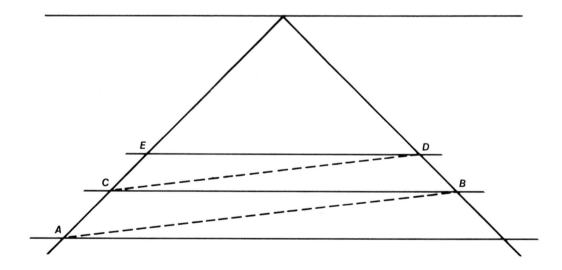

Fig. 16–13.

the trapezoidal shape lying between the tracks and the crossties. Then a line parallel to *AB* is drawn from *C* to where it contacts the right rail at *D*. Using this point, a line is drawn parallel to the crosstie line, *CB*. This line, *ED*, locates the third crosstie. Continuing this procedure upwards to the vanishing point, the result appears as in Fig. 16–14: a systematic diminishment of the space between the horizontals. A system related in kind to this is what Masaccio used to create the convincing diminishment of size of the coffers in the vault of his *Holy Trinity*. The principles of one-point perspec-

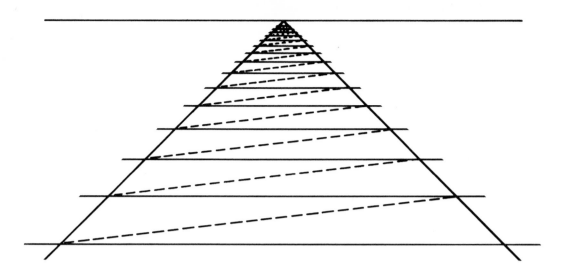

Fig. 16–14.

tive had not been completely formulated at the time this fresco was painted, but Masaccio had studied the works of Giotto; and, although not yet published, talk of Brunelleschi's and Alberti's scientific perspective was in the Florentine air. This means that Masaccio was in command of scientific one-point perspective well over ten years before Alberti's mathematical formulae and model demonstrations appeared.

The discovery of the principles of perspective makes a gripping enough story in itself, but our concern here is only to become acquainted with the kind of spatial unity it made possible in painting. Masaccio's *Holy Trinity* stands in evidence of that achievement. Suffice it to say that this young Italian did, for the first time, accurately produce on a flat surface the illusion of optically correct three-dimensional space. He accomplished this not only by *linear* perspective, but also by light and shade in both the architectural setting of his painting and in the figures. His admiration for the work of Giotto and his allegiance to his own vision result in the solid rounded appearance of the figures. Their clearly established and optically correct positions in the illusory depth of his work owe, of course, to the same principle that established the positions and sizes of the coffers. He has, for instance, painted the figures of the Virgin and St. John smaller in size than the donor figures, which kneel on a plane *outside* the vaulted area and hence appear closer to us. The donor figures are larger than the holy figures, not because they are symbolically more significant, but because Masaccio wanted them to appear closer to us. And throughout the painting he has made use of most of the devices for creating the illusion of three-dimensional space on a flat surface. He has, in fact, created the first work of art which scientifically creates a flat image that appears to be one and the same with the volumetric visual world of men.

But what about the dilemma that Masaccio resolved in such a pointed way? What about this situation in which Masaccio meets the contradictory demands of a supernatural story on the one hand, and a Renaissance humanism on the other? His resolution centers around the figure of God the Father. In earlier representations of the Holy Trinity, the Father was often shown as floating above the cross and supporting it. In Masaccio's painting, the Father

201

is in the right place and doing the right thing, but he is not shown as floating. Rather, he stands quite flatfooted on a sturdy cantilevered plane. Why is this? Maybe because Masaccio preferred to have the Father, here portrayed as a man, *stand* as a man. But the tradition called for the Father to be above the cross; how could He stand on the ground level of the cross and still be above the cross? He could make Him just that much taller—say about nine feet tall—but that would be unnatural. So Masaccio simply creates the plane for the Father to stand on. And since he wanted the illusion of deep space we see here—wanted to demonstrate that he could work it— he makes this plane appear to spring from the back wall of the vaulted area and run clear forward to the cross. In a quite comfortable and convincing way, then, God stands *at* the cross and *above* it on this plane, which is, appropriately, the highest plane in the painting. This solution describes an attitude: the traditional and doctrinal must be harmonized with the experience of men. Masaccio's scientific perspective, put to work with the elements of a supernatural concept, and resulting in this illusion of cubical space peopled with men and women and things of this world, documents this attitude.

Now let us look at two works from the High Renaissance that stand among the highest achievements of this man-centered, human-scaled space illusion. First is a painting often considered to be the first of the High Renaissance, *The Last Supper* by Leonardo da Vinci (Fig. 16–15), begun just three years after the discovery of America by another Italian. From our experience with Masaccio's *Holy Trinity,* we should respond immediately to Leonardo's painting as one based on a centralized one-point perspective. The "picture box" or cube sets the controlling spatial conditions for the mural, and as such works a unifying force throughout. Eye level for *The Last Supper* is at the level of Christ's eyes; the vanishing point is located in the center of the work at the intersection of the diagonals of the painting and behind the head of Christ. All edges and planes perpendicular to our plane of sight (the picture plane) are drawn from that one point. Edges and planes parallel to the picture plane are drawn horizontally across it. In these respects Leonardo repeats the system employed by Masaccio. However, the subject of Leonardo's fresco encouraged him to bring together in one coherent image the metaphysical symbolic import of the Last Supper and the scientific naturalism of one-point perspective. Here is one of those arresting instances of the discovery and expression, through art, of compatibility between the old and the new, in this case the metaphysical and the physical. Just how does this work in *The Last Supper?*

Starting with the religious import of the Last Supper, we remind ourselves that it has to do with the Christian sacrament called the Eucharist. This sacrament was instituted by the action of Jesus Christ at his last supper with his disciples when he gave them bread, saying, "This is my body," and wine, saying, "This is my blood." The traditional interpretation of these words is that in the sacrament the bread and wine actually turn into the

Fig. 16-15. *LEONARDO DA VINCI.* The Last Supper. *c. 1495–1498. Oil tempera on wall,* 10′6″×29′10″. *S. Maria delle Grazie, Milan. Photo: Alinari.*

substance of the body and blood of Christ. This interpretation gives rise to the term transubstantiation. The Eucharist is of essential significance in Christian doctrine, and the picturing of it in a work of art becomes an undertaking of considerable and specific demands. The unique potential of Christ to work this miracle on earth should be made clear pictorially. Because it is through Him and Him only that it can work, He is central to its realization, and in complete control. His divine power as the way from earth to Heaven, and His key position in the Holy Trinity of Father, Son, and Holy Ghost must be given form in any work of art on this subject that would attain anything like adequacy of expression. And then there is the subdominant theme of the Last Supper: the prediction by Christ of his own betrayal, and the shock that this creates among those at the supper. Judas must be present with the others, and he should be separated by Christ's knowing prediction. All this constitutes more than a demand for an *illustration*—for how could one illustrate a miracle? Proof of a miracle, if proof has anything to do with it, is the working of another miracle—or, for us mortals, the making of a physical object which in its own best way analogizes the spirit of the miraculous. This is what the mortal Leonardo, from the little town of Vinci near Florence, did in his fresco *The Last Supper*.

Satisfying all the requirements of script and dramatis personae, Leonardo goes on to analogize the miracle of the Eucharist. Christ is conceived as holding the central station in a perspectival network that radiates from

Fig. 16–16.

him. The controlling force of the vanishing point becomes the controlling force of Christ. His image is conceived as descriptive of a triangle—the tri-partite Holy Trinity—and it dominates as it participates in the constructed space of the room. His utterly human appearance is modified toward the divine by gesture and by the implication of a halo swung from the vanish-ing point as center and leaving only an exact concrete trace in the rounded pediment over the doorway behind him (Fig. 16–16). Leonardo, with a fine sense of the structural unity of scientific perspective, brings that quality into harmony with the meaning of the Eucharist and the Last Supper. Structure and meaning become identified and inseparable. And as for the subdominant theme, Leonardo gives us the illusion of substantial and perfectly articulated figures as disciples engaged in excited concern for the predicted betrayal of Christ by one of them. The figure of Judas, constructed within the outline of a distorted equilateral triangle which reflects his closeness to Christ and the impending betrayal, is dark and bearded black. The disciples may not know who will betray Christ, but Leonardo lets us know quite clearly by Judas' silhouette and by his breaking the plane of the table, as no other figure does.

In coming upon Leonardo's *The Last Supper* in the refectory of the Church of Santa Maria delle Grazie in Milan, we adopt the eye level of the painting even though it is above us on the wall. Not only do we adopt this level of Christ's eyes, we also assume a position directly in front of Christ. This is the result of the directive power of one-point perspective: it causes us to vicariously experience the scene from a single fixed point directly forward of the vanishing point. But this is not all that happens. We are caused, also, to experience *time* as fixed. Leonardo has organized this scene by means of a system that presumes single, simple location and stopped time. Every part of this cubical setting, every position of every figure and object, as well as every subtlety of expression in the faces and hands, has been conceived as being perceived just that way from only one position at only one moment in time. But that position and that moment is ours, the spectators'. This scientific perspective postulates position and time as *ours*—Christ and the disciples must share it with us. This is an anthropocentric work of art. It encourages and documents the scientific humanism of the Italian Renaissance.

The demonstrations and codifications of the new perspective by Brunelleschi, Alberti, and others had made it less difficult for Leonardo than for Masaccio to perform in that idiom with such apparent ease and success. Once such a concept has been reduced to formulae, it becomes teachable. Once teachable, it is more readily learned, and performance in it then often becomes virtuose, with a heavy emphasis on technical display. This is what becomes evident in the other High Renaissance work we will look at—Raphael's brilliant fresco *The School of Athens* in the Vatican, Rome (Fig. 16–17).

Fig. 16–17. *RAPHAEL.* The School of Athens. *1510–1511. Fresco, length 18′. Stanza della Segnatura, The Vatican, Rome. Photo: Alinari-Art Reference Bureau.*

Seventy-three years lie between Masaccio's *Holy Trinity* and Leonardo's *Last Supper;* a mere twelve years separate Raphael's *The School of Athens* from Leonardo's masterwork. But in *The School of Athens* we witness a competence in the manipulation of one-point perspective that is nothing short of virtuosity. Commissioned by Pope Julius II as one of four fresco murals for his library, it is an allegory of Athenian thought and philosophy. This in itself should be of interest to us—that the head of the Roman Catholic Church would commission for the Vatican a monumental work celebrating the achievements of the scholars, scientists, and philosophers of classical times. Indeed, the sixteenth century is the period of the High Renaissance in Italy!

Raphael brings nothing new to the science of perspective. Fundamentally the *cubical space* illusion of *The School of Athens* is no more than what we have already seen in Masaccio and Leonardo, but it is a rich and brilliant display of that. And it is this richness and brilliance that Raphael sought and to which we respond with such admiration. It would not have been possible without its first inventor-geniuses. The simple perspectival system which establishes eye level at the waists of the figures in the higher row, and the vanishing point between the two central figures of Plato and Aristotle, is what Raphael complicates. He does it mainly by multiplication —to the extent of *fifty* figures, more than a dozen figurative sculptures, three huge barrel vaults with *diamond* and *hexagonal* coffers, the drum of a dome, and a variety of invented classical details. And along with these are complex foreshortenings of figures which stand, walk, climb stairs, sit, kneel, lean, and recline, and are viewed from the front, back, and a great variety of in-between angles. These figures are lifelike and they take their places in an equally lifelike space. Together they give us a reality as rational as Copernicus' lectures on mathematics and astronomy delivered in Rome at about the time *The School of Athens* was being painted.

Scientific one-point perspective served to organize the space of rational Renaissance men. It stands as one of the formulations and expressions of man's estimate of himself as determinative in the world he physically inhabits. The humanly scaled reasonable space of Renaissance painting asserts man as the measure of all things. This is the often tacit, always fundamental assumption of Renaissance art. It is given such monumental and eloquent form in Michelangelo's *The Creation of Adam* (Fig. 16–18) that we feel driven by necessity to reverse the scriptural account to read, "God was created in man's image." And this is the motivating assumption behind Renaissance sculpture as well. We see it given form in Pollaiuolo's *Hercules and Antaeus* (Fig. 12–17), Donatello's *Gattamelata* (Fig. 16–19), and Michelangelo's *David* (Fig. 14–7). All have to do with the life and power of man. Pollaiuolo identified the life he knew with the classical myth and gave it a form that interacts with the living space around it. Donatello, commemorating Gattamelata, the recently deceased commander of the Venetian armies, identifies him with the Roman Emperor Marcus Aurelius and all men of brooding power. Gattamelata, huge in size, rides easy in his saddle and still activates the very air around him in the Piazza del Santo in Padua. Michelangelo, in a single figure over three times life-size, creates an image not just of the David who slew Goliath, but of youthful man as champion of causes which his efforts prove to be just. Originally intended to be placed high above the street on one of the buttresses of the Cathedral of Florence, the *David* is proportioned to compensate for the distortions created by the spectators' anticipated low angle of sight. This is why in our photograph, taken from a level near the knees of David, the head appears too large in relation to the rest of the body. Here, again, is a clear example of the Renaissance artist wishing for his work to take its place naturally in the space of the live spectators' world—even to the extent of building spatial illusion into the sculpture itself. And the *David,* with its open negative spaces and its irregular contours, pushes out into the surrounding space and participates with it in an active way.

Fig. 16–18. *MICHELANGELO.* The Creation of Adam, *detail of the ceiling. 1508–1512. Fresco. Sistine Chapel, The Vatican, Rome. Photo: Alinari-Art Reference Bureau.*

ANTONIO DEL POLLAIUOLO. Hercules and Antaeus. *National Museum Florence, Photo: Alinari-Art Reference Bureau. Figure 12–17 repeated.*

MICHELANGELO. David. *Academy, Florence. Photo: Alinari-Art Reference Bureau. Figure 14–7 repeated.*

208

Fig. 16–19. *DONATELLO*. Equestrian Monument of Gattamelata. *1445–1450. Bronze, c. 11'✕13'. Piazza del Santo, Padua. Photo: Anderson-Art Reference Bureau.*

THE PROTRUDING ANGULAR CUBE ILLUSION
AND SCIENTIFIC MULTIPLE-POINT PERSPECTIVE

In our previous considerations of spatial illusion based on the cube, we
have emphasized the illusion of looking into a hollow cubical space from
the center of an open side. Only in the case of eighteenth-century Japanese
block prints did we make a point of the illusion of looking into a cube from
an oblique angle. In that case, the one we referred to as the Japanese corner
illusion, we observed that an angular-isometric perspective was employed.
This perspective is not optically correct, as is the one-point perspective of
Masaccio, Leonardo, and Raphael, as we noted earlier. Now we must consider a type of space illusion that is both angular and scientific, and hence
employs more than one vanishing point. We can begin by looking at Pieter
Brueghel's *Peasant Wedding* (Fig. 16–20).

    With this sixteenth-century Flemish painting we become immediately
aware of a reasonably organized, humanly scaled picture space characteristic

Fig. 16–20. *PIETER BRUEGHEL THE ELDER. Peasant Wedding. c. 1565. Oil on wood.
45×64". Art History Museum, Vienna.*

210

of the Renaissance. Unlike the examples we have looked at, however, this
painting is not based on one-point perspective. First of all, Brueghel has us
look into a space whose descriptive planes create an illusion of looking into
a corner. In this respect it bears some similarity to the Japanese corner
illusion of which we have spoken, but there the similarity ends. Brueghel
employs scientific perspective; his aim is quite different from that of the
Japanese artist's employing isometric perspective in symbolic and decorative
ways. In the *Peasant Wedding* we are made aware, for instance, of the
diminishing vertical dimensions of the enclosing walls as they seem to go
into the far corner. Actually, the long, light plane behind the seated bride is
drawn in such a way as to indicate its relation to a vanishing point. Were it
possible for us to see the line of the bottom of that wall, it would slant
upwards from right to left. The top lines of the wall slant downward from
right to left. If these lines were extended they would converge at a vanishing
point outside the left edge of the painting. Following the same logic, the top
and bottom lines of the other wall plane would converge at another vanishing point beyond the right edge of the painting. Ample clues to this exist
in the timbers of that wall. This, then, would give us two vanishing points
—one far to the left, the other far to the right. This can be illustrated by a
diagram from which all the relieving irregularities have been omitted
(Fig. 16–21). The horizontal upon which both of these vanishing points lie is
the eye level of the painting. It falls a little above the head of the bride. It is
from that level and from a point directly out in front of the largest foreground figure that we seem to be viewing this event.

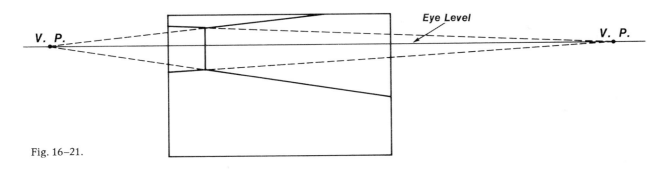

Fig. 16–21.

Now, within this corner of space, Brueghel presents his subject matter
in a very particular way. He has not arranged the figures horizontally across
the format as the earlier sixteenth-century Italians did. Instead he has the
figures and the furniture follow the angular directions of the two enclosing
walls. We understand from the perspectival evidence that the table at which
the bride sits runs parallel to the long, light wall. The ends of this table
parallel the short wall far to the left. The benches at the side and at the near
end of the table parallel the long and short walls, respectively. This can be
diagrammed as in Fig. 16–22. These three shapes, which describe the top
planes of the table and the two benches, are properly called trapeziums since

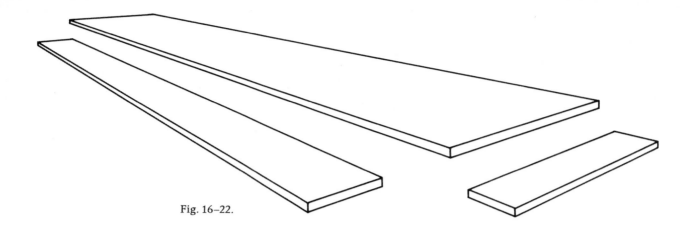

Fig. 16–22.

they are irregular four-sided planes. And just as their shapes and positions in space are determined by the perspective of the enclosing walls, these trapeziums provide the controlling reference for the placement of the figures which sit or stand in close relationship to the table and benches. Finally, this complex of figures and furniture, taken as a mass, roughly describes a cubical solid, a corner edge of which appears to jut out at us (Fig. 16–23). The lines drawn over the painting are intended to define the size, shape, and position of this cubical solid.

Fig. 16–23.

Diagrammatically, then, we have a complex spatial situation that consists of two closely integrated illusions: first, the corner illusion, which suggests *contraction* of size in depth, and, second, the protruding angular cube illusion, which suggests expansion toward the foreground (Fig. 16–24).

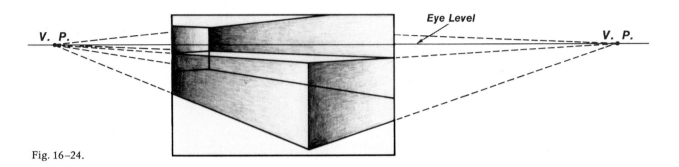

Fig. 16–24.

With certain exceptions, which Brueghel introduces to create a mood of natural informality in the painting, these two spatial illusions are constructed from the same right and left vanishing points. It follows that both assume the same eye level. The space illusion of a painting such as Brueghel's *Peasant Wedding* affects us in ways radically different from those produced by the centralized one-point perspective of earlier Renaissance artists. The employment of the corner illusion based on more than a single vanishing point encourages asymmetrical configurations, and we respond quite differently to the informality of asymmetry and to the formality of symmetry. The balancing of visual forces in an asymmetrical pattern is a much more complicated undertaking in which, as we have pointed out in Chapter 10, unlike elements and qualities must be balanced by largely intuitive means. Perhaps because of the greater visual surprises possible in this way, asymmetrical configurations are much more likely to appear dynamic than are symmetrical ones. The nearly symmetrical works of Masaccio, Leonardo, and Raphael, because of their clear spatial orientation around a single point, are often expressive of a static kind of equilibrium. As we said earlier, they communicate qualities of fixed time and single, unchanging position. And in addition, one-point perspective gives us the illusion of contracting space; all images of figures and objects appear to be shrinking in the direction of a single vanishing point.

What we are saying about the space illusion of the *Peasant Wedding* is simple but of considerable consequence: it communicates qualities of both contraction and expansion in space with an emphasis on expansion; it is more complicated than one-point perspective; it is asymmetrical and dynamic. It is generally expressive of the broader, more involved orientation to life that is characteristic of the sixteenth, seventeenth, and eighteenth centuries. This may be even more clearly evident in paintings that do not include the confining walls of the corner of a cube. Another painting by Pieter Brueghel, *Unfaithful Shepherd* (Fig. 16–25), should serve to illustrate this.

Fig. 16–25. *PIETER BRUEGHEL THE ELDER.* Unfaithful Shepherd. *16th century. Oil on wood, 24¹/₄×33⁷/₈″. John G. Johnson Collection, Philadelphia.*

In this wide and deep landscape, Brueghel creates an illusory space that shrinks toward the horizon. At the same time, however, he manages to give us the feeling of spatial expansion outward toward us. How does he do this? To achieve the shrinking spatial quality he makes use of a flat ground plane upon which we see images of trees, animals, and distant houses, all properly diminished in size, value, and clarity to produce an illusion of great depth. This quality of spatial contraction is heightened by the angling direction of the ground line beneath the trees on the left and by the opposing diagonal direction of the row of light colored animals on the right. He achieves the illusion of expanding space by placing the large, convex, clearly delineated shape of the shepherd low in the format and near the center in such a way that it appears to protrude from the picture plane. This quality of protuberance is enhanced by the fact that the shepherd is in a position of running—as if he were moving out of the picture and hence expanding toward us. But something less obvious is working to encourage illusions of spatial contraction and expansion. Brueghel makes use of the trapezium shape even as he did in the *Peasant Wedding,* only here it is employed more subtly. The front corner of this nearly diamond shape is at the shepherd's right foot. From that point we can move diagonally and upward to his left foot, along the dark shape in the mottled field immediately next to that foot, then past the slanted top of the light-colored plant and through the tree trunk to the strongly functioning shape of the sheep that stands at the extreme right of the format. This implied line, produced by tensions and closures, describes the right front edge of the trapezium. The left front edge runs from the shepherd's right foot, along his lower leg, and across the open terrain to the base of the tree at the far left. The left back edge of the trapezium starts at the base of that tree and runs along the clearly marked ridge to a point near the clump of trees near the horizon. The right back edge of the trapezium connects that distant point along the diagonal line of light-colored sheep with the sheep showing at the extreme right of the format. These four slanting lines give us the sides of the trapezium lying within the painting, as diagrammed in Fig. 16–26. The forward thrust of lines *AB* and *AD* contributes powerfully to the illusion of protuberance to which we respond in the figure of the shepherd. Together, these lines and the figure are principally responsible for the quality of spatial expansion in this painting. Lines *BC* and *CD* augment and support the quality of spatial contraction.

Fig. 16–26.

Fig. 16–27. *PETER PAUL RUBENS.* Peasants' Dance. *1636–1640. Oil on canvas, $28^7/_{10} \times 39^7/_{10}''$. Prado Museum, Madrid.*

Turning to a painting by the seventeenth-century Flemish painter, Peter Paul Rubens—his *Peasants' Dance* (Fig. 16–27)—we experience an even more dramatic display of spatial expansion and contraction. Into a landscape that is otherwise ordinary for that time, Rubens composes a group of sixteen swirling figures. They appear to move toward us, then turn and move quickly away only to return, it seems. This is accomplished partly by the attitudes and gestures of the figures. We can see that the figures on the left are turned and in positions indicating movement in our direction, and that those on the right are making their way back into the space of the painted landscape. The sensations of coming and going in space are specified in the apparent actions of these figures, but Rubens accomplishes this largely by employment of the angular protruding cube as the principal spatial reference of the painting. Going further than Brueghel, who used a flat trapezium in his *Unfaithful Shepherd,* Rubens makes his large group of figures conform to the planes of a rectilinear solid seen from above, with a corner turned toward us. This front corner is defined by the female figure lowest in the format. From the vertical axis of her body, two planes extend in opposite directions, one to her right, the other to her left. They terminate in the bodies of the figures farthest to the right and left in the painting. These planes take

216

on the perspectival character of the sides of a cubical solid seen obliquely. The trapezium-shaped top of this solid is described by the implied lines that connect most of the heads of the group. In diagrammatical form this would appear as it does in Fig. 16–28.

Here, again, we see an asymmetrical pattern, dynamic in character and without the single, contracting spatial quality of one-point perspective. Here we respond strongly to a spatial extension and expansion that relies on multiple vanishing points: the cube alone has two vanishing points, the house in the background has two more, and because each separate figure is turned in its own direction, separate vanishing points must be assumed for them. Still, as in all scientific or optically oriented perspective, there is but one eye level. It lies at the level of the eaves of the house in the background. This continuously functioning eye level serves to associate and integrate all parts of the painting, no matter how many vanishing points might be involved. As in one-point perspective, the painting is conceived as being seen by one pair of eyes, ours, and from a single position. However, the duality of the spatial illusion—as if it were both contracting toward the horizon and expanding along the forward directions of the front planes of the protruding cube—creates an illusion of reciprocal back and forth action that is easy to imagine as *our own bodily movement*. Not only do the images in the painting appear to be in motion, but we ourselves are encouraged to respond as if our viewing position changes with shifts of our attention from the illusion of "going back" to the illusion of "coming forward."

Fig. 16–28

The function of the angular protruding cube is crucial in developing this quality of "pulsating space." And since this richly dynamic spatial quality must have satisfied the tacit requirements of the equally rich and equally dynamic scientific and philosophic experience of the seventeenth century—the *Baroque* period—we find it operative in a great many works of that time. We find it in the meticulously conceived paintings of interiors by Jan Vermeer, which make us aware of a most deliberate exploitation of the reciprocal action of contracting and expanding space. His *A Girl Drinking with a Gentleman* (Color Plate 37) is an excellent example.

JAN VERMEER. A Girl Drinking with a Gentleman. *Staatliche Museen, Berlin. Photo: Steinkopf, Berlin. See Plate 37.*

It is only after Vermeer has gathered us into the mood of this small radiant room that we begin to experience a contrapuntal quality that gives this simple painting its deeply moving character. Against the foil of this room and its occupants—a kind of plainsong—Vermeer plays other fading and forceful melodies. We follow the diminuendos, as it were, into the shadowed depth of the corner of the room, and we are struck by the crescendos coming out to meet us. The shrinking space of the corner is counterpointed by the expanding cube formed by the chair, table, and the two figures. The protruding edge of the cube is deliberately marked by the line of the right back leg of the chair. From that edge two implied planes move diagonally upward to left and right. A surprising forward thrust is developed in the empty chair; it seems to all but push forward through the picture plane, just as the corner of the room pushes backward beyond it. An extremely subtle balance of these illusory and invisible forces is maintained in the picture. This balance, comparable to the systolic and diastolic actions of the most evenly operating heart, is almost at once dynamic and static. It is a measured balance of expanding and contracting spatial illusions.

Perhaps no paintings of the Baroque period better fathom and present the mood of seventeenth-century scientific and philosophical thought than those of Jan Vermeer. Here, in art, is the dualism of Descartes, Vermeer's contemporary in Holland, who based a whole philosophy on doubt and equivocality and performed valuable researches in the reflection and refraction of light. Like Descartes, Vermeer accepts as a fact that what we perceive clearly and distinctly is true—always allowing that truth may be both deceptively simple and deceptively complex, perhaps even simultaneously so. And it is no less than wonderful that Jan Vermeer, a man who earned his livelihood by making and selling picture *frames* and who perhaps accomplished almost all of his paintings in two or three small rooms in the city of Delft,[3] should be the one to give such convincing form to the Protestant Baroque dream of truth. And satisfying, too, is how Vermeer does all this with images of a man and a woman having wine in a quietly radiant room.

But we cannot leave the seventeenth century without contrasting Vermeer's contribution, one of the highest of the Protestant Baroque, with that of Rubens, one of the highest of the Catholic Baroque. Earlier, we spoke of Rubens' employment of the protruding angular cube and of his combining illusions of contracting and expanding space. However, as a Counter-Reformation Catholic, Rubens' tastes were cultivated in a direction which favored pageantry and a kind of sensuous mystical drama. These were often given form in an atmosphere of pagan excitement in some of his greatest works. It is true of his magnificent oil *The Fall of the Damned* (Fig. 16–29).

---

[3] P. T. A. Swillens, *Johannes Vermeer* (Utrecht: Spectrum Publishers, 1950).

In this almost overwhelming vision of hurtling bodies and serpent and animal forms, Rubens frees himself from the regular demands made by a perspectival world of ground and sky. Here the picture space is more akin to free aerial space or the kind of spherical space we sense deep under water. Our reason for discussing this painting (see also Rubens' *Battle of the Amazons,* Color Plate 5) is to make a point of the fact that space illusion in Baroque painting was often of a kind that was concerned with spatial convolutions and involutions. Instead of the clear "coming and going" in space that we saw in Vermeer, Rubens and many Italian and Spanish painters of the time exploited the sinuosity, the twisting and winding together, of the visual elements. The use of diagonal axes, curves, spirals, and serpentine directions serves to produce illusions of knotting and braiding the space of the picture. This character of the Baroque is still concerned with, and expressive of, expansive and dynamic space of which we have spoken, but here these spatial qualities are given free rein with a subject that certainly invites freedom from ordinary control.

PETER PAUL RUBENS. Battle of the Amazons. *Bayer. Staatsgemäldesammlungen. See Plate 5.*

Fig. 16–29. *PETER PAUL RUBENS.* The Fall of the Damned. *1618–1620. Oil on wood, 113×88". Pinakothek, Munich.*

In Rubens' *The Madonna Adored by Saints* (Fig. 16–30) we have a brilliant performance in spiralling space. The total configuration of this painting, which memorializes St. Catherine of Siena, an abortive fourteenth-century force toward Catholic reform, is based on a conical spiral seen from the side. Here Rubens develops an illusion of continuously expanding and contracting space as we experience the swing of the spiral toward us and then away and then toward us again. Our vision is invited with equal promise upward and downward along this dynamic structure that takes on the character of a revolving spiral staircase. And just as in his *Battle of the Amazons, The Madonna Adored by Saints* appears not to be bound by the limits of the picture format. The developed forces of spatial expansion seem to go beyond the frame of the painting—to enter *our* actual world, the world of the living spectator. The lower reaches of the conical spiral, its revolving base, seem to sweep out toward us and we feel as if we ourselves were being caught up in something like centrifugal force.

Fig. 16–30. *PETER PAUL RUBENS*. The Madonna Adored by Saints (The Marriage of St. Catherine). *1628. Oil on canvas, 18'8¹/₂" × 13'2". St. Augustine, Antwerp. Photo: Peter Adelberg, Inc.*

Plate 37. JAN VERMEER. A Girl Drinking with a Gentleman. c. 1660. Oil on canvas, $26^{1}/_{4} \times 30^{1}/_{8}$". It is only after Vermeer has gathered us into the mood of this radiant room that we begin to experience a contrapuntal quality that gives this painting its deeply moving character. Around the foil of this room and its occupants—a kind of plainsong—Vermeer plays other fading and forceful melodies. (Staatliche Museen, Berlin.)

Plate 38. MASACCIO. The Tribute Money. c. 1425. Fresco,
8′ 4″×19′ 7″. Masaccio celebrated not only the physical world
itself, but also the transient quality of that world. The shifting
play of light over the apparently solid shapes of his painting

and the somewhat indefinite boundaries of those shapes encourages responses in us that are related to movement, change, and
transience. (Brancacci Chapel. S. Maria del Carmine, Florence.
Photo: Art Reference Bureau.)

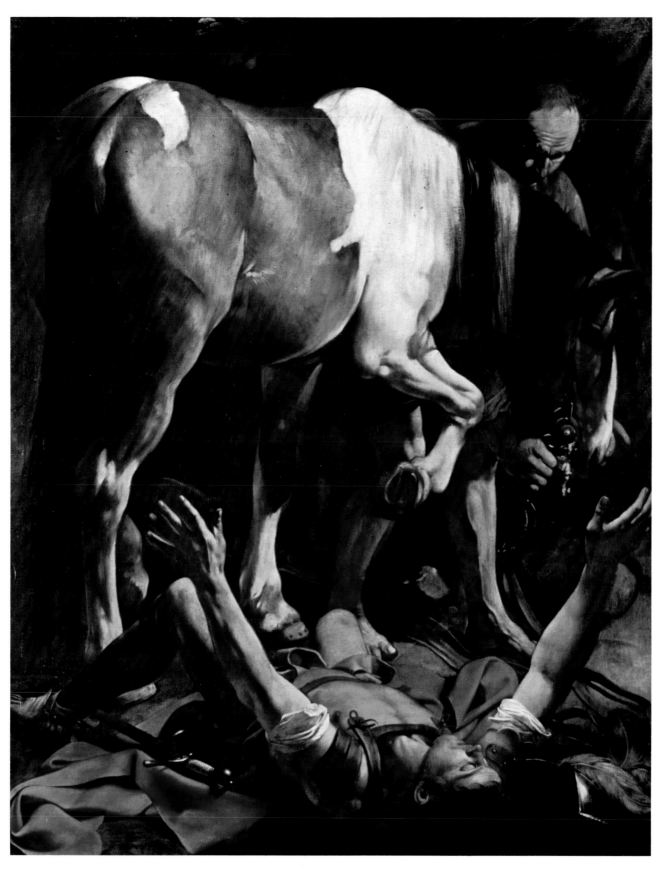

Plate 39. CARAVAGGIO. The Conversion of St. Paul. 1601–1602. Oil on wood, 90¹/₂×69″. The realism of Caravaggio prefers the concrete and the specific, not the elusive and the general. He spotlights the quite concrete *images presented in his paintings; he does not allow them to be dissolved or generalized in a light diffused by a particle-laden atmosphere. (S. Maria del Popolo, Rome. Photo: Art Reference Bureau.)*

Plate 40. WILLEM CLAESZ. Still Life. 1634. Oil on wood, 17×22½". Claesz gives us images of substantial and clearly defined objects as they are revealed by light. Still, even with these very precisely described images of liquid in a glass and oysters on a plate, the pristine space in which they appear to exist is closely related to that of much abstract or nonobjective painting. (Boymans Museum, Rotterdam.)

GIANLORENZO BERNINI.
David. *Borghese Gallery, Rome.*
Photo: Alinari-Art Reference
Bureau. Figure 7–4 repeated.

The space of Baroque painting is an active expanding space. It often does not honor the physical limits of the canvas; it seems to move out into the three-dimensional world of actuality and envelop us. And along with this, the subject matter of Baroque painting, perhaps especially the painted images of figures, often appears to participate in a world of actuality easily identifiable with our own. This is also true of Baroque sculpture. We have already made some reference to the employment of the spiral form in speaking of Bernini's marble sculpture *David* (Fig. 7–4). Turning back to that life-size figure, it should now be easy for us to see how much its actual three-dimensional spatial organization resembles that of the illusory space of Rubens' *The Madonna Adored by Saints.* The *David* does not fold into itself as does much Egyptian sculpture, for instance; it appears to expand in a dynamic way into the air around it. This is even more dramatically apparent

in Bernini's *Apollo and Daphne* (Fig. 16–31). Here Bernini's subject—the pursuit of Daphne by Apollo and Daphne's turning into a laurel tree in order to escape Apollo's love—is one that would attract the talents of a sculptor interested in dynamic action and transmutation of form. Bernini, with an extraordinary will to render qualities of life in lifeless stone, makes full use of all the artifices possible through his craft. His figures are made believable as human forms in actions with which we as live persons are kinesthetically familiar. He bases his structural pattern on a rising spiral form which culminates in an illusion of transmogrification of Daphne's hair and hands. He plays concavities against convexities, rough textures against smooth, positive volumes against negative volumes to produce convincing illusions of spatial contraction and expansion. And over the total configuration of rich sculptural surfaces, he has planned for the play of light to produce an appearance of life and action in the very space and atmosphere in which the sculpture stands. Seeming to move and breathe, and reaching outward from its sculptural core, the *Apollo and Daphne* group becomes part of the same world with which we, as spectators, are coextensive.

SPATIAL ILLUSIONS OF LIGHT AND ATMOSPHERE

In several of our references to spatial illusion in painting we have alluded to qualities of solidity in the images of figures. We said that the illusion of deep space was enhanced by the presence of figures that appear bulky or substantial. Certainly this is true of the works of Giotto, Masaccio, Leonardo, Raphael, Vermeer, and Rubens. Now, besides the character—the linear qualities—of the drawing of such figures, it is the illusion of light shining upon them which creates the appearance of three-dimensional volumes standing in an illuminated space. And because there is a long history of concern for illusions of both light and atmospheric effects, we will consider them as integral adjuncts of pictorial space.

Just as Masaccio was the first painter to produce a thoroughly scientific one-point perspective as the basis for his illusions of measured deep space, he was also the first painter since the days of Pompeii to create illusions of solid bodies existing in lighted atmospheres of one kind or another. His fresco painting *The Tribute Money* (Color Plate 38), completed at the very end of the first quarter of the fifteenth century, manifests an optically logical combination of landscape, figures, and architecture. This logic depends upon the consistency with which Masaccio employs one-point perspective: the fresco is painted as if seen from a single point in space and at a single moment of time. By extending the oblique edges of the architecture to the

Fig. 16–31. *GIANLORENZO BERNINI. Apollo and Daphne. 1622–1625. Marble, life-size. Borghese Gallery, Rome. Photo: Alinari.*

MASACCIO. The Tribute Money. *c. 1425. Photo: Alinari-Art Reference Bureau. See Plate 38.*

point at which they converge, we can locate both the vanishing point and the eye level for the painting. The vanishing point lies behind the head of Christ. The eye level, hence, lies at the level of the heads of all the standing figures. It is in relation to this level and this point that we orient ourselves to the painting. And even though this is a work which employs the old means of *continuous narrative,*[4] all figures and other images are scaled reasonably and in relation to that point and level. Now, with the same consistency, Masaccio develops an illusion of light shining down upon this composite event. No matter at what passage of the painting we look, we see that surfaces that apparently face to the right and upward are light, and all surfaces that face the opposite direction are dark. The surfaces facing in-between directions are painted in a variety of color values between the lightest lights and the darkest darks. This means that Masaccio assumed the existence of a source of light, the sun, as being above and to the right of this scene. Having established this as a control, he then modelled his figures and objects as if they were voluminous and being revealed in the light from that single source. This by itself is not Masaccio's invention. However, the somewhat substantial quality of the atmosphere—as if it were damp or slightly dusty—which seems to envelop all the figures and objects is distinctly Masaccio's. As we look from figure to figure, or from the figures to the landscape, we are made conscious of a sparse but effective influence surrounding and uniting every part of the painting. This phenomenon is often referred

---

[4] This is a means used to show a sequence of events separated in actual time, but brought together in a single configuration. It was employed as long ago as in the painting and relief sculpture of ancient Egypt. In *The Tribute Money* Masaccio combines three related events: Christ telling Peter to catch a fish which will hold in his mouth the tribute money demanded by the tax collector (left center of the painting); Peter extracting the money from the fish (at the far left); Peter paying the tax collector (far right).

to as *aerial perspective*. In *The Tribute Money* it is accomplished primarily through the consistent quality of the illusory light, by the merging of less than brilliant colors, by the not always clear contours, and by the somewhat granular surface of the fresco, which diffuses the actual light of the Chapel which strikes the painting.

MASACCIO. The Holy Trinity with the Virgin and St. John. *Photo: Alinari. See Plate 36.*

With the exception of some of Masaccio's other frescoes, notably *The Holy Trinity with the Virgin and St. John* (Color Plate 36) and *The Expulsion from Paradise* (Fig. 16–32), this highly successful illusion of a substantial atmosphere remains unique in painting for the next half-century. Masaccio, an avant-garde artist of his time, celebrated not only the physical world of which he must have deemed himself an integral part, but also the transient quality of that world. The shifting play of light over the apparently solid forms of his painting and over the somewhat indefinite boundaries of those forms encourages responses in us that are related to movement, change, and transience. We can take this to be expressive of an attitude toward the world, an attitude quite different from that expressed by works which give us uniformly delineated sharp contours and which appear to exist outside the natural world of atmosphere and ever-changing light.

Fig. 16–32. *MASACCIO*. The Expulsion from Paradise. *c. 1425. Fresco. Brancacci Chapel, S. Maria del Carmine, Florence. Photo: Alinari-Art Reference Bureau.*

In a host of works produced after Masaccio's masterpieces we see more and more refined exploitations of means for producing illusions of light in painting. Few, however, go beyond what Masaccio accomplished with illusions of *atmosphere*. Caravaggio, a century and three-quarters after Masaccio completed *The Tribute Money* and *The Expulsion from Paradise*, gives us works that attain something like maximum illusions of dramatic spotlighting. His *Conversion of St. Paul* (Color Plate 39) strikes us as utterly natural in its single source, stagelike lighting. Every apparent volume in the painting, from the huge body of the horse to the smallest folds in drapery, is rendered as if being revealed to us in the beam of a powerful light source to the right and above the painting. These illusory volumes appear to come forward from the dark areas that surround and weave in and out of the painting. For the most part, all the lighted passages are given in clear, sharp contours, and we tend to extend these even into the shadows. It is only light that modulates the apparent volumes. We do not sense the presence of an *atmosphere* acting to obscure and unite them. Compared to Masaccio's *The Expulsion from Paradise,* Caravaggio's painting is either without the qualities of an earthbound atmosphere or with the qualities of an atmosphere so rare it approximates those of a vacuum. The realism of Caravaggio is one that prefers the concrete and the specific, not the elusive and the general. He spotlights the quite concrete images presented in his paintings; he does not allow them to be dissolved or generalized in a light diffused by a particle-laden atmosphere.

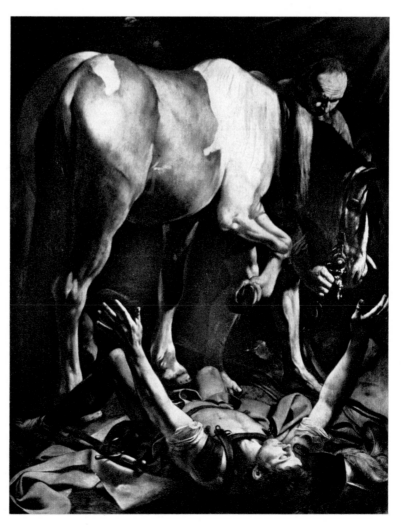

CARAVAGGIO. The Conversion of St. Paul. *Photo: Alinari-Art Reference Bureau. See Plate 39.*

WILLEM CLAESZ. Still Life. *Boymans Museum, Rotterdam. See Plate 40.*

This is also true in such works as *Still Life,* by the Dutchman Willem Claesz (Color Plate 40). With the possible exception of the area occupied by the drapery in the lower part of the painting, we are given images of substantial and clearly defined objects as revealed by light. No matter if the illusion is one of transparency or opacity, of roughness or smoothness, we find ourselves responding as if to magnificently clear objects standing in a single constant light beaming down through an airless atmosphere. The spatial quality produced by this must be akin to the space of the stars— intangible, incapable of diffusion or friction. And even with these precisely described images of liquid in a glass and oysters on a plate, the pristine space in which they appear to exist is closely related to that of abstract or nonobjective painting. The lines, shapes, colors, and textures of Joan Miró's *Composition* (Color Plate 41) find place in an illusory space little different from that of Claesz's *Still Life.* But Claesz, different from Miró, is concerned with the objective world and employs his skills in producing such illusions of light that will give us the utterly concrete quality of dishes and glasses, fruit and nutshells. In a sense, he delivers these objects into our hands and we are caused to *feel* their substance and weight rather than to *see* them as momentary intervals in an inconstantly lighted atmosphere. These paintings by Caravaggio and Claesz persuade us into an uncompromising world of material substance laid bare in light. And even though Caravaggio's painting is concerned with the mystical conversion of St. Paul while he was on the road to Damascus to suppress Christianity there, and even though this conversion was worked by a miraculous flash of light which blinded St. Paul while a bodiless voice questioned him from out of space, still Caravaggio

230

Plate 41. JOAN MIRO. Composition. 1933. Oil on canvas, 51¹/₄×63¹/₂″. The lines, shapes, colors, and textures of Miró's painting take their places in an illusory space. They mark off intervals of that space in ways as far removed from ordinary visual experience as is the space between the stars or the space between amoebae under the microscope. (Wadsworth Atheneum, Hartford.)

Plate 42. J. M. W. TURNER. Burning of the Houses of Parliament. c. 1835. Oil on canvas, 36¼×48½″. This is hardly a portrait, so to speak, of the Houses of Parliament—or of the river or the bridge. It is a painting primarily concerned with the behavior of light and atmosphere under extraordinary conditions. For Turner it must have been the dramatic pattern of such behavior that moved him to create an analogy of it in paint. (Philadelphia Museum of Art. John H. McFadden Collection.)

Plate 43. CLAUDE MONET. Morning Haze. Date? Oil on canvas, 29¹/₈×36⁵/₈". Monet is concerned with suggesting the encompassing atmospheric conditions that the presence of various different objects makes perceivable to us. It is true that we can see images of a field and a row of trees in this painting, but these serve mainly as passages in a continuous net for catching light. (National Gallery of Art, Washington, D. C. Chester Dale Collection, 1958.)

Plate 44.   *CLAUDE MONET*. Rouen Cathedral, Early Morning. *1894. Oil on canvas, 41³/₄×29¹/₈". In his efforts to present the elusive face of reality in the flux of time and space, Monet made twenty-six paintings of the light and* atmosphere showing upon and around Rouen cathedral. *Each of these paintings was accomplished at a different time of day and under different aerial conditions. (Museum of Fine Arts, Boston. Tompkins Collection.)*

presents the event as if composed of static material elements standing separately in a steadily lighted vacuum. Nothing of the action, change, or transmutation inherent in an act of conversion is communicated by Caravaggio's painting. There is no attempt to temper the material substance of apparent things by the intercession of illusions of atmosphere. There is light and shadow; there is no intimation of flux, mystical or natural. And what we say about the *Conversion of St. Paul* is also true of the utterly material and tactile quality of the inanimate objects imaged in Claesz's properly titled *Still Life*.

Now all this is not to say that either Caravaggio or Claesz failed in what he set out to do, or that these are poor paintings. What we are trying to do is call attention to some of the means that work to give us what we see and feel in relation to these paintings. In the early part of this discussion of spatial illusion in painting we said that the way the artist contends with space in his works is indicative of his larger orientation to life in general. And both Caravaggio and Claesz, it would appear, are oriented to a world of deep, mathematically logical, tridimensional space. For them, this space is marked off by the presence and particular location of solid substances in various forms. The shapes of these substances are thought of as separate from each other and clear—even when enveloped in shadow. Theirs is a

JOAN MIRÓ. Composition. Wadsworth Atheneum, Hartford (Ella Gallup Sumner and Mary Catlin Sumner Collection). See Plate 41.

clear world of bounded objects, and light exists to reveal these objects and so prove and guarantee that sort of world. Neither Caravaggio nor Claesz appears deeply concerned or even artistically aware of aerial conditions in nature which cause objects to lose their boundaries and merge. For them, there are objects—and the role of light is to make them clear. Neither light nor atmosphere is thought of, or perhaps even *seen,* as a phenomenon having its *own* role to play among objects. Perhaps this will become better understood if we turn to some works which rather obviously reveal the artist's concern for both light and atmosphere as prime subject matter.

In J. M. W. Turner's *Burning of the Houses of Parliament* (Color Plate 42), it would appear that it is the visually perceivable *conditions of burning* which most interest the artist. This is hardly a portrait, so to speak, of the Houses of Parliament—or of the river or the bridge. It is a painting primarily concerned with the behavior of light and atmosphere under extraordinary conditions. For Turner it must have been the dramatic pattern of such behavior which moved him to create an analogy of it in paint. And hardly ever modest in his means, Turner invents as well as selects the terms of this extraordinary situation which allows for a maximum staging of that drama. Against a dark lavender-blue field, a starry night sky, he paints illusions of smoke and steam-filled air within which the firelight wavers and takes on qualities of material substance. It is the *incandescence* of the buildings of

J. M. W. TURNER. Burning of the Houses of Parliament. *Philadelphia Museum of Art (John H. McFadden Collection). See Plate 42.*

CLAUDE MONET. Morning Haze. *National Gallery of Art, Washington, D.C. (Chester Dale Collection, 1958). See Plate 43.*

Parliament, the *reflections* of colored atmosphere in the river, the *shadows* of smoke along the bridge, the *merging* of individual figures, boats, water, sky, and shore—all brought together in a dynamic pattern—which commands our eyes and engages our mind. The buildings, the river, the bridge, and all the other images presented exist for purposes of giving body to something else. These images, thought of as obstructing objects, are merely the necessary means to reveal the unifying and pervasive qualities of light and atmosphere. And those qualities, not the objects, are the prime subject matter of Turner's painting.

Now, this shift of emphasis from objects standing in space to the visually perceivable qualities of space itself is no less than profound in its implications. But before we attempt any generalizations, let us look at a few works which most fully epitomize the achievements of this shift.

With the possible exception of certain contemporary works, it is the painting of the French Impressionists during the late nineteenth century which gives the most persuasive form to concerns for light and atmosphere, as such. And of all Impressionists, it probably is Claude Monet who most completely succeeds in giving form to the evanescent conditions in which all the furnishings of our visual world exist. In his *Morning Haze* (Color Plate 43), Monet deserts all concern for historical, allegorical, religious, or literary subjects. Actually, he also moves away from preoccupations with the traditionally accepted descriptive clues to such subjects: his emphasis is not upon depicting objects but upon suggesting the encompassing atmospheric conditions which the presence of objects makes perceivable to us. It is true that we can see images of a field and a row of trees against the sky, but these serve mainly as passages in a continuous fabric for catching light. It is the specific quality of this fabric, or net, which, by artifice, "re-presents" the colors and textures of light and atmosphere which Monet visually perceived as he sat facing this motif across a particular field at a certain time on a certain day in the year 1892.

It is the pervasive qualities of light and atmosphere which, properly speaking, are the subject and the subject matter of Monet's paintings. And for Monet, as for the other Impressionists, it was required that these qualities be perceived with perceptual unity and *directly*—that he must sit *in*, not just *in front of,* his motif—and as rapidly as possible analogize these qualities that change with every fractional turn of the earth and every subtle change in the composition and movement of the atmosphere. In his efforts to present

CLAUDE MONET. Rouen Cathedral, Early Morning. *Museum of Fine Arts, Boston (Tompkins Collection). See Plate 44.*

CLAUDE MONET. Waterloo Bridge. *Worcester Art Museum, Massachusetts. See Plate 45.*

the elusive face of reality in the flux of time and space, Monet made 26 paintings of the light and atmosphere showing upon and around Rouen Cathedral (Color Plate 44) and 16 centered around Waterloo Bridge (Color Plate 45). Each of the paintings in these series was accomplished at different times of day and under different aerial conditions. It appears that Monet wished to record and understand the nature of these differences which exist among the same set of material substances simply because of differing conditions of light and atmosphere. His primary interest appears to have lain in the changing conditions and not in the objects or surfaces providing traces of these conditions. These paintings, which make use of most of the devices for creating illusions of depth on a flat surface, make special and telling use of color. The temperature phenomenon of color, and how it functions to produce illusions of nearness or farness, is employed in consistent but not always obvious ways. We find, for instance, bluish colors in areas suggestive of shadows even when those areas lie low in the format of the painting and hence should appear close to us—which, in most cases, they do. This is accomplished partly by the Impressionists' use of what has been called "divided color," or by a process of "divisionism." In this technique the whole range of the spectrum colors is used over the *whole* canvas, but they are applied in small short brush strokes or daubs in close proximity to each

235

other and they are distributed in different quantitative relations to each other. For instance, the background area of an Impressionist painting may contain separate red, orange, and violet daubs of color, but the cooler violet daubs will predominate in quantity and hence determine the apparent temperature of the entire area. Likewise, a foreground area composed of blue, violet, yellow, and red brush strokes will, in most cases, reveal a preponderance of yellow and red. These two colors, being the warmest on the spectrum, will then work to cause the area to appear close to us. By this method of building *more* cool than warm colors into certain areas of the painting, and *more* warm than cool colors into other areas, the Impressionist painter produced illusions of recession into space. However, with his attention focused on the all-pervasive phenomena of light and atmosphere, we find a greater tendency to merge foreground and background in the common fabric of space characterizing Impressionist paintings. This is true, for instance, in Monet's *Rouen Cathedral, Early Morning* (Color Plate 44) in which we see the blue of the sky area almost duplicated in the deeply shadowed recesses of the foreground architecture. And the light yellow color of the base of the façade—apparently quite close to us—is identical to the light yellow painted high in the towers of the Cathedral, which are apparently quite distant from us.

Some of what we have been saying may strike us as contradictory. On the one hand we are saying that illusions of light and atmosphere are integral adjuncts of space illusion in general, and that Impressionist painting achieves maximum illusions of light and air. On the other hand we are saying that Impressionist painting evidences tendencies to compress space— to confuse the space-implying powers of color, to compromise those forces and so diminish illusions of deep space. All that can be said of this contradiction is that it does exist, and that from the standpoint of color *alone* the space of Impressionist painting is sometimes equivocal in character—certainly if we compare it to that of Claesz's *Still Life* (Color Plate 40) or Raphael's

WILLEM CLAESZ. Still Life. Boymans Museum, Rotterdam. See Plate 40.

RAPHAEL. The School of Athens. *Photo: Alinari-Art Reference Bureau. Figure 16–17 repeated.*

The School of Athens (Fig. 16–17). However, in this very contradiction lies a key to what we have been saying all along—that Impressionism is not primarily expressive of a world of clearly bounded objects standing still at easily measurable distances from each other in deep space. Rather, Impressionism is expressive of a world in which force or energy pervades all space, inside and outside of what we call objects, and which is never at rest. In such a world, energy is expended in all directions and in all patterns, continuously. Objects become concentrations of forceful patterns which interact with and are coextensive with all other patterns.

This is not to say that Claude Monet or any of the Impressionists were knowingly concerned or dedicated to formulating and expressing such a world. All we are saying is that the paintings themselves give rich evidence of sympathy for, and engagement with, visual phenomena that intimate a dynamic and insubstantial world. It is almost as if the Impressionists, in their uncomplicated desire to record nature as it came to their eyes, discovered that matter appears to dissolve in the agent that reveals it—the illuminated atmosphere. Under the eye and the brush of the Impressionists the object-centered world established during the Renaissance gives way to a world in which all objects have their significance mainly as traps for the immaterial qualities of light. We can say that with all the self-evident beauty of Impressionist painting, it still stands as expressive of a crucial shift in the minds and hearts of men—a shift from static matter to dynamic energy. And how this relates to the urbanization and the industrialization of the nineteenth century, to the disintegration of old social, political, and religious institutions, is not easy to say. But it happens to be true that while the last vestiges of the closed and self-sufficient systems of Europe were being attacked or crumbling, the Impressionists were quietly painting images of the open air in which boundaries between things disappear and all things participate in a common radiance.

Earlier, when we were discussing the works of Giotto, we said that his paintings made us aware of the past out of which they come—primarily the Byzantine—and the future to which they point—the High Renaissance. We said that Giotto's concern for a pictorial unity based on illusions of three-dimensional space and his preoccupations with verisimilitude in the shape, bulk, and expression of his figures are indicative of humane interests that will later culminate in the destruction of the medieval world of Divine Law and metaphysical conviction. Later, in commenting upon the achievements of Renaissance art, we noted the fruits of Giotto's and Masaccio's work. We said that scientific one-point perspective served to organize and present the space of rational Renaissance men. We said that that perspective stands as one of the formulations of man's estimate of himself as determinative in the world he physically inhabits—that the humanly scaled, reasonable space of Renaissance painting asserts man as the measure of all things.

Now we are saying that a concern for illusions of aerial space, first adumbrated in post-classical times by Masaccio and forcefully embodied by Turner, is brought to its final, or most recent, expression in the paintings of the Impressionists. And the only reason we make a point of any of this is to reinforce one of the things we said at the very outset of this discussion of space and spatial illusion—that how men cope with space in works of art is indicative of their larger orientations to the world in general. And in the work of the Impressionist painters we can see how they depended on the achievements of those who went before. Masaccio is alive, so to speak, in their works; and so is Leonardo, Vermeer, Rubens, Rembrandt, and Turner, to name only a few. For when we stop to analyze the space illusion of Impressionist painting, we see that it makes continual use of most of the preceding accomplishments in *linear* perspective from the early Renaissance through the Baroque to the nineteenth century. Although the Impressionist painters may have compressed pictorial space and brought a new emphasis to the *fabric* of visual reality by admitting the pervasive conditioning forces of light and atmosphere, their works are still of Renaissance lineage. They are, in fact, its consummation. And it should strike us as being somewhat ironic—but perhaps no more so than the outcome of many of man's imperfectly anticipated adventures—that a search for the form of objective reality should result in images expressive of the dissolution of matter itself. That this is the case, however, becomes more certain when we see what Auguste Rodin, the greatest of Impressionist sculptors, did with the recalcitrant medium of stone.

In his marble portrait *Puvis de Chavannes* (Fig. 16–33), first developed in clay and then translated into stone by the most skillful of stonecutters, Rodin succeeds in producing the image of a specific person as if only partly rescued out of the wavering continuum of light in atmosphere. By avoiding sharp transitions from the hollows and bosses of interior volumes—as in the areas of the eyes, cheek, and forehead—light is allowed to flow rather continuously over these and contiguous areas. This serves to unify all surfaces of the sculpture as if we were seeing them through a gossamery veil. Along with this, Rodin has kept the surface of his sculpture unpolished; he has avoided producing abrupt and clear differences between the limits of the stone and the surrounding air. The rough and granulated texture of the surface serves to reflect, diffract, and diffuse light in ways that produce a radiance among, rather than a separation between, the volumes of the sculpture. It is this veiled radiance which brings to the hard, unmoving stone qualities of change and resilience. With Rodin, the solid forever-unchanging "Rock of Ages" becomes a means for making manifest the flux and energy that permeates and defines all matter.

Fig. 16–33. *AUGUSTE RODIN*. Puvis de Chavannes. *1910. Marble, height 29⁵/₈". Rodin Museum, Paris.*

CHAPTER SEVENTEEN

Illusions
of
Ambiguous Space

In just about everything we have so far said about space and spatial illusion we have implied a continuing quest for means by which men might adequately and with grace formulate their relation to the world in which they live. The Egyptians accomplished this in their way, Renaissance and Baroque men did it in ways at least satisfactory to them, and so did the Impressionists. It is no more than fair to say that each in his own time and place was right in both the nature and results of his quest. The whole truth never lies in one place or in one time, and one truth does not necessarily invalidate another. The history of art is less a simple story of rejecting one truth for another than it is a comprehensive indication of the changing demands for truth that man's existence calls forth. And although no simple evolutionary theory will suffice to describe or explain the relationships among the varieties of truth called forth at different times and places, still, such relations do exist.

The conditions of early fifteenth-century Florence and the occurrence of a man called Masaccio somehow came together in ways that resulted in the first full statement of mathematically and optically correct one-point perspective—an arresting truth. With this as a basis for organizing and presenting space, variations and expansions were made possible all over the Western world during the ensuing five hundred years. What we saw of the angular protruding cube and multiple-point perspective, as well as of illusions of light and atmosphere are all, in some way, related to the clear statement made by Masaccio in the Church of Santa Maria Novella in 1425. Throughout these hundreds of years the most insistent demand appears to have been for increased and more complex means of creating convincing illusions of space seen or conceived as receding with measurable regularity away from the spectator. In the work of Raphael and Rubens we are struck

by both the depth and complications possible within this front-to-back order.
In the modest paintings of the Impressionists we are given a world partially
disembodied by effects of light and atmosphere. But in all this great variety
of painting one common assumption is evident. This assumption is that
whether we concentrate on objects or on the agents which reveal them,
man sees (experiences) his world from *a single position at a single moment
in time.*[1] This is what lends a simplicity and clarity to even the most complex
compositions of the Baroque painters. For all the convolutions of a gigantic
Rubens painting, the subtle spatial contractions and expansions of a Vermeer, or the coalescing shapes of a Monet, it is still true that the overall
images are presented as if seen from a fixed location at a fixed time. The
post-Renaissance exceptions to this are relatively few in number but of
more than ordinary importance to what we will have to say later in this
section.

Against the Renaissance tradition of a generally clear pictorial space
based on an assumption of fixed time and single location, there is another.
Specifically, it had its quite self-conscious beginning in the first decade of
the twentieth century in a style of painting we call *Cubism.* However, long
before that there existed paintings whose creators, by all evidence, were
concerned with something outside of limited time and place. This is true,
for instance, in the late sixteenth-century painting *Christ at Gethsemane*
(Color Plate 46), by Domenikos Theotocopoulos, known to us by his nick-
name El Greco.

Few of us, perhaps, are not moved by the splendor, power, and drama
of this painting. Even if we are not familiar with the scriptural account of
Jesus' going into Gethsemane to pray for understanding and strength in the
face of impending betrayal and crucifixion, we are still positively affected
by the unsettling dynamism of the total configuration of the painting. This
is the quality in which El Greco conceives of this crucial event in the life of
Christ; and if we respond to that we then have a promising entree to its
more specific import. This is an event which involves a troubled and uncertain Christ, his disciples, and his anxious prayers to the Father in the Garden
of Gethsemane. During this event Christ prays more than once; he leaves
the Garden and returns more than once; he reports to his disciples more
than once; and he finds them asleep and awakens them more than once. It
is the sort of serial event that could be given pictorial form by using the
device of continuous narrative; but El Greco does not make use of that
device. Instead he gives us single, unrepeated images of the disciples and
of Christ and the Garden and the answering angel. And still, El Greco

---

[1] This would appear to be true even in cases where the device of "continuous narrative"
is employed, as in Masaccio's *The Tribute Money* (Color Plate 38). For even though we
are given images of three events that we know from Scriptural account are separated
in time and place, still these images are presented as if seen simultaneously in a single
continuous landscape from a single point of view at a given moment in time.

manages to communicate something of the fact that this event, as a whole, exists outside of simple time and place. He succeeds in intimating more than one time passing in more than one specific place, and he does this in a single configuration. How is this accomplished? To answer that question we must look closely at the painting and ask some other questions.

First, let us ask ourselves where is the eye level for this painting? Ordinarily we might look to a horizon and declare that the eye level. In this painting, however, there is no clear horizon; at the far right we look past a series of apparently overlapping hills, the highest of which merge with unusual cloud shapes. This will not help us much in discovering the eye level of the painting. So, next, let us look at how the figures are drawn—

EL GRECO. Christ at Gethsemane. *The Toledo Museum of Art (Gift of Edward Drummond Libbey, 1946). See Plate 46.*

maybe the manner and degree of their foreshortening will establish the level from which they were conceived. The figure of Christ is given as being almost entirely *below* eye level, for we can see the top of his left shoulder passing behind his neck. The figure of the angel, even though its lower one-third lies below the upper part of Christ, is shown as entirely *above* eye level. It appears that the figure of Christ is presented as being seen from one eye level while the figure of the angel is seen from another. In other words, these figures, as they exist in this painting, could not be seen from a single eye level; they could not be seen this way from a single fixed position.

Now, what about the matter of vertical position in the format as indicative of the nearness or farness of images from us? When we look at the sleeping figures of the disciples, Peter, James, and John huddled in the mysterious egg-shape at the far left, they appear very small—as if at a considerable distance back of Christ. However, when we take note of the position of these figures in the format, they appear too low to be consistent with the smallness of their size. In other words, from the standpoint of size relationship the disciples appear rather far off in the distance, but their position low in the format causes them to appear much closer to us. We could say that depending on how we shift our attention, these figures appear close to us and then farther away. We can also say that they appear close and far from us at the same time, but that would be a rather ambiguous statement.

Our main point in all this is very simple. We intend only to establish the fact that between the Renaissance and the twentieth century there were artists who did not employ the principles of mathematically correct perspective in the tradition of the Renaissance. El Greco's *Christ at Gethsemane* is evidence of that. Upon examination many of El Greco's works reveal the assumption of more than one eye level and more than one position from side-to-side or front-to-back in relation to the images presented. His paintings often communicate qualities of existence which are not limited to a single moment in time or to a fixed position in space. As a result, paintings such as the *Christ at Gethsemane* present us with a kind of pictorial illusion which is *spatially ambiguous*.

Now, when we describe anything as ambiguous, we mean that it is capable of being understood in two or more ways. So when we use the term *ambiguous space* we mean that the space illusion is indeterminate, that it is doubtful or uncertain and that it can be interpreted in a number of ways. Earlier, when we were discussing Leonardo da Vinci's *The Last Supper* (Fig. 16–15), we said that it created an illusion of looking into that room from a single position directly forward of the vanishing point. Every part of that painting is conceived as being seen from that one fixed point in space and time. The spatial illusion in Leonardo's painting is *clear,* not ambiguous. It is free from doubt; it is certain, single, and without equivocation of any kind. This, we must assume, is precisely how Leonardo wished to organize and present his image of the Last Supper; this is at the core of

LEONARDO DA VINCI. The Last Supper. *Photo: Alinari. Figure 16–15 repeated.*

what the painting still expresses to us after almost five hundred years. But, as we have just observed, this is not how El Greco presented his image of Christ's agony in the garden. He chose to present that as residing in more than one moment and as if viewed from more than one position—simultaneously. And we can assume that El Greco chose, by whatever means, to do this for his own reasons of expression—in order to persuade the viewer into the mood of uncertainty and doubt that was with Christ in Gethsemane and which, in a more general sense, accompanies all men of wisdom wherever they may be.

So, we are saying that ambiguous spatial illusion exists in paintings accomplished after the great discoveries of perspective were made in the fifteenth century—and even after those discoveries were known and understood, as in the case of El Greco. That it existed in works prior to the Renaissance, we know through our references to Egyptian and Byzantine art. However, it was not until the twentieth century that spatial ambiguity, *as such,* becomes a prime concern of artists. Early in this century it was Pablo Picasso the Spaniard who presented for the first time a full image of spatial ambiguity itself. But before we speak of him and his invention of *Cubism,* we must acknowledge the work of his great predecessor, the French painter Paul Cézanne.

In such modest appearing paintings as Cézanne's *The Gardanne* (Color Plate 47), painted toward the end of the nineteenth century, there already

244

exists some of the evidences of an interest in indeterminate space. This painting, which most of us see first as a quite uncomplicated and clear picture of buildings on a hillside, takes on other aspects the longer we dwell in our perception of it. The longer we look at it, the less clear certain passages appear—the more ambiguous its illusion of space becomes. If, for instance, we look at the area above and right of the center of the painting,

PAUL CÉZANNE. The Gardanne. *The Metropolitan Museum of Art, New York (Gift of Dr. & Mrs. Franz H. Hirschland, 1957). See Plate 47.*

Fig. 17–1. *PAUL CÉZANNE.* The Gardanne, *detail above center right. 1885–1886. Oil on canvas, 31¹/₂ × 25¹/₄". The Metropolitan Museum of Art, New York (Gift of Dr. & Mrs. Franz H. Hirschland, 1957).*

enlarged here in Fig. 17–1, we discover that it is not at all clear where houses, hillside, and shrubbery begin or end. Starting just below the brow of the hill upon which the two small one-window buildings stand, we feel comfortable enough in our interpretation of this expanse as the side of a hill that faces toward us. Moving our eyes slowly downward, however, leads us into a lighter area which flows to right and left into and among darker shapes, the identities of which are not clear. Because the contours of these shapes are highly irregular and because most lines are discontinuous or broken, we can interpret the surrounding light area as descriptive of either parts of buildings or extensions of the hillside *into* and *through* those buildings. The hillside, buildings, and shrubbery appear to *interpenetrate* each other. We cannot be sure which is which, where one ends and another begins, or which of these, in this position or that, is intended to appear close or far from us. The separate identities of object-images appear to interact, and along with this interaction—which is reinforced by Cézanne's purposive use of the temperature qualities of color—a spatial ambiguity is produced.

The same phenomenon is clearly evident in the area to the left and above center of this painting (Fig. 17–2). Here, as in several other passages,

Plate 45. CLAUDE MONET. Waterloo Bridge. 1903. Oil on canvas, 25³/₄×36³/₈. By virtue of Monet's use of color in broken patches rather than in flat areas, by his avoidance of clear divisions, and by his skill in analogizing the elusive fabric of light, which dissolves as it pervades these momentary vistas, we are made aware of a continually changing and insubstantial world. (Worcester Art Museum, Massachusetts.)

Plate 46. EL GRECO. Christ at Gethsemane. 1590–1598. Oil on canvas, $40\frac{1}{4} \times 44\frac{3}{4}''$. El Greco manages to communicate something of the fact that this event, as a whole, exists outside of simple time and place. He succeeds in intimating more than one time passing in more than one specific place, and he does this in a single visual configuration. (The Toledo Museum of Art. Gift of Edward Drummond Libbey, 1946.)

Plate 47.   *PAUL CÉZANNE*. The Gardanne. *1885–1886. Oil on canvas, 31¹/₂×25¹/₄″. This painting,
which first appears as a quite uncomplicated and clear picture of buildings on a hillside, takes on
other aspects the longer we dwell in our perception of it. The longer we look at it, the less clear
certain passages appear—the more ambiguous its illusion of space becomes. (The Metropolitan Museum
of Art, New York. Gift of Dr. & Mrs. Franz H. Hirschland, 1957.)*

Plate 48. PAUL CÉZANNE. The Basket of Apples. 1890–1894. Oil on canvas, 25×32″. Cézanne labored almost ritualistically in creating such paintings as this one. Throughout his long efforts spent before such familiar objects as these, he sought to give form to a visual reality that would go beyond fixed time and fixed location in space. (Courtesy of The Art Institute of Chicago.)

Fig. 17–2. *PAUL CÉZANNE*. The Gardanne, *detail above center left.*

it is possible for us to interpret the spatial illusion in more than one way. At times one area appears closer to us than other areas; at other times, that same area will appear farther away. And as we continue to look at the painting, we experience something like a backward and forward motion taking place. The different color and shape patterns seem to exchange places and sometimes merge within the relatively shallow pictorial space. Here the security and stability of Masaccio's and Leonardo's space is lost. As beholders of Cézanne's art we lose the feeling of standing continuously in one place, for at times we seem to be closer, at other times farther away from his paintings.

Now Cézanne accomplished more than illusions of indeterminateness or of shifting *in depth* as we have just indicated. He produced paintings in which we sense shiftings *across* the plane of the picture—as if different passages of the painting were being seen from different positions *parallel* to the picture plane. This can be exemplified in Cézanne's *The Basket of Apples* (Color Plate 48). For those of us who are sophisticated in photography or in scientific perspective, this still life painting may appear disjointed. Something about the table top makes it appear optically incorrect, or out of kilter. Too, there appears something "wrong" about the saucer in which the cookies

PAUL CÉZANNE. The Basket of Apples. *Courtesy of The Art Institute of Chicago. See Plate 48.*

are piled. Yet we know that even though Cézanne was competent in the use of Renaissance perspective, he still insisted upon these kinds of "distortion" in a great number of his works; we assume he intended to do pretty much what he did do. Let us see if we can discover what that was from the evidence he has given us.

First of all, but only after we have enjoyed the robust monumentality that surrounds this small group of ordinary objects, let us agree that in one way or another Cézanne was concerned with objects arrayed on a table. All of us are intimately familiar with that situation and we recognize it here. We see the painted shapes of the lower supporting part of the table, and the top which we assume to be rectangular and upon which the objects rest. We assume that this particular table, like almost all the tables we know, stands upon a more or less level floor and that the top of the table is parallel to the floor. But if this is all so familiar, why does it leave us with an unsettled feeling? What is it about this particular situation of objects resting on a plane that leaves us in doubt? The answer is simple: Cézanne did not paint this still life as if he could see it all at once from a single point of view. He painted it part by part from different points of view in the same manner in which he perceived the actual objects he had set up before him. It is the simultaneous presentation of these separate and uncompromised views which unsettles us. It leaves us in doubt as to which of several views is the controlling or "correct" one. It creates an illusion of space that is ambiguous.

We know that in any split second we see sharply only a pinpoint of the visual field into which we look. Wherever the lines of our two-eyed vision converge is the location of what we see sharply in focus; all else, though available to our vision, is blurred. In such an instantaneous and single fix of the eyes, however, the total configuration of the visual field *does* come through to us as we pointed out earlier. An *acquaintance* with the *pattern* of the whole visual field is accomplished in this initial contact. However, if interest in the *constituents* of the visual field is encouraged, we *scan* the field by making many separate visual fixes. It is the data perceived in these subsequent "looks" that are put together and justified in relation to whatever prior experience we have had with situations similar to the one we are looking at. This is, in fact, what we mean when we say that we *recognize* things and situations. What Cézanne does in his painting *The Basket of Apples* is to skip the step in the process of perception-recognition-representation that would have brought his separate perceptions together under some known, traditional control. Had Cézanne been Raphael or Vermeer, he would have compromised the differences of his separate perceptions by recourse to the principles of Renaissance or Baroque perspective. But Cézanne was Cézanne; he did not submit the data of his perceptions to the requirements of any such theories of perspective. Nor did he compromise the fruits of his perceptions in order to square them with what he *knew beforehand* about the objects and situations before him. He stayed with his perceptions and configured them with but one goal in mind—to create out of them the most personally satisfying and significant *visual structure* he could. That the result was often spatially ambiguous was of no special concern to him. He was after trying to image his perceptions of nature in ways that those perceptions *themselves* seemed to be asking for.

But we have come too far without pointing out some of the specific causes of spatial ambiguity in Cézanne's still life. Let us look first at the saucer holding the cookies. It is a very special image of a saucer, for were we to continue the line of its rim around and behind the cookies, it would not meet itself! In the case of a circular shape—as this saucer is certainly meant to be—we see it as an ellipse when it lies on a table in front of us, as shown

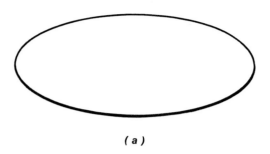 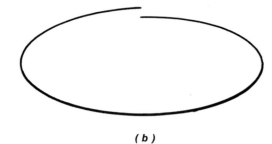

(a)   (b)

Fig. 17–3.

in Fig. 17–3 (a). Cézanne's saucer, however, would look like Fig. 17–3 (b) if
we continued the rim behind the cookies. Now, what about this? We know
too much of Cézanne's procedures to dismiss this as a simple error in drawing or just plain ignorance of such visual phenomena. What we actually
have here are two views of a single saucer. These separate views are joined
in the continuously running front edge. If we hold our hand over the left
half of the saucer, then the right half looks entirely convincing as one half
of a circular shape lying out in front of us and somewhat below the level of
our eyes. When we hold our hand over the right half of the saucer, then the
left half also appears convincing as one half of a circular shape. However,
this half appears to lie farther below our eye-level than the other.

It would appear that Cézanne painted the separate halves of this saucer
from different points of view—one higher than the other. That the separate
halves of a circular shape can be seen from different points of view is no
more than common fact; but to present in a *single* image more than one
view of an actually *observed* object is far from common. It becomes extraordinary when, to all evidences, this is done in contradistinction to known
prevailing facts and tradition. We must assume that Cézanne knew what he
was doing, and that, for whatever reasons or intuitions, he found it right to
do just what he did. His own visual experience, it would appear, proved to
his satisfaction that we see only *facets* or parts of objects at a time and that
each of these facets should be presented in its own right. Cézanne not only
exercised *facet vision,* as all of us regularly do, he presented the results of
such vision without compromising the differences produced by his changing
point of view. As a result, many of his paintings give clear evidence of what
we call *mixed perspective.* This term has its meaning only in reference to
the clear, "unmixed" perspective we have known since the Renaissance.

Even more dramatic evidences of facet vision and mixed perspective
exist in Cézanne's *The Basket of Apples.* If, for instance, we look at the front
edge of the tabletop we see that this edge cannot be interpreted as being
continuously straight as it passes behind the overhanging cloth. The edge to
the right of the cloth is much lower than the edge to the left. There are at
least two ways in which this can be interpreted: either as some odd kind of
split-level tabletop, or as a single plane seen from two different points of

250

view. The latter would seem more reasonable in light of the total context of the painting, but it is still true that ambiguities do exist here. Likewise, we sense spatial ambiguities along the back edge of the table. We see three sections of that edge—one to the right of the saucer, one between the saucer and the bottle, and the third at the far left of the painting. Each of these sections is horizontal, but they lie at different levels in the painting. We cannot interpret them as integral parts of a continuously running straight line or edge. They appear to step down from right to left. Again, if we assume that any one of these sections is drawn "correctly" according to the principles of scientific perspective, then the other two sections must be in "error." But if we assume different points of view for each of these sections, then each, in itself, appears consistent. Certainly, in Cézanne's mode of perception, these separate views appeared worthy in themselves; they became more than that when they were brought together not for reasons of simple perspectival accuracy, but for reasons of creating a painting which, in itself, possessed a commanding visual structure. This structure, we are saying, is one which depends upon facet vision and employs multiple points of view. Paintings arrived at in this way give evidence of mixed perspective and hence are spatially ambiguous. And it is the paintings of Paul Cézanne which first make express point of the equivocality of space.

Before objects such as the ones we see in many of his still lifes and landscapes, Cézanne labored almost ritualistically. He never set out to be an "abstract" painter; he was seeking visual reality, but a reality transcending the traditional one based on fixed time and single location in space. Throughout his long efforts to isolate and present that reality, he was convinced that the only way this could be done would have to be based principally upon what he could learn through direct observation of the world around him. For Pablo Picasso, Cézanne's great successor, it was a different story: Picasso saw Cézanne's *paintings* and he observed them with an intensity equal to Cézanne's observation of *nature*. In them he saw how Cézanne produced shiftings in depth and lateral alignment across the plane of the painting. The spatial ambiguity produced by these shiftings fascinated the young Picasso. He became interested in these visual phenomena for their own sakes, as *ends in themselves*. Then, it was almost as if Picasso

Fig. 17–4. *Mask, from Torres Straits area, New Guinea. Mid-19th century? Wood, string, cotton, shell inlay, shells, painted, height 19⁷/₈".* The Museum of Primitive Art, New York.

Fig. 17–5. *Figure Supporting a Chief's Stool, Baluba tribe. 19th century. Wood, 23³/₈×13³/₄". Copyright 1970 by The Barnes Foundation, Merion, Pa.*

decided, sometime around 1906, to create pictures of spatial ambiguity itself. And having been previously conditioned to a nonnaturalistic art by his study of primitive Oceanic and African sculpture (Figs. 17–4 and 17–5), he produced his *Les Demoiselles d'Avignon* (Color Plate 49) in 1907.

Here the interpenetrations of background and foreground planes, the indeterminateness in space of convex and concave shapes, the spatially illogical employment of illusions of overlapping, and the use of color for its decorative rather than for its space-implying qualities—all these mark this as the first self-consciously and purposively conceived image of spatial ambiguity. Today we know *Les Demoiselles d'Avignon* as the first *Cubist* painting. The style we know as *Cubism* was, in fact, invented by Picasso in the process of creating this very painting.

PABLO PICASSO. Les Demoiselles d'Avignon. *The Museum of Modern Art, New York (Acquired through the Lillie P. Bliss Bequest). See Plate 49.*

PABLO PICASSO. Ma Jolie. *The Museum of Modern Art, New York (Acquired through the Lillie P. Bliss Bequest). See Plate 50.*

Fig. 17–6. *PABLO PICASSO.* Les Biscuits. *1924. Oil and sand on canvas, 32×39". Private Collection.*

By 1912 Picasso had painted his *Ma Jolie* (Color Plate 50). When we compare it to a detail of Cézanne's *The Gardanne* (Color Plate 47) we can see how Picasso, the great prestidigitator, transformed the primitive, experimental art of Cézanne into the classical art of Cubism. We can see now that the transformation was worked in a surprisingly simple way—by shifting the emphasis from an *equivocal mode of perception* to the *free invention of equivocal images.* Picasso did not derive his *Ma Jolie* from direct observation of objects in nature. *Ma Jolie* resulted from his intellectual concern for equivocality—for the *idea* of ambiguity. This is why the art of Cubism is so often referred to as an intellectual sort of art.

In subsequent paintings, Picasso often makes use of mixed perspective in ways that are quite familiar to us today. For instance, in his *Les Biscuits* of 1924 (Fig. 17–6) he not only repeats the ambiguous saucer image which we saw first in Cézanne's *The Basket of Apples,* but he also deliberately combines *top* and *side* views in the image of the large dish near the center of the painting. And although Picasso's cubist inventions are not limited merely to combining separate views in single images, he still depends to a large degree on such combinations to produce spatial ambiguity. The union in one image of obviously different views of the same object clearly contradicts the tenets of scientific perspective. The presentation of such images is one of the surest ways of throwing into question the whole concept of fixed time and fixed position. Let us see just how this works. In Fig. 17–7

255

Fig. 17–7.

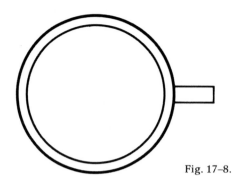

Fig. 17–8.

we see a mug drawn as if we were seeing it from a position above and in front of it. We interpret this drawing as if it were a mug in a position below our eye level because we can see partly into it. And we interpret it as being at some distance in front of us because we see the circular opening as an ellipse. Now, this same mug can be drawn as if from a position directly above, as if we were looking down into it (Fig. 17–8). In this case, the outer circle indicates the top edge of the mug, while the inner circle describes the limits of the surface at the bottom and inside the mug. The latter circle is smaller because it is further away from our eyes. The horizontal shape at the right indicates the top of the handle. This is a *top* view of the mug. A *bottom* view of the mug would look very much the same except that it would not include the smaller circle simply because we cannot see inside (Fig. 17–9). And in the case of a direct *side view,* we would see the top and bottom only as very slightly curved lines, the sides as straight lines, and the handle as a clear profile (Fig. 17–10).

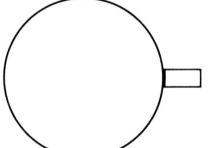

Fig. 17–9.

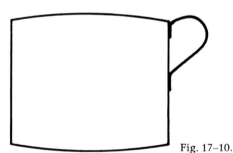

Fig. 17–10.

It should be obvious that each of these views is consistent in itself and entirely within the conventions of scientific perspective. Each of these views is developed as if from a single, unmoving position. Now, if we make any *combination* of these views, we necessarily imply more than one point of view; we mix the separate perspectives. In Fig. 17–11, *a* combines top and side views; *b* combines bottom and side views; and *c* combines all three views—top, bottom, and side. All three of these composite images, *a, b,* and *c,* leave us with doubts as to just how we are seeing this mug. There is more than one way in which we can interpret each of these drawings. They are, we say, drawn in ways that create qualities of spatial ambiguity.

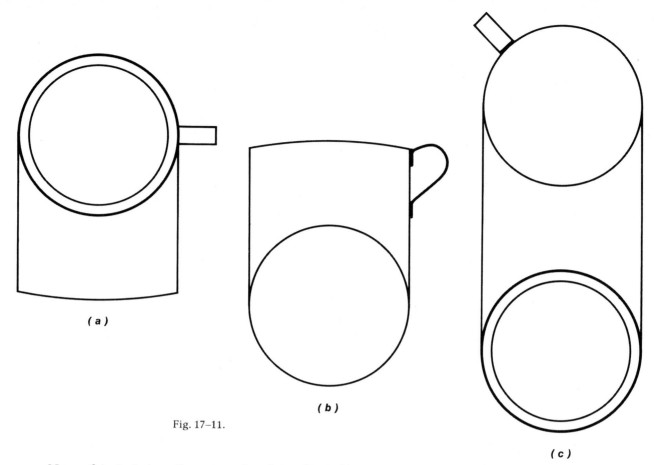

(a)

(b)

(c)

Fig. 17–11.

Now, this is interesting enough when the subject matter is a simple mug; it becomes fascinating, however, when the human figure is employed, or referred to. For it is a simple fact that we identify ourselves much more fully with images of the human figure than with images of anything else— animate or inanimate. The composite views of a mug, a chair, or even a flower can entertain us from a distance, impersonally, as it were—but when we see various views of the human figure in simultaneous combination we feel an actual bodily wrench within us. The ambiguity of such images comes home to us with extraordinary force. Picasso's painting *Figure Seated in a Wicker Chair* (Fig. 17–12) exerts that kind of force on us. For even though all of us have seen people from the front, back, and from all sides, we can see only one such view at a time. But when these views are combined, the effect is unreal and real at the same time—we recognize the views, but only with what feels like a muscular effort of mind can we compromise them.

When we come upon an image such as Picasso gives us here, we are thrown into doubt as to where we are in relation to the figure to which it refers. Or to put it the other way, we cannot be sure where or in what attitude the figure continually exists. The head can be interpreted as being seen from the front, or just as easily from the left or right side. Two profile views are intermingled to create a front view, and depending upon how we fix our eyes and focus our attention, we can see any one of these views as *the* view —but only momentarily. With each new fix of our eyes our attention shifts, and in response the image appears to shift, to turn or to oscillate. And no matter where we look in this painting, whether at the noncontinuous chair back or the complicated intermingling of the figure and its ground, this

257

Fig. 17–12. *PABLO PICASSO*. Figure Seated in a Wicker Chair. *1943. Oil, 40×32¹/₂″. Formerly Collection Louis Carré, Paris.*

uncertain shifting continues to affect us. Here, then, is a variety of spatial ambiguity made the more forceful because of its power to involve us personally with the human image.

Since the great pioneering works created by the Cubists, especially by Pablo Picasso, Georges Braque, and Fernand Léger, a tremendous body of work in which spatial illusion is purposely ambiguous has been produced. Just as with the great discoveries of Masaccio, and as is true for every great generic idea, the discoveries of the Cubists were rapidly exploited and systematized in the works of their followers. More and more sophisticated images of spatial ambiguity continue to be produced right up to the very present. Besides extremely convolved perspectives and complicated interpenetrating images, the spatial functions of color and shape have come to be better understood and more subtly employed in the works of contemporary painters. Without attempting to concern ourselves in any complete way with the variety and intricacies of this later work, we still should take note of one of the methods by which illusions of spatial ambiguity are now being systematically achieved. This particular and widely used method is a simple one. In a word, it operates by virtue of employing the regular optical functions of the visual elements and their qualities in *contradictory* ways. In order to understand just what we mean by this, it will help to refer to the table of space-implying visual phenomena presented earlier in this discussion.

APPEARS CLOSE TO US	APPEARS FARTHER AWAY
Large size	Small size
Overlapping	Overlapped
Low in format	High in format
Convex shape	Concave shape
Clear edge	Unclear edge
Rough texture	Smooth texture
Light value	Dark value
Intense color	Dull color
Warm color	Cool color

Now, if our aim were to create on a flat surface an illusion of regular and clear recession into space, we would employ this table in a consistent manner. In other words, we would make use of the visual characteristics listed in the left-hand column in all those passages of our picture or pattern that we wished to appear close to us. For all those passages we wished to appear farther away from us, or deeper in space, we would employ the visual characteristics listed in the right-hand column. In a general way, this is the method used to create illusions of clear deep space in most Western painting from the time of the discovery of scientific perspective right up to the present.

Now, to create illusions of spatial ambiguity on a flat surface, this table must be used in an inconsistent or contradictory way. In other words, visual characteristics which imply closeness in space must be mixed with other visual characteristics which imply the opposite. For instance, in Color Plate 51 we see two rectangular shapes. The smaller one is drawn so as to appear to overlap the larger one. On the basis of the phenomenon of overlap, the smaller shape appears the closer to us. However, the smaller shape is a cool blue in color, and the larger shape is a very warm red. This relation of colors causes the overlapped shape to appear the closer to us. A contradiction is created here. The space-implying powers of the overlap and of warm and cool colors—as well as of large and small size—are here pitted against one another. The result is a visual situation in which it is not clear which shape is closer and which is farther away from us. Spatially, this is an ambiguous situation.

Fig. 17–13.

In Fig. 17–13 we see a black convex shape lying in a white field. The convexity of the interior shape creates an illusion of expanding size and, hence, of closeness to us. The concavity of the surrounding field creates an illusion of shrinking and of being pinched out of existence and, hence, of being farther away from us. However, the black of the convex shape causes that shape to appear to recede, while the white concave field appears to advance. Here the space-implying powers of shape and value are at odds with each other. They work against each other to the extent that at one moment the black shape appears to float above the white field and at the next moment it appears to be a dark hole in the white field—as if the convex shape were behind the concave shape. Spatially, this is an ambiguous situation because it can be interpreted in more than one way.

These simple examples may suffice to indicate how the traditional space-implying devices can be used in a contradictory manner to produce illusions of ambiguousness in space. Still, this is by no means all there is to it. Everything we have said from the very beginning of this discussion of space and space illusion has implications for spatial ambiguity as well as for spatial simplicity and clarity. One of the ordinary wonders of the human experience teaches us that every invention of man, no matter how complete and seemingly ultimate its integrity, bears within it the description of, if not the powerful yearning for, its opposite. In the way that is the hallmark of the human adventure, Masaccio—almost five and a half centuries ago—made Cubism possible by his work on the wall of a Florentine church.

Now, at the close of this summary discussion, which leaves us in what is still our own time, we must say something about how this concern for ambiguous space in painting is indicative of larger orientations to life in general. For after all, that is one of our principal aims: to know again that the art of men is more than a private, isolated concern unrelated to the life men lead in the street, their meeting rooms, their beds, and their courts of law. In order to suggest some of these relations it may help to remind ourselves of some things we have already said.

Earlier, when we were speaking about "The Protruding Angular Cube

Illusion and Scientific Multiple-Point Perspective," we spoke of two closely integrated spatial illusions that appear simultaneously in many Baroque paintings. One was the corner illusion, which suggests *contraction* of size in depth; the other was the protruding angular cube illusion, which suggests *expansion* into the foreground and out toward the viewer. We likened the reciprocal phenomena of these spatial illusions to the intellectual dualism of René Descartes, the great seventeenth-century thinker, who based a whole philosophy on doubt and equivocality and who, at the same time, believed that what we perceive clearly and distinctly is true. And without attempting to say how or to what extent the painting of Vermeer relates to the complexities of such seventeenth-century thought, we still wished to suggest the existence of a real relationship between them. Certainly, we are impressed with the assumption of Descartes and Vermeer that truth may be both deceptively simple and deceptively complex—perhaps simultaneously. This kind of assumption has been fully domesticated since then. None of us is any longer surprised by the assumption of duplicity—or even multiplicity —in matters of human existence. It seems that now we *know* that nothing is simple, single, static, or clear. This is the way of our time, and it was Cubism which first created the emblem of that way.

Today, after Sören Kierkegaard, Sigmund Freud, Albert Einstein, James Joyce—and Cubism—we experience our lives in terms of the simultaneity of the contents of consciousness. It seems we know now that we live in more times and in more places, even more guises, than those of the *here* and *now*. A past, by virtue of memory and history, is forever with us; a future, by virtue of anticipation, can never be avoided. And the present in which, instant by instant, we stand changing, can hardly be experienced as simple or certain. Even so simple an act as looking at the objects on the table before us—the typewriter, ash tray, books, the vase of flowers—is now thought of as the complex experience that it is. For when we look at those familiar objects, our past experiencing of them, in no matter what contexts, functions in our present perception of them. Having seen the bottom of the ash tray when we washed it yesterday functions in our vision of it today— even though at the present moment we cannot actually see the bottom. And in a much more subtle way, all of our past feelings and imaginings about these objects condition how we perceive them at any single moment in time. The past functions in the present, and the present is pregnant with our expectations of a future. The simple mixed perspectives of Cubism work to create images of this ambivalence and simultaneity.

Far from being illogical or crazy, the ambiguous images and ambiguous space of Cubism are indicative of contemporary man's desire for a coherency that exists outside the old assumptions of fixed time and simple location. Cubism is part of this century's effort to cope with, to give form to, what each of us suspects is true: that human beings live in more times and in more places than the here and now—and simultaneously. In its own way, Cubism is saying that we live in the present, the past, and the future—the present plus memory and anticipation, all at once and never for long. It is saying that, as in the life of the mind, we are not fixed in place or in time, and that in a deep sense we are homeless, or, to put it another way, free. It is saying that whatever "home" we may have is described by the "success" we have in integrating our past with the present, as we relate both to anticipations of a future. I sit here, in this place, now, talking with you; and you are in the place you are, and in your time. But as I sit here I am aware of my life as it ran yesterday, last year, and when I was a boy of ten or twelve far from this room and the surrounding hills now being drenched in a late afternoon rain. And I, just like you, am aware of the possibility of tomorrow and even next year. I am not only here and now, and you are not only there and now. And though that sounds doubtful and unclear, it is part of the human experience which all of us share—and that is what ambiguous space illusion is all about.

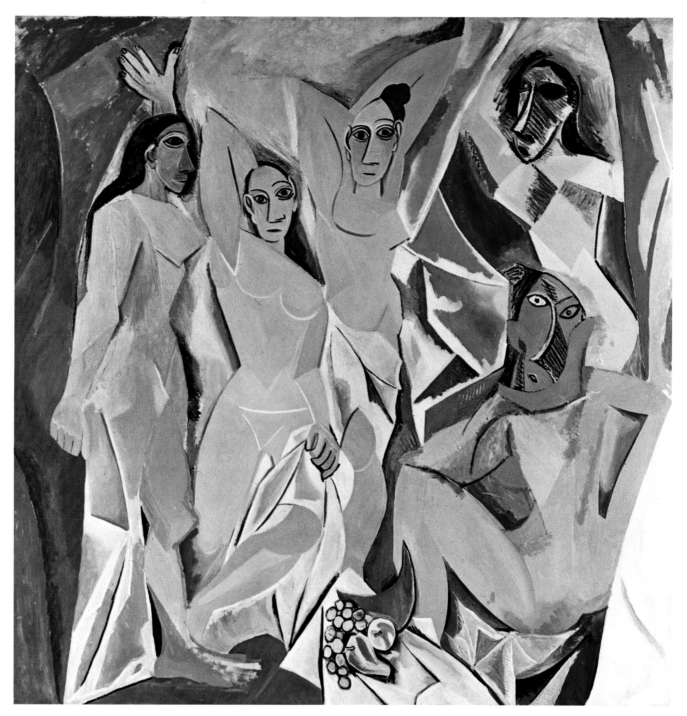

Plate 49.   *PABLO PICASSO. Les Demoiselles d'Avignon.
1906–1907. Oil on canvas, 96×92″. Interpenetrations of
background and foreground planes, indeterminateness in
space of convex and concave shapes, spatially illogical
employment of illusions of overlapping, and the use of*
*color for its decorative rather than for its space-implying
qualities—all these mark this painting as the first purposively conceived image of spatial ambiguity. (The
Museum of Modern Art, New York. Acquired through the
Lillie P. Bliss Bequest.)*

Plate 50.   PABLO PICASSO. Ma Jolie. *1911–1912. Oil on* canvas, *39³/₈×25³/₄". Picasso did not derive this painting from direct observation of objects in nature. It results from his intellectual concern for equivocality—for the idea of* ambiguity. This is partly why the art of Cubism—Picasso's own invention—is so often referred to as an intellectual sort of art. (The Museum of Modern Art, New York. Acquired through the Lillie P. Bliss Bequest.)

Plate 51.

Plate 52.   *JOSEF ALBERS.* Study for an Early
Diary. *1955. Oil on masonite, 15¹/₂×15¹/₂″. Just
as a set of parallel bars in a gymnasium invites
us to exercise our large muscles, this painting* *invites us to exercise our vision and to pleasure
in it. First and foremost, this painting constitutes
an exercise in optics, in visual perception. (Nebraska Art Association, Lincoln.)*

CHAPTER EIGHTEEN

Perception
and
Conception

In our discussions of space and space illusion we have been concerned both with visual perception and with the selection, organization, and presentation of whatever is provided and valued in such perception. The ancient Egyptian looked at and saw the world in which he lived; and so did Masaccio, El Greco, and Picasso see theirs. But from the worlds they perceived they garnered different clues to the character of the lives that were theirs from day to day in body and mind.

We say that men visually perceive the world of objects in space and that their perceptions are patterned into the concepts which at any one time tend to characterize the society in which those men live. This is true up to a point as we have indicated earlier in our discussion of the visual elements. But the matter of perception and conception is both more subtle and more complex than that statement would make it seem.

Now, because our discussion of ambiguous Cubist space illusion dramatized the roles of visual *perception* and intellectual *conception* in the creation of art, it appears in place to make a further note concerning these two terms and the activities to which they refer. In general, we accept the dictionary definitions of the words perception and conception. We accept as adequate the definition by which perception means *the direct acquaintance with anything through the senses*. And since we are dealing with the visual arts, we adjust that definition to read: *direct acquaintance with anything through the eyes,* even though our sense of touch is often brought into play in our perception of primarily visual phenomena. Likewise, we accept as adequate the definition by which conception means *the power of mind to form ideas or devise schemes or designs*. If we take these two definitions as they stand here, we are encouraged to think of the phenomenon of perception as radically different from that of conception. In fact, it has for a long time been assumed, or at least continuously implied, that these two phenomena can exist almost independently of each other. This traditional separation of the activities of the senses from those of the intellect is related to the old dichotomy of body and mind. More and more, however, we are coming to recognize the unity of body and mind to the extent of hyphenating those terms into a single term: *body-mind*—even as we have recognized the unity of space and time by the term *space-time,* or even *spacetime.*

The acceptance of such a term as *body-mind* should, it would appear, argue for the acceptance of such a term as *perception-conception* or, as Arnheim suggests, *"perceptual concepts."*[1] However, before we attempt further comment on the unity of body and mind—and hence on the unity of perception and conception—let us see what these latter two terms have traditionally stood for.

In the case of visual perception the term has stood for a process involving a viewer and an object in light. In the first instants of the viewing process the viewer becomes aware of exclusively visual qualities in a particular configuration. He sees certain shape and size and color qualities in some kind of pattern. At this stage of the process—and perhaps for only a small fraction of a second—we say that his awareness of such visual stimuli is merely sensuous. We say that the viewer has as yet done nothing *about* or *with* the pattern of visual stimuli: he has not become cognizant of it; he has not "re-cognized" it as an object of experience; he has not "understood" it nor has he named it. In the simplest traditional terms of one school of psychology it is said that he has merely undergone a sensuous response to a visual stimulus. Unfortunately, this sort of response is sometimes construed as an act of perception. However, even if we remain within the limits of our stated definition of visual perception: "the direct acquaintance with anything through the eyes," this simple stimulus-response description of perception is at least incomplete. It is true that in the situation we have described there has been a direct confrontation of viewer and object. But what about the word "acquaintance" in our definition? Is it only after some passage of time—say five or ten seconds, or a few minutes—that this acquaintance is accomplished? And more importantly, how is it accomplished?

First of all it must be said that the amount of time required for an act of visual perception is not of crucial importance; it is always short and varies from perhaps as short a time as 1/150 second. Next, we must acknowledge the difference which exists between becoming acquainted with visual phenomena and becoming acquainted with any set of abstract facts or with, shall we say, a neighborhood in a city. The way we become acquainted with abstract facts is by a part-by-part process. We are told, or we read and interpret the signs of those facts; they come to us discursively, over a period of time. With some exceptions, such as the *visual appearance* of certain solutions to algebraic equations (how the total configuration of the mathe-

---

[1] Rudolph Arnheim, *Art and Visual Perception* (Berkeley: University of California Press, 1954), pp. 34 ff.

matical functions *looks* as a visual pattern when written out on the black-
board), we cannot immediately grasp the overall structural character of
groups of abstract facts or the features of a neighborhood. We know, how-
ever, that we can immediately take in the basic structural pattern of a paint-
ing *along with* its individual features. This is the fundamental nature of
presentational form, which characterizes the visual arts and which we
discussed in Chapter 3, "Total Configuration." And not only is this total
and immediate availability of structure characteristic of the visual arts, it is
characteristic of the very nature of vision itself. In looking at an object or
at any configuration of visual elements and qualities we do not first see
details and then proceed to see the whole. Quite the opposite, it is the overall
structure or pattern that comes first to us. And, very significantly, *it is the
grasping of these basic visual structures that constitutes our acquaintance
with whatever it is we are looking at.*

Here, then, we have the basis for a broadened understanding of the
traditionally accepted definition of visual perception: direct acquaintance
with anything through the eyes. It should be clear now that the process of
visual perception involves both a direct confrontation of the object and an
acquaintance with that object. It should also be clear that this confrontation
and acquaintance take place instantaneously and *simultaneously.*

Now we must take the next major step by asking whether or not
the process of visual perception partakes of the qualities of conception.
So, let us look back to our traditional definition of conception, which
reads: the power of mind to form ideas or devise schemes or designs.
We note that in this definition the word *mind* is employed, and that what-
ever that word signifies it has *power* to accomplish things such as the
formation of ideas and the devising of designs. Now, even though the
nature and functions of what is called the mind are still highly speculative
and uncertain matters, let us agree to accept the traditional definition of
mind. In the first instance it is defined simply as "memory." It is further
defined as "the seat of consciousness, thoughts, volitions, and feelings."
In these terms we can now revise our definition of conception to read as
follows: *the power of memory* (which is the seat of consciousness, thoughts,
volitions, and feelings) *to form ideas or devise schemes or designs.* With this
definition we are able to understand that a crucial and extended element of
time is introduced, since we are dealing with *memory* and its powerful
actions concerned with thoughts and feelings as well as with wishes. It
appears that this definition means that the process of conception requires
much more time than does perception; that, since memory is richly involved,
direct observation of the objects of interest is not necessarily required as in
perception, and that in the process of conception one's own wishes and
feelings are brought into play.

It is from precisely the sort of interpretation we have just made
that many psychologists attribute to the process of conception an activity
they call "generalization." Let us see how this works. They say, in effect,
that first we *perceive* an object or any visual situation. This first step, they
say, is limited to the level of direct sensuous awareness—a primitive sense

265

*Perception
and Conception*

response to mere visual data. This process of perception, as they call it, is repeated with other visual stimuli, and the successive perceptions of visual data are received into the mind where they are recorded and remembered. Then and only then, according to the psychologists, can the qualities of these separate perceptions be brought together, sorted, thought about, and generalized into a concept. What these psychologists are saying is that concepts depend for their formulation upon a process of logical abstraction accomplished in the mind, or memory. Notice in this that clearly separate functions are attributed to the senses on the one side and to the mind on the other: the eye perceives; the mind conceives. And the manner in which this theory of the "division of labor" has so often been put forth has tended to encourage the supposition that there is, in fact, a real separation between the body and the mind. This, of course, is not true. Today we know too much about *psychosomatic* (mind-body) symptoms and conditions to continue to believe in a life of the mind separate from that of the body. However, the psychological theory of the "division of labor" is in error precisely because it tacitly makes this assumption of a partition of the body-mind unit. This assumption continues in theory even though there exists ample evidence that the mind functions with the senses in any act of visual perception. When, for instance, we look at an object, it is not at all certain that there is first a short period of only passive response to the specific visual qualities. For, as we have already said, an *acquaintance* with the object, as well as a simple awareness of it, is accomplished right from the very beginning. This acquaintance, it seems, consists in our managing to fit visual qualities to the pattern suggested by the object before us. This acquaintance amounts to a discovery of pattern or structure among the visual stimuli. It is this pattern which to a large extent determines what we see. We cannot, after all, receive the raw material of the stimuli—we cannot take colors or shapes, as such, into ourselves; for this reason it seems plausible that they enter in the form of patterns different from, but *analogous* to, the structure suggested by the stimuli. This must involve a process of conversion which, to all evidence, is a function of vision.

Now if vision itself is capable of discovering patterns among visual stimuli and of creating new analogous patterns, then we must recognize that there is indeed a similarity between the activities of vision and those of the mind. For it would seem that vision itself can "generalize"—by what other means could it discover and create patterns? Would this mean, then, that vision duplicates some of the conceptualizing activities of the mind? Perhaps not so. It would appear much more plausible to settle for the possibility that vision is a creative activity of the mind. This would have the advantage of leaving the body-mind, sense-intellect unity unviolated and would encourage acceptance of the possibility that there are such phenomena as "perceptual-concepts." And it could then follow that even at what has traditionally been called the primitive "level of sense" a real kind of *understanding* can be achieved.

Our aims in all this discussion of perception and conception can now be made clear. First of all, we wished to become familiar with the generally accepted meanings of those two terms; that is why we began with their traditional definitions. Second, we wished to point out that if these definitions are taken in a literal rather than a permissive way, they are apt to suggest the existence of a radical division between our senses and our mind or intellect. We wished, rather, to emphasize the natural unity that exists in the processes of perception and conception and so bring our thinking around to a kind more sympathetic to our own personal experience of the unity of body and mind. This was accomplished by making a point of visual activities that resemble those of the mind. With this as evidence we could recognize that vision is a creative activity of the mind and that, as such, vision can achieve a kind of understanding traditionally attributed only to high-level intellection.

One of the important dividends of our discussion should be an increased estimate of the role of vision in all of our lives and, perhaps, a greater respect for the visual artist who relies so heavily on the understanding he gains principally through his eyes. But no matter how much the artist relies on his eyesight for gaining insight into the nature and meaning of his world, he also relies on his memory. For it is plainly a fact of life that we remember a great deal of what we see from minute to minute and year to year, and that we generalize and transform those "perceptual concepts" into concepts arrived at primarily by intellectual activity. The artist, as well as the mathematician and the philosopher, arrives at concepts by the intellectual processes of logical abstraction and generalization.

Some works of art give evidence of their creator's greater concern for what is directly seen. Other works give evidence of a greater concern for concepts arrived at by prolonged intellectual activity. Because of these different and varying emphases there is a temptation to classify some works as perceptual and others as conceptual. We will avoid that temptation; first, because there exists no such clear difference—not even between the most extreme examples—and, second, because our bias in favor of the unity of body-mind experience disallows it. However, the history of art is characterized by varying degrees of preference for what can be known by seeing and what can be known by logical abstraction and intellectual formulation. It is worthwhile for us to become familiar with works that exemplify these preferences.

In all the history of art it is perhaps the work of the French Impressionists that provides us with the best examples of an art concerned with what comes directly to our eyes. We think of such late nineteenth-century painters as Camille Pissarro, Auguste Renoir, Alfred Sisley, and Claude Monet as the most radical and consistent of the Impressionists. All of them, as a matter of fundamental principle, worked directly from nature. They did not *invent* the landscapes they painted: they *selected* them from the panorama of nature. They took their painting materials out into the landscape itself and began and completed their paintings by direct visual reference to the particular passage they had selected. They worked in the conviction that, for the painter, the world of physical reality comes through his eyes and that his work is a celebration of human vision. They

Fig. 18–1. *CLAUDE MONET.* Boulevard des Capucines. *1873. Oil on canvas 31$^1/_2$ × 23$^5/_8$". Marshall Field III Collection, New York.*

were against the older procedure that involved making only sketches from nature and then creating paintings in the studio where direct perception of the subject was not possible. More than this, their procedure was one encouraging an immediate and instantaneous registration of the total subject on the retina. Partly because of this, typical Impressionist paintings give us the feeling, or the *impression,* of seeing the subject as if in a single glance.

When we look at Monet's *Boulevard des Capucines* (Fig. 18–1), we experience something of the quality of the artist's own instantaneous perception of the subject. No part of the painting is given in clear contours or sharp edges. The images of people, cabs, trees, and buildings are indistinct; they are suggested rather than elaborated. We sense a pervasive quality of light mingling among and partially revealing these images. It is almost as if we had not been afforded enough time to focus on the individual parts of this scene—as if our eyes had been suddenly and only momentarily confronted by these stimuli. It was this very fleeting aspect of observed reality that the Impressionists sought to represent in oil paints on canvas. And all their researches into color theory and their study of works by earlier artists such as John Constable and J. M. W. Turner were aimed at discovering how best they could make paintings that presented the character of primary optical contact with the surrounding world.

It is not surprising, then, that the Impressionists were not concerned with creating paintings that made intellectual comments upon the battles of the Franco-Prussian War, classical myths, or the political life of Paris in the late 1870's. They were not concerned with using their art to tell anecdotes or to argue for any sort of morality. These Impressionists were interested in the kind of understanding that could come through their eyes. As one of Claude Monet's contemporaries once said, "Monet is just an eye—but what an eye!" If it can be said of any group of painters that they dealt in "perceptual-concepts," it can be said of the Impressionists. And as for those who might say that the work of the Impressionists is superficial, that it gives us only passing glimpses of a world that can be known only through sustained intellectual effort, we must answer that the world can be known in many ways.

Whether we are looking at Monet's *Boulevard des Capucines* (Fig. 18–1), his *Waterloo Bridge* (Color Plate 45), or Pissarro's *The Meadow and the Great Walnut Tree in Winter, Eragny* (Fig. 18–2), we are caused to experience these images of the world in a particular way. By virtue of the spectrum colors, which are employed in broken patches rather than in flat areas, by the avoidance of clear divisions between whatever images are presented, and by the creation of an elusive fabric of light which dissolves as it pervades these momentary vistas, we are made aware of a changing and insubstantial world. The vision of the Impressionists is one in which the world and man appear as phenomena in a state of constant flux and transition. It is a vision in which everything coalesces and in which there are no other differences but the various approaches and points of view of the beholder. Far from being superficial or insignificant, the "perceptual-concepts" imaged by the

CLAUDE MONET. Waterloo Bridge. *Worcester Art Museum, Massachusetts. See Plate 45.*

Fig. 18–2. *CAMILLE PISSARRO.* The Meadow and the Great Walnut Tree in Winter, Eragny. *1885. Oil on canvas, 23¹/₄×38¹/₂″. Philadelphia Museum of Art (W. P. Wilstach Collection).*

Impressionists are witness to the fleeting and transitory nature of life. Impressionist art, by the very passive attitude from which it springs, persuades belief in chance as the principle of all being and in the truth of the moment as invalidating all other truths.

Certainly with the Impressionists it is clear that they were primarily concerned with the world as directly perceived. They enjoyed exercising their vision in the world as it existed in Paris, along the Seine, in the south of France, or wherever they turned their eyes. They were interested in visual perception and they celebrated it by creating images that analogized their immediate awareness of the natural world.

Now, there are other ways in which artists have given evidence of an overriding concern for what is directly perceived through the eyes. For instance, an artist such as Josef Albers *constructs* visual phenomena instead of *selecting* passages from the already existing visual world. Whereas the Impressionists created analogies of their perceptions of the natural world, Albers works with the visual elements and their qualities to produce exquisite experiences for the eyes. His *Study for an Early Diary* (Color Plate 52), regardless of the title, which could have only some highly personal and metaphorical meaning for Albers himself, gives us colors, shapes, sizes, and textures in relationships that engage our vision in a precisely directed way. We see these squares and almost-squares, their warm and cool colors with their differences of value and intensity; we see clear and unclear edges, and we experience illusions of space and movement of very particular kinds. As a set of parallel bars in the gymnasium invites us to exercise our large muscles, this painting invites us to exercise our vision and to pleasure in it. First and foremost, this painting constitutes an exercise in optics, in visual perception. Whatever "deeper" intellectual meaning it might have would be related not so much to the painting *itself*, but to the whys and wherefores of its creation and admiration in late twentieth-century America.

In recent years we have witnessed the appearance and wide acceptance of a kind of painting called *Op* or *Op Art*. The name is short for *Optical Art* and it is intended to suggest an almost exclusive preoccupation with the functions of human vision. Another name for this kind of painting is *Retinal*, and works created in its extreme mode are sometimes called *Retinal Art*. But whether it is called *Op* or *Retinal*, the intention is clear: to indicate an approach to painting that attempts to limit all concern to how the eye reacts to specific configurations of visual stimuli.

JOSEF ALBERS. Study for an Early Diary. *Collection of the Nebraska Art Association, Lincoln. See Plate 52.*

An excellent example of Op Art is Bridget Riley's black and white painting titled *Current* (Fig. 18–3). Whatever interest this work holds for us must surely result from the specific sort of visual excitement created in us by this particular combination of thin wavy shapes. It must have been the discovery of this excitement in the process of creating this pattern which sustained the artist through the labor of covering this area of almost 25 square feet. It is from the visual excitement caused in us by this completed pattern that we as viewers must take our satisfaction; no more than this was intended and no more should be expected.

This is truly a matter of the retina—of visually experiencing the effects of these varying undulations of shape. The longer we stare at the pattern, the more it seems to move, shift, and vibrate. Secondary directions seem to appear and the dimensions of the black and white shapes appear to change —now wider, now narrower—and illusory gray passages come and go. If we tip our heads to bring our eyes into any relation to the painting that is other than horizontal, then the whole pattern appears to change and begins to vibrate as if in accordance with another quite different program. And during all our savoring of changing optical excitements we never once catch ourselves engaged in high-level intellectual conduct. We keep responding to a pattern of stimuli and changing our position in relation to it in order to maintain visual interest. It is only when we begin to wonder what makes this thing work, when we become concerned with how the artist made his painting, that we begin to richly indulge ourselves in memory, logical abstraction, and intellectualized generalizations. And this, we would submit, is

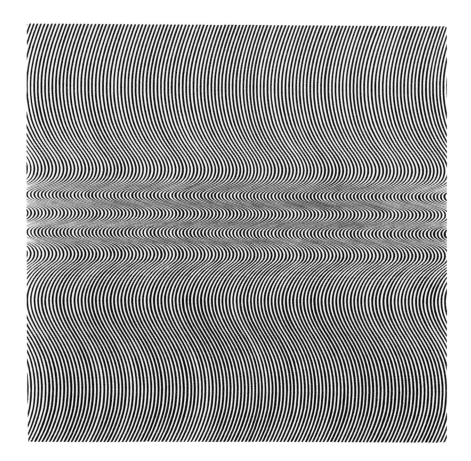

Fig. 18–3. *BRIDGET RILEY.* Current. *1964. Synthetic polymer on composition board, 58³/₈ × 58⁷/₈″. The Museum of Modern Art, New York (Philip Johnson Fund).*

similar to looking at Leonardo's *Mona Lisa* and then becoming concerned with how much of what kind of varnish he used with his pigments and to what exact degree the Mona Lisa's mouth turns upward at the ends.

As we said earlier, the very unity of body and mind makes a totally perceptual visual art an impossibility. Conversely, it is also impossible for the same reason to have a totally conceptual visual art. What we are making a point of here are degrees of emphasis: some art emphasizes the optical or perceptual qualities; other art emphasizes the intellectual or conceptual. We have referred to Impressionism and to Op Art as examples of strong emphases of the perceptual. Now let us move to the other extreme and consider some examples of visual art which evidence a strong emphasis on the conceptual.

Fig. 18–4. *PIERO DI COSIMO*. The Discovery of Honey. *c. 1498. Oil on panel, 31¹/₄×50¹/₄″. Worcester Art Museum, Massachusetts.*

When we look at Piero di Cosimo's painting *The Discovery of Honey* (Fig. 18–4), our first split-second perception of its purely visual qualities is immediately followed by *questions*. These questions have to do with the painting's own invitation to *understand* what it is that it is alluding to. These questions have to do with the *meaning back of the painting*. We wonder who and what these images are meant to represent, why they are together in this landscape, what they are doing and why. And no matter how finely our visual sense has been developed, none of these questions can be answered from the evidences of the painting alone. Nor was this painting ever intended to convey its complicated meaning directly through the eyes—or through what we have been calling "perceptual concepts." Any adequate response to this painting depends in large degree on historical, philosophical, religious, and artistic concepts lying entirely outside the work itself. Unless we have in mind and at our command a range of specific concepts concerning, among other things, classical and Renaissance philosophy, pagan mythology, "culture heroes," fifteenth-century Flemish painting, and Florentine humanism, then Piero di Cosimo's painting must remain largely outside our experience—no matter how long we look at it. And this is because the painting took its beginning not from the perceived visual world, but from conceptions concerning the history, beliefs, and conduct of men and societies.

Let us see just how complicated in concept this painting is. First it is important that we know that this painting was made at the very end of the fifteenth century and that Piero di Cosimo was a Renaissance Florentine who admired the realism of such Flemish painters as Hugo van der Goes.[2] Equally important to know is that classical subjects inspired by ancient literature and monuments were adapted to Christian purposes by the Italians. By the fifteenth century the Florentines had become extremely able in identifying classical gods and goddesses such as Hercules and Venus with the Christian figures of Sampson and the Virgin Mary. As a respected Florentine painter of the time, Piero di Cosimo as a matter of course became familiar with classical mythology and with analogous Christian allegories. And not only did he possess this fashionable knowledge, he was also aware of a philosophy called *Neoplatonism* which was then best represented by another Florentine, Marsilio Ficino, who headed the new Platonic Academy in Florence.

This philosophy, based on the works of Plato and Plotinus, as well as

---

[2] The highly influential *Portinari Altarpiece* (Color Plate 53), by van der Goes, had arrived in Florence about 18 years before Piero di Cosimo painted *The Discovery of Honey.*

HUGO VAN DER GOES. The Portinari Altarpiece *(open). Uffizi Gallery, Florence. Photo: Gabinetto Fotografico, Florence. See Plate 53.*

others, held that there is an utterly transcendent One from whom all come by a process of emanation. In effect, Neoplatonism held that all wisdom or revelation emanated from the same source—the One. Logically, then, all revelation, whether it is found in the Holy Bible, the writings of Plato, Plotinus, or Philo, or in ancient mythology, was equally true. It was this all-encompassing tenet of Neoplatonism that made it not only possible, but right and good to justify any and all pagan and Christian thought as mere variants of revelation accomplished by the same One. More than this, there went along with the assumptions of Ficino's Neoplatonism a mysticism that tacitly encouraged presentations of individually experienced truths. This recognition of the crucial role of the individual, no matter how indirect, documented and supported Italian humanism. Italian Renaissance artists were respected as special manifestations of genius who, through divine inspiration, could create works of divine revelation.

Coming back to the work of Piero di Cosimo, let us see how some of this relates to his curious painting. As a Florentine who lived into the sixteenth century, it is not unusual that he often employed pagan gods in his paintings. Hence we see Bacchus and Ariadne standing together in the lower right, and throughout the landscape we see more than a dozen mischievous pagan gods or demons (satyrs) in partly human and partly bestial form. In appearance and gesture these gods and satyrs are far from spiritual. Somehow, Piero di Cosimo has failed to conceive of these pagan figures as godly in the sense that the Neoplatonic ideal would have them. Yet, by this negative statement of their character he gives us evidence of his conversance with Neoplatonic thought and ideals. Also, he gives us evidence of exercising his own individual genius for interpreting the gods; he is practicing the freedom that is his as a late fifteenth-century Italian humanist. Instead of idealizing the incorporeal essence of these gods, he shows them as being closer in physical form and attitude to the animal world. These figures look more like monkeys than like gods. And what might Piero di Cosimo mean by presenting us with such a concept? Very likely he wished the viewer to recognize that ancient men, as well as their gods, were primitive in comparison to men of his own time; that man had risen from barbarism by his own efforts. And how does Piero di Cosimo tell us that man has risen by his own ingenious efforts? Simply by how he depicts the central theme of the painting: the discovery of honey. He shows ancient men around an old tree making noise in order to drive a swarm of bees to settle in one place so that the honey they deposit can be efficiently collected. We know that what they are after is the wine they will eventually make from the honey. In a sense, then, these figures represent "culture heroes"—personages who have advanced their race by causing nature to work for them. The different landscapes to the right and left of the central tree represent respectively the earlier barbaric life and the civilized life of Italy in the fifteenth century.

Now, even though what we have said comes nowhere near a complete inventory of the ideas upon which an understanding of this painting depends, it should still serve to point out its predominantly conceptual character. That we can experience some purely visual satisfaction from *The Discovery of Honey* goes without saying. However, the meat of this work is of an intellectual kind; this is a primarily conceptual painting.

It should be clear now that the same is true for Eugène Delacroix's monumental painting *The Massacre of Chios* (Fig. 18–5). Rich as this work is in perceptual qualities, it still depends to a large degree upon an intellectual grasp of specific concepts for its complete effect. Based upon reports of an event in the Greek-Turkish War of 1822, it refers to the ruthless massacre of Chian Christians on the island of Chios. Our more exclusively visual response to this painting is quickly diverted into thoughts related to Delacroix's poetic concept of the tragedies of this war for Greek independence: the death of lovers, the ravaging of beauty, the separation and death of mothers and children, and the waiting of survivors only to be delivered into slavery.

Fig. 18–5. *EUGÈNE DELACROIX.* The Massacre of Chios. *1822–1824. Oil on canvas, 13′10″ × 11′7″. The Louvre, Paris. Photo: Giraudon, Paris.*

Fig. 18–6. The Banker Lucius Caecilius Secundus, *from Pompeii. c. A.D. 50. Bronze, life-size. National Museum, Naples. Photo: Anderson-Art Reference Bureau.*

Fig. 18–7. *CONSTANTIN BRANCUSI.* Mademoiselle Pogany. *1913. Bronze, first stage after a marble of 1912, height 17¼". The Museum of Modern Art, New York (Acquired through the Lillie P. Bliss Bequest).*

Just because we have referred to paintings representing figures and objects in a more or less natural environment does not mean that conceptual emphases can be made in only that mode. We will remember that in speaking of Picasso's *Ma Jolie* (Color Plate 50) we made note of the fact that Cubism is often referred to as an intellectual sort of art. We said that *Ma Jolie* resulted in large part from Picasso's intellectual concern for equivocality—for the *idea* or *concept* of ambiguity. Along with the fact that Cubist paintings provide some of the most engaging visual experiences, they still depend for their full enjoyment on our familiarity with complicated and often subtle and even humorous concepts.

To reinforce the fact that degrees of perceptual or conceptual emphasis are not necessarily determined by the level of naturalism in a work of art, we have only to look at two portrait busts. Figure 18–6, a Roman portrait *The Banker Lucius Caecilius Secundus,* is certainly closer to observed reality than Constantin Brancusi's *Mademoiselle Pogany* (Fig. 18–7). Yet it should be obvious that if conceptual interests in art are evidenced by an emphasis on the role of the mind to devise schemes or designs, then the Pogany portrait is certainly a more conceptual work. On the other hand, the Roman portrait engages us in a way comparable to the way in which we would be engaged by the actual presence of the living banker. It appears that the artist has been concerned almost entirely with only those transformations of perceived visual data that are required for their representation in bronze. In the terms we have been using, the Roman portrait is a more perceptual work.

In all that we have been saying about perceptual and conceptual emphases there has been no question that in every case the examples we have used are genuine works of art. Whether a painting, an etching, or a sculpture succeeds as a work of art does not depend on whether it is primarily perceptual or primarily conceptual. Deep, moving and memorable experiences of art have been and perhaps always will be available to us in both modes of emphasis. And the invitations to these experiences are extended to us in different proportionate relationships in single works of art. Some of the most consummate works are those in which perceptual and conceptual qualities are so thoroughly intermingled and interdependent that their separation and identification are difficult if not impossible. One such work is Rembrandt van Rijn's *The Three Crosses* (Fig. 18–8).

Fig. 18–8. *REMBRANDT*. The Three Crosses *(3rd state). 1653. Etching 15^{1}/$_{4}$×17^{3}/$_{4}$". The British Museum, London.*

Plate 53. *HUGO VAN DER GOES. The Portinari Altarpiece (open). c. 1476. Panel, center 8′ 3¹/₂″×10′, wings 8′ 3¹/₂″×4′ 7¹/₂″ each. This huge altarpiece, a most remarkable combination of realism and the supernatural, arrived in Florence about 1480 from Flanders. Its characteristically precise Flemish realism greatly affected the Italian artists of the late 15th and early 16th centuries. (Uffizi Gallery, Florence. Photo: Art Reference Bureau.)*

Plate 54. *MATTHIAS GRÜNEWALD.* The Resurrection, *open wing of the* Isenheim Altarpiece. *c. 1510–
1515. Oil on wood, 106×60¹/₂″. This panel, which
comes into view when the* Isenheim Altarpiece *is
opened, contrasts dramatically with* The Crucifixion
*(Color Plate 15), which is painted across the outer
wings. Here Grünewald presents the risen Christ,
not in pitiful defeat, but in a brilliantly lighted and
explosive image of victory over death. (Unterlinden
Museum, Colmar, France.)*

Plate 55. *JOHN CONSTABLE. Stoke-by-Nayland. 1836. Oil on canvas, 49½×66½". Constable, one of the first painters to work out-of-doors directly from nature for prolonged periods of time, was a precursor of Impressionism. He developed a strongly scientific interest in color, and even this carried forward into the concerns of such Impressionists as Monet, Pissarro, and Sisley. (The Art Institute of Chicago.)*

Plate 56. *IVAN LE LORRAINE ALBRIGHT.* That which I should have done I did not do. *1931–1941. Oil on canvas, 97×36". This image of a closed door bearing the traditional crape of mourning is developed in such exaggerated detail that it takes on an air of the supranatural. This, in conjunction with the long interpretive title that must be considered an integral part of this work, invites the viewer of the painting to philosophical contemplation. (Courtesy of The Art Institute of Chicago.)*

For those of us familiar with the Christian tradition, recognition of the event to which this etching refers comes almost instantaneously: it is the Crucifixion of Jesus Christ. We know of it from four rather similar accounts in the gospels of Matthew, Mark, Luke, and John. Rembrandt knew of it from the same sources. His experience of this tragic event was vicarious—just as is ours. So, from the very outset *The Three Crosses* was not a matter of direct visual perception. It derives from highly abstract written accounts which abound in allusions to Christian and other concepts. Because, of the four accounts, the one made in Luke (23:33–49) appears to have been most relied upon by Rembrandt, let us remind ourselves of it:

> And when they were come to the place, which is called Calvary, there they crucified him, and the malefactors, one on the right hand, and the other on the left.
>
> Then said Jesus, Father, forgive them; for they know not what they do. And they parted his raiment, and cast lots. And the people stood beholding. And the rulers also with them derided him, saying, He saved others; let him save himself, if he be Christ, the chosen of God. And the soldiers also mocked him, coming to him, and offering him vinegar, and saying, If thou be the king of the Jews, save thyself. And a superscription also was written over him in letters of Greek, and Latin, and Hebrew, THIS IS THE KING OF THE JEWS.
>
> And one of the malefactors which were hanged railed on him, saying, If thou be Christ, save thyself and us. But the other answering rebuked him, saying, Dost not thou fear God, seeing thou art in the same condemnation? And we indeed justly; for we receive the due reward of our deeds: but this man hath done nothing amiss. And he said unto Jesus, Lord, remember me when thou comest into thy kingdom. And Jesus said unto him, Verily I say unto thee, Today shalt thou be with me in paradise. And it was about the sixth hour, and there was darkness over all the earth until the ninth hour. And the sun was darkened, and the veil of the temple was rent in the midst.
>
> And when Jesus had cried with a loud voice, he said, Father, into thy hands I commend my spirit: and having said thus, he gave up the ghost. Now when the centurion saw what was done, he glorified God, saying, Certainly this was a righteous man. And all the people that came together to that sight, beholding the things which were done, smote their breasts, and returned.

Here, then, is just about all of the scriptural account from which Rembrandt worked. He has been faithful to it. Here is the place, Calvary—Golgotha; Jesus is under the superscription and flanked by the malefactors, the two thieves; the soldiers are here with the centurion; the people are gathered around. More than this, Rembrandt has created the place as if the sun was indeed darkened and the veil rent by a powerful light from above. He identifies the thieves according to their faith and lack of faith in Jesus. The one on the left is in darkness—without faith. The one on the right is in light—with faith; he will join Jesus in paradise. The centurion, stooping before the cross and raising his arms, is glorifying God in an act of conversion and comprehension of the Christian meaning of Jesus' death. The people respond dramatically, and some begin to leave the place.

Rembrandt succeeded eminently in giving visual form to the highly intellectual concepts of the scriptural account of the Crucifixion. In a sense, he has given the abstract a concrete form. And more than just making a translation from discursive to presentational form—an admirable achievement in itself—he has managed to create a visual configuration which analogizes a certain phase of the verbally reported Crucifixion. Rembrandt analogizes the *mood* of the time between the sixth and the ninth hours. He must have sensed that mood as compounded of tragic exhaustion and marvelous exhilaration, of beginning out of ending: the very *structure* of *The Three Crosses* bears a visual resemblance to an opening chrysalis.

In the simplest structural terms, this etching amounts to an irregularly egg-shaped light mass almost entirely surrounded by dark grays and black—an encasing shell or cocoon. The strongest focus in the light area is concentrated around the figure of the crucified Christ—the dynamic nucleus or living germ. It describes a triangle riding on its apex, and it induces in us a feeling of rigid suspense immediately prior to a violent upward thrust. For us of the late twentieth century, it encourages comparison, if only of the pictorial qualities, to the moment of ignition of a rocket missile. The missile stands vertically on its pad; the smoke and gasses issue in a boiling ring around its base—blast-off is a second or two away. And above Christ the cocoon of heavy dark air is already broken by a glittering shaft of light. The *rigor mortis* of earthly death will launch Christ into a spacious life. And whether or not we are familiar with the scriptural history of the Crucifixion and its meaning for Christian faith, we still respond to the visual metaphor which Rembrandt has created here. He has managed to render in direct perceptual terms an experience heavy with conceptual involutions. Here, by deep personal identification with both the propositional logic of this event and the fruits of his own experiencing of the infinite among the finite world of sense, he has caused the perceptual and conceptual to exist in inextricable combination.

From our reading of the account of the Crucifixion, entombment, and Resurrection of Jesus Christ, we know that Christ did not ascend directly from the cross. He was buried, and only later did he arise from the tomb. But this Resurrection was assured in his death by crucifixion, and Rembrandt chose to identify death and rebirth in this version of the etching. Visually, this is what the etching accomplishes by visual analogy. For an equally moving "perceptual-concept" of the event of death-into-life, and one which has Christ rising from the tomb, there is *The Resurrection* (Color Plate 54) painted more than a hundred years before by Matthias Grünewald. And, perhaps not without reason, this image can again be compared to a violent launching by rocket. We even see in Grünewald's version the effects of the concussion accompanying the blast-off: the soldiers are knocked down by it.

Now, we must not leave this discussion of perception and conception without clearly acknowledging the fact that with the visual arts *high level* intellectual conception *follows* our direct perception of the art object. No matter what depth of acquaintance may be gained in the very act of seeing,

MATTHIAS GRÜNEWALD. The Resurrection, *open wing of the* Isenheim Altarpiece. *Unterlinden Museum, Colmar, France. See Plate 54.*

the experiences of our successive perceptions are funded in us; they go into a kind of memory bank and are held for extension and transformation. It is this store of prime experiences which can be "re-membered" either while we are still looking at the object or much later when we are no longer in its presence. In memory these perceptual experiences can be arranged in sequences and patterns *unlike* those in which we actually perceived the object or situation. Our memory-converted perceptions have a plastic quality; they are capable of change and distortion, combination and separation. We made a special point of this in what we said about Paul Cézanne. We said that he looked at actual objects from different points of view—that he experienced a series of different perceptions and then brought them together in patterns which, in fact, did not exist until he painted them. This is, of course, not only possible for all of us, it is characteristic of the life of the body-mind.

These new patterns derived from our stored, converted, and generalized percepts are most commonly called *concepts*. Our concepts of *tree, house,* or *man* are based in our direct perceptions of those phenomena. This being true, it is of utmost importance that we credit and value the means of perception—our senses, our eyes—even though we know they can err. In order to experience a work of art we must become sensuously aware of it. In a real way we must surrender to it; we must open ourselves to it. With a minimum of prepossessions, we must make ourselves available to whatever the object offers. That there exist dangers in this open, receptive attitude goes without saying—after all, we can be fooled, cheated, taken for a ride. But in the long run there is less danger in risking our open surrender to the visual world than there is in going about behind an armored vision. The poverty or richness of our concepts is determined by the depth and quality of our perceptions. Only through an ever increasing perceptual awareness can our concepts and our whole conceptual life attain to more than mere adequacy in a world that is forever ready to reveal more of itself to us. And in this adventure, art proves a model of this perception-conception relation. As Herbert Read has said, "Art excites the senses and engages the mind."

CHAPTER NINETEEN

Form
and
Content

The temporal character of language, as we said earlier (Chapter 2, "The Visual Arts and Language") requires that we string out reports of our reactions, feelings, and ideas even though they may, in fact, exist simultaneously. In speaking or writing about anything, the medium of language requires that we name the objects or concepts of our interest in a separate, discrete, and unilinear way. This requirement often causes us to misrepresent the nature of the phenomena we wish to present. To some extent our discussion of perception and conception suffers from this kind of distortion. We could not, for instance, present at one and the same time the simultaneous character of the first stages of the perception-conception experience. And now in this closely related discussion of *form* and *content* we will again be forced to treat interdependent and simultaneously functioning phenomena *as if* they could be separated, and *as if* their functions could continue in isolation. It is hoped, however, that we understand that such separation is in the nature of language and not in the nature of the actual phenomena of which we speak.

Before we get down to considerations of the highly integrated matter of form and content, we had better make certain that two terms we have already introduced casually are clearly defined and understood. These terms are *subject* and *subject matter*. When we use the term *subject* we refer to the *theme* or the *topic* of a work of art. If we ask, what is the subject of Toulouse-Lautrec's painting reproduced here as Fig. 19–1, the answer is: the circus. This is the theme of the work; it is the topic of the artist's concern, his admiration, animadversion, satire, mockery, or other treatment. The subject of Henry Moore's sculpture *Family Group* (Fig. 19–2) is the family.

Fig. 19–1. *HENRI DE TOULOUSE-LAUTREC.* In the Circus Fernando: The Ringmaster. *1888.*
Oil on canvas, 38¹/₄×63¹/₂″. The Art Institute of Chicago (Joseph Winterbotham Collection).

Fig. 19–2. *HENRY MOORE. Family Group. Cast 1950. Bronze, height 59¹/₄". The Museum of Modern Art, New York (A. Conger Goodyear Fund).*

The range of possible subjects that one can deal with in the visual arts is just about unlimited. A simple exemplification of sample categories of subject should serve to indicate the variety:

ALLEGORICAL: Prud'hon, *Justice and Divine Vengeance Pursuing Crime* (Fig. 19–3)
ART ITSELF: Vantongerloo, *Construction of Volume Relations* (Fig. 19–4)
CURRENT EVENTS: Copley, *Watson and the Shark* (Fig. 19–5)
GENRE: Rogers, *Checkers up at the Farm* (Fig. 19–6)
HISTORICAL: Roman, *The Battle of Issus* (Fig. 19–7)
LANDSCAPE: Constable, *Stoke-by-Nayland* (Color Plate 55)
LITERARY: Daumier, *Don Quixote Attacking the Windmills* (Fig. 19–8)
PHILOSOPHICAL: Albright, *That which I should have done I did not do*
  (Color Plate 56)
RELIGIOUS: Michelangelo, *Pietà* (Fig. 19–9)
PORTRAITURE: Bronzino, *Portrait of a Young Man* (Color Plate 57)
STILL LIFE: Harnett, *Old Models* (Color Plate 58)

Fig. 19–3. *PIERRE PAUL PRUD'HON.* Justice and Divine Vengeance Pursuing Crime. *1808. Oil on canvas. The Louvre, Paris.*

Fig.19–4, *from p. 289.*

Fig. 19–6, *from p. 294.*

Fig. 19–5. *JOHN SINGLE-TON COPLEY.* Watson and the Shark. *1778. Oil on canvas, 72¹/₂×90¹/₄". Museum of Fine Arts, Boston.*

Fig. 19–7, *from p. 288.*

JOHN CONSTABLE. Stoke-by-Nayland. *The Art Institute of Chicago. See Plate 55.*

Fig. 19–8. *HONORÉ DAUMIER.* Don Quixote Attacking the Windmills. *c. 1866. Oil on canvas, 22¹/₄×33″. Private Collection.*

IVAN LE LORRAINE AL-BRIGHT. That which I should have done I did not do. *Courtesy of The Art Institute of Chicago. See Plate 56.*

WILLIAM HARNETT. Old Models. *1892. Museum of Fine Arts. Boston (Charles Henry Hayden Fund). See Plate 58.*

Fig. 19–9, *from p. 290.*

AGNOLO BRONZINO. Portrait of a Young Man. *The Metropolitan Museum of Art, New York (Bequest of Mrs. H. O. Havemeyer, 1929). See Plate 57.*

287

This list of categories could, of course, be much extended, and other hybrid categories could be established. For instance, Daumier's *Don Quixote Attacking the Windmills,* which we placed in the literary category, could also have partial claim to a place in the landscape category; Copley's *Watson and the Shark* might share in a category of *seascape.* So, what this points up is the fact that subjects can be combined; religious subjects can be, and often have been, presented in terms of current events; philosophic subjects have often been supported by portraiture of a very specific sort. But no matter the purity or the mixed quality of whatever the subject might be, the term *subject* will still mean theme or topic.

The second term we mean to clarify is *subject matter.* Simply, it is the matter of the subject. In the case of Michelangelo's *Pietà* it is comprised of the figures of Christ and Mary. The *subject* is religious; the subject *matter* is that which Michelangelo employed to embody and convey the religious subject. In the case of the historical subject of *The Battle of Issus* (Fig. 19–7), the artist employed horses and riders, weapons and armor as the subject matter. In the case of the *Construction of Volume Relations* (Fig. 19–4), the subject is, as we said, *art itself.* This work is a self-referring work; it makes no attempt to refer to any thing or any situation outside of itself. It exists for its own sake; it is its own subject and its own subject matter. All we can say of its subject matter is that it consists of its own particular elements and qualities—those we can see: vertical and horizontal cubical solids and their integrated voids. Subject matter, then, consists of those *specifics that the artist visually presents as means for the embodiment of his subject.* From this definition it should be clear that anything that serves the purposes of the artist can be employed as subject matter in his work. And by the same token, anything that serves the purposes of the artist can be used as the subject of his work.

Fig. 19–7. The Defeated Persians under Darius, *detail of* The Battle of Issus, *from Pompeii. Mosaic copy of a Hellenistic painting. National Museum, Naples. Photo: Alinari-Art Reference Bureau.*

Fig. 19–4.
GEORGES VANTONGERLOO. Construction of Volume Relations. *1921. Mahogany, height 16¹/₈". The Museum of Modern Art, New York (Gift of Miss Silvia Pizitz).*

A term more difficult to define and understand than either subject or subject matter is *form*. This is true because it is in fact more than a simple term; it is the name for a complex concept. Perhaps we can get at it through an example outside of what is usually considered art.

Most of us are familiar with what we call *form* in athletics. The athlete, in striving for excellence in throwing the javelin or the discus, or in swimming or diving, develops a *form*—an integrally related series of movements by which the action is carried forward to completion. In a diving competition those experts responsible for judging the events are concerned not only that the participants complete one and one-half turns in the air, shall we say, but also with *how* a diver begins his spring from the board, *how* he leaves the board, *how* he executes the turns, and *how* he enters the water. In other words, the judges of such an event are concerned not only with *what* the participant does, but also *how* he does it. The ideal form for any athletic event is one by which that event is most efficiently and most gracefully accomplished by the action of a particular human being—all under specific conditions.

In the case of the diving event, we could say that the one and one-half dive is the *subject* or the *subject matter;* this particular kind of dive is the *what* of the event. On the other hand, the way in which the dive is executed is the *form* of the event; it has to do with the *how* of the dive. And in athletics as well as in art there is a close relationship between *what* is done and *how* it is done.

When we speak of *form* in the visual arts we are referring to the total organic structure of the work and to the quality of relationships existing among all of its elements. The unique form of a work of art results from how the subject was construed by the artist; how the chosen subject matter was employed; how the particular medium (clay, paint, stone, etc.) was used; and how specific visual elements and their specific qualities were configured into the work we see. This is a very inclusive definition of form. It appears to cover almost everything we have mentioned up to now. What it does not cover is the phenomenon we call *content,* although, as we shall see later, it too is integrally related to, and a concomitant of, form. But before we speak of content, let us see what we mean by our definition of form. Looking back to Michelangelo's *Pietà* (Fig. 19–9), we can compare it to another *Pietà* (Fig. 19–10) created by an unknown German sculptor of the fourteenth century. The subject of both of these sculptures is religious. The

Fig. 19–9. *MICHELANGELO.* Pietà. *1498–1499. Marble, height 69″. St. Peter's, Vatican, Rome. Photo: Alinari.*

Fig. 19–10. Pietà, *by an un-known German sculptor. 14th century. Wood, height 34¹/₂". Provincial Museum, Bonn.*

subject matter is almost identical: images of Christ and Mary, drapery, and a bench on which Mary sits. Even the relative positions of Christ and Mary are closely comparable. But the ways in which these sculptors construed their subject is far from similar. How the subject matter was employed is radically different. Differences of media—white marble in the case of Michelangelo's carving, wood in the case of the German's—and how they were employed make for great differences in the forms of these two works. And certainly there is a world of difference between the configurations of the visual elements in these two sculptures. The element of size, alone, is crucial in determining their respective forms: the Michelangelo is near life-size; the German piece is less than three feet tall. So, here we have a situation in which the religious subject matter of two sculptures is just about identical, but the forms in which the works are presented are at great variance: the *what* is the same, the *how* is radically different.

Other great differences in form become evident if we compare either or both of these sculptures to another work of the same religious subject. The *Avignon Pietà* (Color Plate 59), because it was realized in oil paint and gold leaf on a wooden panel, gives us an appreciation of the determinative role

291

The Avignon Pietà, *by a southern French master. The Louvre, Paris. Photo: Giraudon, Paris.*
See Plate 59.

of the medium in the visual arts. Certainly the fact that the creator of this painting worked in two rather than three dimensions and that he employed devices of spatial illusion to create an environment for the figures makes a very different thing of his presentation. Again, the *what* is similar but the *how* is quite another matter.

Now, if we say that subject and subject matter have to do with *what* a work of art is *about,* and that form has to do with *how* a work of art *is,* then what can we say about *content?* Does it help to remind ourselves that in regular usage the word means *that which is contained in a vessel?* Yes, to some extent it does help, but only if we remember that when we speak of a work of art we are not dealing with something as simple as a hollow kitchen utensil. If a work of art can be compared to a vessel of any sort, it would perhaps suffer least if compared to a blood vessel, or to one of the membranous canals in which the fluids of the body are contained and by means of which they are circulated. Thinking of the work of art as this kind of vessel would at least admit of the fact that both the vessel and the fluid it contains are inseparably part of the same, identical life—just as the form and content of a work of art are inseparably of one and the same thing. But perhaps more fruitful for our discussion would be another part of the dictionary

definition of content. That part says that content is *that which is contained*
in a conception. This is nowhere near as simple as the first definition, for
instead of referring to a simple material thing such as a jug or a jar and
whatever it might hold, this definition requires that we deal with a conception. And the words *content of a conception* make reference to a much
more elusive reality than, shall we say, jam in a jar or helium in a tank.

In our discussion of perception and conception, specifically when we
were speaking of high-level intellectual activity, we said that conception is
the power of mind to form ideas, or devise plans, schemes, or designs. And
it is understood that what is produced by this means are called conceptions.
It would then follow that *content* is whatever such conceived ideas, plans,
schemes, or designs contained. Now when we try to get at the content of
these—when we try to describe what an idea, scheme, or design *contains*—
we must take into account everything that goes to make up that idea,
scheme, or design. Therefore, if we were looking at a painting and responding to its content, we would be sensuously aware of it—of its colors, shapes,
textures, its spatial qualities, balance, and unity. We would be aware of *how*
it is: we would be sensitive to its *form,* its unique total configuration of
visual elements and qualities. We would also be aware of the subject matter,
and through that, the subject, providing that the subject did not lie entirely
outside our personal knowledge or experience. And since the work we are
looking at is a successful one, all of these factors as conditioned by, and
realized through, the medium of oil paint and the artist's technique would
give us the clues relevant to the content.

So, content is not just the subject or the subject matter; it is not merely
the configuration of visual elements and their qualities (called by some the
"formal elements"). Content is what all these factors, by nature of their
working together as a single coherent unit, manage to show, describe, sig-
nify, and suggest. In this sense, content is the *import* or meaning of the
work of art.

Since the late nineteenth century, and especially since the early part of
this one, there has been a tendency for writers on art as well as artists themselves to devaluate content as a legitimate concern in art. In the first instance,
this came about as a reaction to the most popular nineteenth-century painting
and sculpture. An overwhelming amount of the work of that time concerned
itself almost exclusively with the anecdotal and suggestive possibilities of
naturalistic subject matter presented without any real knowledge or concern
for form. Almost all emphasis was on the *what;* the *how* was neglected. And
not only was this true; almost worse was the preference for subjects and
subject matter of a shallow and meanly sentimental variety. John Rogers'
Checkers up at the Farm (Fig. 19–6), which we saw earlier, is a modest
American example of this sort of thing. So is Thomas Hovenden's *Breaking
Home Ties* (Color Plate 60), which was reproduced in color (at that time a
very expensive process) in *The Art of the World Illustrated in the Paintings,
Statuary and Architecture of the World's Columbian Exposition* of 1893.

Fig. 19–6. *JOHN ROGERS. Checkers up at the Farm. 1877. Plaster, height 20". The New York Historical Society.*

THOMAS HOVENDEN. Breaking Home Ties. Philadelphia Museum of Art. Photo: A. J. Wyatt. See Plate 60.

Plate 57.   *AGNOLO BRONZINO.* Portrait of a Young Man. *1530–1532. Oil on wood, 37⅝×29½". That portraiture is an art concerned with more than the simple re-presentation of the observable features of a particular person is made eminently clear in a* painting such as this. It is as much a portrait of an entire exalted social caste of a given era as it is the portrait of a certain young man. (The Metropolitan Museum of Art, New York. Bequest of Mrs. H. O. Havemeyer, 1929.)

Plate 58. *WILLIAM HARNETT. Old
Models. 1892. Oil on canvas, 54×28″.
The heightened realism of William Harnett is such that it all but fools the eye
into mistaking these painted images for
actual three-dimensional objects. As a
painter of still life, Harnett is of the
lineage of men like Willem Claesz (see
Color Plate 40), the seventeenth-century
Dutch painter. (Museum of Fine Arts,
Boston. Charles Henry Hayden Fund.)*

Plate 59. *Southern French Master. The Avignon Pietà. c. 1470. Panel, 64×86". Here the time-honored theme of the Pietà is given form in an otherwise deserted landscape. The illusory depth of the bleak setting serves both to isolate and to heighten the highly expressive character of the dead Christ, Mary, and the mourning figures. (The Louvre, Paris. Photo: Giraudon, Paris.)*

Plate 60. THOMAS HOVENDEN. Breaking Home Ties. 1890. Oil on canvas, 52¹/₂×72¹/₄″. That this sort of storytelling picture was very much in vogue in the late nineteenth century is evidenced by the fact that this very painting was acclaimed by popular vote the prizewinning work of art at the World's Columbian Exposition held in Chicago in 1893. (Philadelphia Museum of Art. Photo: A. J. Wyatt.)

The article of appreciation that accompanied the reproduction of the painting spoke only of the subject matter, as we would expect. In the last paragraph the unknown "critic" wrote:

> This is one of the compositions which tells its own story. The young man, already taller than his mother, and dressed in his best, is about to leave home. His sister—or possibly his sweetheart—holds in her lap some precious last gift. The mother's anxious look shows the distrust she feels for the great world outside. The old grandmother sits at the table; while the father is ready with the carpetbag, and frets for fear that the stage or train may be missed.

That this sort of painting (often with an accompanying "I'll-tell-you-the-story-of-the-picture" type of commentary) was strongly in vogue at the time is evidenced by the fact that *Breaking Home Ties* was acclaimed by popular vote the prize-winning work of art in that International Exposition of 1893. And equal acclaim came to works of this general sort all over western Europe, as well as in America. An emphasis on sentimentalized subject matter, melodrama, and a neglect of almost everything except the story-telling potential of pictures characterized much of the work produced during the last part of the nineteenth century. The great popular success of William Bouguereau in France (Color Plate 61) still advertises the mode of painting prevalent during the 1880's and 1890's.

WILLIAM A. BOUGUEREAU. Whisperings of Love. *Isaac Delgado Museum of Art, New Orleans (Mr. & Mrs. Chapman H. Hyams Collection). See Plate 61.*

But no matter the excesses of that period, subject matter is still a legitimate concern of painting; it *does* function as an integral force in the projection of content. And who would devalue the content of a work of art? To do that would be to devalue *form* as well, for they are inseparable. As Edmund Spenser, in a somewhat different context, put it long ago:

> *For of the soule the bodie forme doth take;*
> *The soule is forme and doth the bodie make.*

In those two lines we have the whole story of form and content: one cannot exist without the other and, in fact, each determines the other. In the finest works of art these become one. In the case of Rembrandt's *The Three Crosses* (Fig. 18–8), we said that the perceptual and the conceptual qualities are so thoroughly intermingled and interdependent that their separation and isolation are just about impossible. Just as easily and just as truthfully we can say the same about the form and content of that etching.

REMBRANDT. The Three Crosses. *British Museum, London. Figure 18–8 repeated.*

But in all our talk about form and content we have not come out and said just what the content of some particular work of art might be. If content is that which was intended to be or actually is expressed by the work of art, we ought to be able to identify it, or at least *point* to it. This, we can say now, is what we were doing in a general way in our earlier discussions in Chapter 6, "The Visual Elements and Expression," and Chapter 7, "Expression: General and Specific." With the material of those chapters again in mind, along with what we have just been saying about form and content, we can make some specific comments concerning the contents of individual works

EDWARD HOPPER. Early Sunday Morning. *Whitney Museum of American Art, New York. See Plate 62.*

of art. Let us first turn our attention to Edward Hopper's painting *Early Sunday Morning* (Color Plate 62).

In our first visual encounter with this work we become aware of a predominantly rectangular structure with strong differences of generally rich color. We respond to an overall format that impresses us as being almost two times as wide as it is high. The powerful horizontality of this enclosing shape is reenforced by long horizontals running clear across the painting. In turn, these are reenforced by scores of shorter horizontals. Against the restful effect of this dominant horizontality there is played the subdominant role of scores of shorter, or broken, verticals. Together they actually form, or visually imply, rectangular shapes that form a gridlike pattern of color over the surface of the painting. The effect of this pattern upon us is one of rigidity, relieved by only relatively few slanting directions or lines, some wavy and some obscured contours, and the quietly pulsating quality of contiguous color areas. Because this painting emphasizes the flatness of the canvas by its reliance on the horizontal and the vertical, we experience a quality of direct confrontation. There is nothing oblique about this; we come upon it as if squarely from the front and we are, so to speak, stopped and held still in that position. A condition of stasis obtains in us and in the painting, but for some inexplicable reason we do not expect this abruptly induced condition of stoppage to last for long. Because of the radiance of the color, we sense the suspension of deep and powerful forces existing among the other structural components of the grid. We sense qualities of impendence, of imminence—as if something extraordinary was about to happen. This sensing, this feeling, is directly communicated to us, or induced in us by the very form of the painting.

But the form of the painting is made visible to us in the terms of recognizable subject matter, and visually they cannot be separated. The subject matter comes to us in the form Hopper gave it as a result of his own interaction with the specific objects depicted in the painting, the medium of oil paint, and his own techniques as a painter. It consists of a two-storey building with small stores and shops on the lower level, the street in front, a barber pole, a hydrant, and the side of another building showing against the sky. The utterly ordinary situation from which Hopper developed this painting is part of almost everyone's experience. This sort of flat array of banal objects and detail exists along the actual streets of New York and San Francisco, as well as the streets of Delphos, Ohio, and Deadwood, South Dakota. But here in Hopper's painting it has been transformed and made into a deeply moving emblem of the nondescript. The feeling of impendence generated by the form takes on a mysterious quality when experienced in relation to the slanting light of early morning as it strikes across awnings, window shades, pink bricks, and a solitary barber pole. The threat or promise of an immediately impending event of extraordinary magnitude has here been domesticated in these images. By the way in which they have been perceived and presented they become effulgent—more than may ever be possible in actuality—and we are moved to experience a pervasive mystery and a quiet magnificence in what strikes us as the utterly real, the utterly ordinary. And if this does not precisely name the content of this painting, then surely, at least, it must point in its direction.

And perhaps we can also point in the direction of the content of Donatello's *St. Mary Magdalen* (Fig. 19–11). In this case we are concerned with a piece of freestanding sculpture carved from wood. This means that its projection of content can never be completed for us until we have seen this three-dimensional work from a great variety of positions and angles. We will be able to suggest the quality of its content only as it comes through to us from the specific views we are given in two photographs.

The *St. Mary Magdalen* is life-size. It occupies the same kind of space we occupy as we stand in its presence in the Baptistery of the Cathedral of Florence. This, as we noted earlier, contributes to a very different kind of experience than is ours when we stand before a flat painting. Most of us feel a closer personal identity with figures existing in the round, since we do actually share the space in which they exist. And when such figures are of a size equal to our own, an even closer identification takes place. So, in this close association of the actual and the imaged we see Donatello's conception of the prostitute who bathed Christ's feet, who was naturally of the faith, was present at the Crucifixion and at the emptied tomb, and who exiled herself into the desert.

There she stands, a furrowed column in shape, leathery brown in color. Most of the surface appears to move as if covered with living serpents. It does not immediately invite our touch. Only those much smaller volumes of a contrasting smoothness suggest qualities of sympathetic life. Almost nothing in the complex of sculptured volumes suggests active participation with the surrounding space. For the most part, the sculptural form completes itself within itself. It is these qualities of the form of the sculpture that are

Fig. 19–11. *DONATELLO. St. Mary Magdalen. c. 1454–1455. Wood, height 74". Baptistery, Florence. Photo: Brogi-Art Reference Bureau.*

identified with the attitude of this image of a woman. Together, the form and the subject matter project a quite specific content.

Mary Magdalen stands in a position suggestive of taking a step forward, but suggestive also of that step being impossible to take. The hands appear unfeeling, numb—as if Mary had intended to bring them together in a position of prayer, but stopped short of contact because there was no way of feeling whether or not they had actually touched. And then there is the head and the face—one of the most haunting faces in all of art (Fig. 19–12). Old, it is, haggard and toothless—and the eyes no longer gaze upon the outward world. They, like the sculptural form of the whole, turn more in than out. The hair falls stiff and ropelike from her head, divides and metamorphoses into the shaggy coat of an animal, a coat that hides her body from both herself and us. Only the lower arms and hands, which carry the gesture of prayer, appear delicate enough to have once been exquisite. The legs and feet are those of a once fleet predatory animal. This is not the voluptuous blonde prostitute of hundreds of other images of this woman; this is Mary Magdalen, the desert ascetic, giving proof of the condemned bodily estate. The decay of the once seductive form is of no consequence to her now. The pride and pleasures of the body have given way to contemplation of a vision of God. The form and content of this image are as closely identified as the medieval concept of *culpa* and *poena*. Donatello chose to project the quality of the *poena*—penitence—and not the sin. The content of his sculpture has to do with redemption through loss, victory through surrender—and this content can come through only in those experiential terms in which the spectator is able to receive it.

The content of a work of art is always difficult to identify and describe. That this is true should be clear after our experiences with the Hopper painting and with Donatello's sculpture, both of which make generous reference to the familiar world of objects. Even more difficult, perhaps, is to cope in words with the content of nonobjective works of art—works that make minimal reference to the world of objects and which have no subject matter in the traditional sense of that term. So difficult has this task loomed since the first purely nonobjective works were created in this century, that most writers on art have avoided all allusion to content—almost as if it did not exist in such works. Instead, these writers have dwelt rather exclusively on the phenomenon of form. But as we have pointed out, form and content exist inseparably. With form there must be content; with content there must be form, no matter how open or untraditional.

In quite incidental ways we have already recognized the historically uninterrupted lineage of the form-content complex with our earlier comments concerning the nonobjective paintings of Kandinsky and Picasso. And in our concluding remarks concerning Cubism and its preoccupation with the concept of ambiguity, we were actually speaking about the content of nonobjective works of art. We said, "Far from being illogical or crazy, the ambiguous images and ambiguous space of Cubism are indicative of contemporary man's desire for a coherency that exists outside the old assumptions of fixed time and simple location. Cubism is part of this century's effort to cope with, to give form to, what each of us suspects is true: that human beings live in more times and in more places than the here and now —and simultaneously. In its own way, Cubism . . . is saying that, as in the life of the mind, we are not fixed in place or in time, and that in a deep sense we are homeless, or . . . free. It is saying that whatever 'home' we may have is described by the 'success' we have in integrating our past with the present, as we relate both to anticipations of a future.'' So let us continue in this vein and try to be even more aware in recognizing and responding to the often neglected content of contemporary nonobjective work. And let us try to be as fair to that content as we have been to the content of Hopper's *Early Sunday Morning* and Donatello's *St. Mary Magdalen.*

Fig. 19–12. *DONATELLO.* St. Mary Magdalen, *detail. c. 1454–1455. Wood, height 74". Baptistery, Florence. Photo: Brogi-Art Reference Bureau.*

In 1948, three years after the close of World War II, Jackson Pollock, then thirty-six years of age and at the height of his development as a painter, created his *Number 1* (Color Plate 63). Upon the fifty square feet of this raw cotton canvas, Pollock poured, dripped, and swept on a variety of colored paints and enamels. In the process, the canvas was kept flat on the floor of his studio and he worked at it from above. He worked from the edges, and he stood and knelt upon the canvas as he worked. He walked and danced upon the canvas while trailing the records of his movements from cans of syrupy medium. At the point where the growing pattern felt complete and "right" to him, he stopped, and the painting was declared finished; he signed it in English letters at the bottom, and with his handprints at the top. In actual size it is over five feet high and more than eight feet across—a maze of wiry and cloudy passages that leads forever to itself. Its unity results from being so much like itself all over, and as we stand before it in the quiet room in Manhattan where it now resides we feel the aerial maze come around us like a million overtones of an unidentifiable melody. We feel incapacitated —able only to lose ourselves to a druglike trance that floats us unendingly through the detached beauty of this clouded network. But is this enough to *say* about this painting? Does its form and content end with that? What if we look, and look again at it, and see what it is showing?

It is showing us the actions of one man. The trails of poured and dripped paint and the smudges of paint-filled rags trace his seemingly random movements as if through mirrored labyrinths within a confining

JACKSON POLLOCK. Number 1. *The Museum of Modern Art, New York. See Plate 63.*

Plate 61.   *WILLIAM A. BOUGUEREAU*. Whisperings of Love. *1889. Oil on canvas, 62×36¹/₂". An emphasis on sentimentalized subject matter characterizes much of the work produced in Europe and America during the late nineteenth century.*

The great popular success of Bouguereau in France still advertises the mode of painting prevalent during the 1880's and 1890's. (Isaac Delgado Museum of Art, New Orleans. Mr. & Mrs. Chapman H. Hyams Collection.)

Plate 62. *EDWARD HOPPER. Early Sunday Morning. 1930. Oil on canvas, 35×60". A feeling of impendence generated by the form of this painting takes on a mysterious quality when experienced in relation to these banal objects in this particular light. The threat or promise of an immediately impending event of extraordinary magnitude has been domesticated in these images. (Whitney Museum of American Art, New York.)*

Plate 63. *JACKSON POLLOCK. Number 1. 1948. Oil on canvas, 68×104". It has often been said that this sort of painting has no meaning: perhaps this no-meaning is meaning. And it may well be that this painting is not merely the private report of a single man, Jackson Pollock, but a statement from the society itself. (The Museum of Modern Art, New York.)*

Plate 64.   *JACKSON POLLOCK.* Number 1, *detail.*
Here we can see the evidences of a technique that
does not so much depend on accident as on inevi-
table happenings—how the paint will drip, flow,
harden. It is a technique that is willing to forgo
the various choices that are inherent in drawing
and in the deliberate brush stroke. (The Museum
of Modern Art, New York.)

JACKSON POLLOCK. Number 1, *detail. The Museum of Modern Art, New York. See Plate 64.*

area of canvas (Color Plate 64). It is showing us a pattern without focus, a pattern depending on saturation of the area for its unity. It is showing us the evidences of a technique that depends not so much on accident as on inevitable happenings—how the paint will drip, flow, harden—but which in any case is willing to forgo the choices inherent in drawing or in the brush stroke. It is showing us something directly related to the inner world of the artist, something which has to do with the flux of man's psychobiological states, but prior to, or with minimum concern for, rescuing anything purposive except the flow or texture of that flux. In this we are presuming that an artist like Pollock somehow managed to go so deep into himself that he was able to tap the flow of raw inner experience prior to its conceptualization or symbolization—that a painting like *Number 1* is a more or less direct transcription of that running, "pre-cognized" inner experience. Herbert Read respects the value of this possibility when he says that inasmuch as our old symbols have been emptied out, it is bootless to attempt to reuse those shells for contents which in any case would not fit. To his way of thinking, the Pollock kind of externalization of pre-conscious experience may be essential so that its record might gradually jell into the new symbols now urgently required to continue civilized life.[1] And Pollock himself, in speaking of what he called the "good European moderns" said that he was "particularly impressed with their concept of the source of art being the unconscious."[2]

---

[1] Herbert Read, *Icon and Idea* (Cambridge, Mass.: Harvard University Press, 1955). See especially Chapters VI and VII.

[2] "Jackson Pollock," *Arts and Architecture,* LXI (February, 1944), 14.

Now if this is so—if we have in *Number 1* an expression of the inner, unconscious world of the artist—then there is a content, a meaning, an import inherent in its form. It has often been said that this sort of painting has no meaning: perhaps this no-meaning *is* meaning. And it may well be that *Number 1* is not merely the private report of one man, Jackson Pollock, but of men in this society. And because we have trouble perceiving any meaning in this sort of painting and resent this kind of performance (Why should we resent a thing which has no meaning?), it behooves us all the more to consider what this meaning or content is.

In much the same way that ancient Egyptian art made statements about the human condition of its time, so did the art of Masaccio, Michelangelo, Vermeer, Watteau, Goya, and Cézanne make statements about the human condition through which they lived. And so does the art of Jackson Pollock. By its abandonment of all except the wish to act out a record of the individual's interior states, it bears witness to contemporary man's attempt to desert the cultural past in favor of a more primitive past—a past that lives on in us as instinct and muscle. It bears witness to an emphasis on the inner world of secluded experience, now so often confused and indifferent that it is neither creative nor destructive. It attests to the existentialist engagement of contemporary man with solitary torment or uneasiness whenever he comes against the problems and responsibilities of man's situation.

The content of *Number 1* is of a kind that bears witness to a resignation in favor of inevitable forces—in favor of fate and uncontrollable processes. And this in turn may attest to the failure of contemporary man to regard the necessity, or even the possibility, for making significant choices—the kind of choices that affect the very heart of whatever stake men have in this life. Its content has to do with the cavities in the substance of our society that were once filled with functioning symbols that have now all but disappeared. And it bears witness to an attempt to encompass contemporary experience with no more than our own human nature, and then, by some enchantment or dance, to pass into and through it. It bears witness to each contemporary man's concept of himself as an entirely lonesome agent for discovering his own truths and creating his own myths while considerations of value are lost in a shadowy civilization. And this in turn attests to a tacit assumption that the process of painting—the creative act—is a spiritual one, capable of appropriating the functions of exhausted spiritual institutions.

In the context of the history of art forms, this painting makes a statement about the abandonment or devaluation of the role of human will. Its content has to do with the displacement of man as a purposive being and the admission of saturation and randomness as transcendental determinants. The content has to do with a state of affairs in which life can be lived, or at least conceived of as, outside man's conscious control and responsibility. This painting is not a record of escape from the "uncelebratable" values of our time: its form is a virtual diagram of them, and that is what its content is about.

CHAPTER TWENTY

The Creative Process:

A SUMMARY OF ITS NATURE

Every work of art, from the first moment of its realization, stands as something unique in the world. It is a new thing. Yet every artistic creation begins its formation out of the old, the commonplace; the germ of its life is to be found in its beginnings, in a past. Because this appears indisputable—unless we can believe that some things come from nothing—a statement concerning the nature of the old and its operation toward the new should be made.

To survive in this world, man, a sensitive organism, makes adjustment to a hostile environment. The life of any man is characterized principally by the quality and extent of the adjustment he finds it possible and good to make. This adjustment is made slowly and on many levels by acquiring the abilities necessary to meet purposively the myriad situations of his environment. The acquisition of these abilities over time constitutes his learning, and what he wrests from that process we often call knowledge.

In the beginning the human organism is apprised both of himself and his environment on the level of sensation. At birth the organism is bombarded with sensations of light, sound, smell, touch, temperature, and taste. These are the beginnings of knowledge, the direct and immediate contact of organism and environment. At this level, both organism and environment are undefined, and no adequate adjustment is possible. But in the human organism these sensations soon begin to integrate; they begin to pattern. A small, round, smooth, cool, red, odd-smelling pattern that yields to pressure in the hands becomes a rubber ball; the large, soft, white, fuzzy pattern that touches the neck and arms becomes the woolen coverlet in the crib. Gradually, by experience, and out of the chaos and confusion of sensation, patterns that stand for objects are formed. The awareness of these patterns as objects constitutes perception. With this new perception the perceiving self is given its first consciousness. Whatever it is that works to patternize sensations into unified objects, it is more than the chaotic stimulation alone. This stimulation is given, but what is prehended is a unity that is more than sensuous and which includes ourselves as part of that unity. With awareness of objects in an external world there grows awareness of ourselves.

Objects are differentiated one from another; they are perceived as form with content in the context of the individual life. But to progress to the *meaning* of these forms and this order requires more than sensation and more than simple perception. Retention in the organism of perceived form is necessary to its subsequent recognition, and *meaning* is dependent on the perfection of recall, in order to free the organism from a role as slave to direct perception. The human organism is so freed when, by virtue of recall, it can re-experience past events and situations when the concomitant physical stimuli of those events, objects, and situations are no longer physically present.

But to be able to recall, even *in toto,* the stuff of an object or an event now removed in time and place—to make that event or object live again as if in the present—is only to bring up a copy of the original. More than this is necessary to begin the transformation of the old, so that it can operate toward the new in artistic creation. Manifold memory must work to collect out of the past everything associated or connected with an object, event, or feeling. It must range through the past, collecting from many times and places, many things and events, and many situations and conditions, in order to bring into the present the kind of pattern or meaning that had not existed until these many formerly disassociated parts were brought together. In this sense memory is more than simple recall. It can select and combine from a past all those experiences of a common quality and hold them for examination, addition, deletion, speculation, change, and finally as material for the foundations of new meanings. It is this plastic quality of the pattern of memory-evoked images that allows for their shaping and patterning into something quite different from their beginnings in actuality. Here, fantasy becomes possible, as well as new, practical knowledge insofar as the substitution of plastic images for percepts encourages invention and new insights.

The nature of the conditions that cooperate to set the creative process in motion has for a long time been a subject of deep concern to specialists in many fields. Although we have the informal and intimate descriptions offered by creative persons themselves, we lack a clear explanation of exactly what takes place at that point which is so often alluded to as the "inspiration." The most persuasive reports, however, tend to make its description within limits of normal human conduct and to eschew any descriptions that tend toward making of it some kind of "divine afflatus." Generally speaking, scientific explanations of the mechanics of inspiration have not been especially helpful since these rarely, if ever, are put forth with any real bearing on the creation or nature of art. One is inclined to favor an explanation that would not limit the operation of this inspiration to the very first stages of the creative process, but that would admit of its operation at every stage, following every temporary stoppage. Inspiration, it would appear from almost all reports of highly creative persons, is a condition which approaches optimum awareness of possibilities for unity, for coherence, in the material at hand. It seems that anything that the human organism can entertain—in any mode—is capable of becoming inspirational in effect when what it brings into the complex of the creative artist is strongly suggestive of an act toward evolving a desirable order. In this sense, inspiration is required at each new beginning and at each new phase of engagement of a large continuing undertaking. It is a continuing occurrence, which, by repeated incursions of immediate or intuitive cognition, judgment, or prehension, throws new light on old material.

It is an unfortunate tradition that speaks of inspiration as a flash rather than as a deep breath, and that limits its occurrence to a single point at the very inception of a creative process. However in error that tradition may be, we must respect its regard for the primogenitor and admit of its importance as a determiner of a line. The best evidence would have us think of this first inspiration as being in a pretty raw state and as something not to be in any way confused with the completed work of art.

From the raw state of inspiration or the initial impulse, the creative process moves forward to a definition in the chosen medium. And though we may never fully come to know or verbalize the exact nature of the impulse to create, it appears important that this perhaps intuitive beginning be recognized as a crucial element in the whole creative process. It is also important that this impulse to create should not be confused either with the fully realized work of art or with art in general. For it must be true that many who experience this impulsion do not, or cannot, carry forward the usually protracted and technical operation which resolves this beginning in a work of art.

This protracted operation, the creative process, deals with the artist as a focus of experience of his age and locale. It deals with the manner of seeing and responding to the world about him. It is concerned with symbolizing insights, of objectifying his particular concept of reality. The creative process consists of a series of interactions between the complex of the artist and the material in which he works. Whatever the nature of the first impulse, if he acts upon it, he does so by beginning to shape his medium—to give it form. In the case of the painter, he begins to paint; in the case of the sculptor, he begins to model. He may work from sketches or diagrams previously made; he may go through any number and variety of preparations, but *at a point* he begins the actual struggle with his medium. In the activity that follows, his aim is always to make his creation communicate a feeling of "rightness" to him: to define, summarize, and present the quality and strength of his initial impulse in terms of a personally satisfying artistic unity. In fulfilling this aim, he uses all means at his disposal: the whole life of his personal experience, the special means and qualities of his medium, the skills and techniques he has acquired, and all the traditions of his craft that he has incorporated into his personal procedures.

Both the era and locale in which he works will limit him to certain kinds of solutions to the problems he meets in the process of creating his work, for at any given time and place the artist has only so much experience out of which he can create. Likewise, he has only so much tradition, technical skill, physical endurance, knowledge of his medium, and power of conceptualization at his command at a particular time. In the matter of personal experience, Goya may have been poorer at the age of twenty-five than he was at the age of fifty-five. And in matters of tradition and power of conceptualization, it may be argued that Gilbert Stuart lived at a less advantageous time than does Robert Rauschenberg. Such considerations of age and tradition, however, are not of first importance in matters regarding the creative process. What is of first importance is the *intensity* with which these factors operate in the process of creating. Because of these peculiar and epochal limitations, it is axiomatic that all things are not possible at all times.

But no matter the natures of the limitations, the artist will still move forward among them to create a work that communicates a feeling of "rightness" to him, that continues to isolate and objectify the quality of the new thing he first vaguely sensed existing in the old. If he is a painter he will brush-in areas in different relations to one another, and he will change these relationships; he will first use this color and then that color within certain areas of his growing composition, and he will keep changing these—one in relation to the other, all in relation to the whole configuration, until, finally, this looks right to him. His operations with whatever he "puts down" are always provisional. They are put down in order that he can see them, savor them in relation to everything else that has been managed up to that point. The whole process of artistic creation moves forward by steps first taken provisionally, then either verified and incorporated into the growing whole or found false and abandoned. In the same manner subject matter, whether it be angels or tenements or color-shapes, is continually being altered, emphasized here and deemphasized there, destroyed and reconstructed until that, too, looks and feels right. It is this basic nature of the creative process that caused Picasso to remark that a painting moves forward to completion by means of a series of destructions. Such destructions are found necessary by the artist as some new notion, fact, feeling, mood, or promise is revealed to him as he works. This new element enters first as a stranger to the developing unity, and if it insists on remaining it necessitates a destruction equivalent to its strength as measured by the artist. Part or, in some cases, all of the unity managed to that point must be destroyed to make place for the new element, which in turn will function to build another unity partaking of the strength of the new element and such others as will subsequently cluster about it. This is the manner in which the more vital

supersedes the less vital. At every stage of the process of creating a work of
art, the artist is making decisions in favor of those colors, those images,
those shapes, those textures that best suit his constantly sharpening discern-
ment of what his finished work must be.

Creating is no such simple process as getting an "idea" and then casting
it in some medium. No idea or concept is complete until it has been embodied
in some objective form, and in a very real sense the idea or concept is itself
created as it takes form. The whole creative process is one of interaction of
the experience of the artist with the medium in which he chooses to work.
And not only does he administer the objective conditions of his medium, but
the general recalcitrance of his medium tends to administer his experience,
in fact to mold his whole life. His initial hunch, notion, or idea is defined as
it is disciplined by what the artist finds possible to accomplish in a certain
medium and still have his work result in a satisfying unity.

Characteristic of the whole creative process is the general movement
from a state of uncertainty or chaos to one of order. It is disorder that
mothers the desire for order and that generates the heat necessary to fire
the relentless effort that characterizes the creator in dealing with the materials and tools of his craft. For the most part, this chaos cannot be induced
artificially: it must come organically as evidence of a new insight struggling
out of the old. It must be integral with the state of the artist's experience. It
must be recognized as the manifestation of a need for order; its character
must be so credited, and action in that direction must be taken if the artist
desires resolution. Taking action—beginning to paint or draw or carve—
can then formally set the creative process in motion.

Fig. 20–1. *HIRAM D. WILLIAMS. Challenging Man.*
1958. Oil and enamel on canvas, 96¹/₄×72¹/₈". This
image of a man rising from a chair, stepping forward
and advancing along the line of his gaze, is fraught
with the spirit of action required of any artist—of any
man—to set any creative process in motion. (The
Museum of Modern Art, New York. Fund from the
Sumner Foundation for the Arts.)

The means required by the artist to progress from stage to stage toward an order objectively embodied in a work of art are evolved from the most recent stage. In this respect, his moving toward completion of his work is similar to physical or chemical chain reactions. But in differentiation to these senseless reactions, the progressive stages in the process of creative activity are managed through laborious effort and often painful toil. The intermittent rewards come with the knowledge of each successive stage achieved toward unity. And with the final work of embodiment and order achieved, with objective form at last given to what started as a shapeless ghost, the artist experiences the joy of equilibrium existing between the old and the new. Yet if he really be an artist, his completed work will suffice only as another experience that will serve to reactivate him toward a renewed vision and the embodiment in artistic form of still another unique insight.

Bibliography

The following very abbreviated list is of titles that bear more or less directly on subjects discussed in this book. It is given in the hope that it may assist the reader in his explorations beyond those entered upon in the preceding pages.

ALBERS, JOSEF, *Interaction of Color*. New Haven, Conn.: Yale University Press, 1963.

ARNHEIM, RUDOLPH, *Art and Visual Perception*. Berkeley: University of California Press, 1954.

BERGSON, HENRI, *The Creative Mind*. New York: Philosophical Library, Inc., 1946. Wisdom Library Paperbacks.

BERKMAN, AARON, *Art and Space*. New York: Barnes & Noble, Inc., 1949. Social Science Paperbacks.

BIRREN, FABER, *The Story of Color*. Westport, Conn.: The Crimson Press, 1941.

CHAET, BERNARD, *Artists at Work*. Cambridge, Mass.: Hill & Wang, Inc., 1960. Webb Books.

CLARK, SIR KENNETH, *The Nude: A Study in Ideal Form*. New York: Pantheon Books, Inc., 1956.

DEWEY, JOHN, *Art as Experience*. New York: G. P. Putnam's Sons, 1934.

DIBBLE, GEORGE, *Watercolor: Materials and Techniques*. New York: Holt, Rinehart & Winston, Inc., 1966.

DOERNER, MAX, *The Materials of the Artist and Their Use in Painting, with Notes on the Techniques of the Old Masters*. New York: Harcourt, Brace, and World, Inc., 1949.

DURST, ALAN L., *Wood Carving*. New York: The Viking Press, Inc., 1938. Studio Books.

EHRENZWEIG, ANTON, *The Psychoanalysis of Artistic Vision and Hearing: An Introduction to a Theory of Unconscious Perception*. New York: Julian Press, Inc., 1953.

EVANS, MYFANWY, ed., *The Painter's Object*. London: Howe, 1937.

EVANS, RALPH M., *An Introduction to Color*. New York: John Wiley & Sons, Inc., 1948.

FOÇILLON, HENRI, *The Life of Forms in Art.* New York: George Wittenborn, Inc., 1948.

GHISELIN, BREWSTER, *The Creative Process.* Berkeley: University of California Press, 1952.

GIBSON, JAMES J., *Perception of the Visual World.* Boston: Houghton Mifflin Company, 1950.

GIEDION, SIGFRIED, *Space, Time and Architecture.* Cambridge, Mass.: Harvard University Press, 1954.

GIEDION-WELCKER, CAROLA, *Contemporary Sculpture: an Evolution in Volume and Space.* New York: George Wittenborn, Inc., 1955.

GILSON, ETIENNE, *Painting and Reality.* New York: Pantheon Books, Inc., 1957.

GOLDWATER, R. J. and M. TREVES, *Artists on Art.* New York: Pantheon Books, Inc., 1945.

GOMBRICH, E. H., *Art and Illusion: A Study in the Psychology of Pictorial Representation.* New York: Pantheon Books, Inc., 1960.

————, *The Story of Art.* New York: Phaidon Press Ltd., 1958.

GREENOUGH, HORATIO, *Form and Function.* Berkeley: University of California Press, 1947.

GREGORY, R. L., *Eye and Brain, The Psychology of Seeing.* New York: McGraw-Hill Book Company, 1966.

HALL, E. T., *The Silent Language.* Garden City, N. Y.: Doubleday & Company, Inc., 1959.

HAMLIN, TALBOT F., *Forms and Functions of Twentieth Century Architecture.* New York: Columbia University Press, 1952.

HAUSER, ARNOLD, *The Social History of Art.* 4 vols. New York: Random House, Inc., 1958. Vintage Books.

HELLER, JULES, *Printmaking Today.* New York: Holt, Rinehart & Winston, Inc., 1958.

HILDEBRAND, ADOLF, *The Problem of Form in Painting and Sculpture.* New York: Stechert-Hafner, Inc., 1945.

HILL, EDWARD, *The Language of Drawing.* Englewood Cliffs, N. J.: Prentice-Hall, Inc., 1966.

HOLT, ELIZABETH G., *A Documentary History of Art.* 2 vols. Garden City, N. Y.: Doubleday & Company, Inc., 1957. Anchor Books.

HUYGHE, RENÉ, *Ideas and Images in World Art: Dialogue with the Visible.* New York: Harry N. Abrams, Inc., 1959.

JANSON, H. W., *The History of Art.* Englewood Cliffs, N. J.: Prentice-Hall, Inc., and New York: Harry N. Abrams, Inc., 1962.

JENKINS, IREDELL, *Art and the Human Enterprise.* Cambridge, Mass.: Harvard University Press, 1958.

JENSEN, LAWRENCE N., *Synthetic Painting Media.* Englewood Cliffs, N. J.: Prentice-Hall, Inc., 1964.

KANDINSKY, WASSILY, *Concerning the Spiritual in Art.* New York: George Wittenborn, Inc., 1947.

KEPES, GYORGY, *Language of Vision.* New York: Paul Theobold, 1944.

KOESTLER, ARTHUR, *The Act of Creation.* New York: The Macmillan Company, 1964.

KOFFKA, KURT, *Principles of Gestalt Psychology.* London: Routledge & Kegan Paul Ltd., 1935.

LANGER, SUSANNE K., *Problems of Art.* New York: Charles Scribner's Sons, 1957.

LE CORBUSIER, *New World of Space.* New York: Reynal & Co., Inc., 1948.

LEE, SHERMAN E., *A History of Far Eastern Art.* Englewood Cliffs, N. J.: Prentice-Hall, Inc., 1964.

MAYER, RALPH, *The Painter's Craft.* Princeton, N. J.: D. Van Nostrand Co., Inc., 1948.

McLUHAN, MARSHALL and EDMUND CARPENTER, *Explorations in Communications.* Boston: Beacon Press, 1960.

MOHOLY-NAGY, LASZLO, *The New Vision.* New York: George Wittenborn, Inc., 1949.

OGDEN, C. K. and I. A. RICHARDS, *The Meaning of Meaning.* New York: Harcourt, Brace, and World, Inc., 1930.

PANOFSKY, ERWIN, *Meaning in the Visual Arts.* Garden City, N. Y.: Doubleday & Company, Inc., 1955.

PETERDI, GABOR, *Printmaking: Methods Old and New.* New York: The Macmillan Company, 1959.

READ, HERBERT, *The Meaning of Art.* Baltimore: Penguin Books, Inc., 1964.

RICH, JACK C., *The Materials and Methods of Sculpture.* New York: Oxford University Press, Inc., 1947.

ROBB, DAVID M. and J. J. GARRISON, *Art in the Western World.* New York: Harper and Row, Publishers, 1963.

RODMAN, SELDEN, *Conversations with Artists.* New York: G. P. Putnam's Sons, 1961. Capricorn Books.

———, *The Eye of Man.* New York: Devin Adair Co., 1955.

SCHOEN, MAX, *Art and Beauty.* New York: The Macmillan Company, 1932.

SEITZ, WILLIAM C., *The Responsive Eye.* New York: The Museum of Modern Art, 1965.

SHAHN, BEN, *The Shape of Content.* Cambridge, Mass.: Harvard University Press, 1957.

SINNOTT, EDMUND W., *The Biology of the Spirit.* New York: The Viking Press, Inc., 1955.

STRUPPECK, JULES, *The Creation of Sculpture.* New York: Holt, Rinehart & Winston, Inc., 1952.

TOMAS, VINCENT, *Creativity in the Arts.* Englewood Cliffs, N. J.: Prentice-Hall, Inc., 1964.

URBAN, WILBUR MARSHALL, *Language and Reality.* New York: The Macmillan Company, 1939.

VERNON, M. D., *A Further Study of Visual Perception.* Cambridge: Cambridge University Press, 1952.

WATROUS, JAMES, *The Craft of Old Master Drawings.* Madison: University of Wisconsin Press, 1957.

WEISMANN, DONALD L., *Language and Visual Form: The Personal Record of a Dual Creative Process.* Austin and London: University of Texas Press, 1968.

WENGENROTH, STOW, *Making a Lithograph.* New York: The Viking Press, Inc., 1936. Studio Books.

WEYL, HERMANN, *Symmetry.* Princeton, N. J.: Princeton University Press, 1952.

WHITE, J., *The Birth and Rebirth of Pictorial Space.* New York: Thomas Yoseloff, Publishers, 1958.

WHORF, BENJAMIN LEE, *Language, Thought and Reality.* New York: Technology Press and John Wiley & Sons, Inc., 1956.

WHYTE, LANCELOT, *Accent on Form.* New York: Harper & Row, Publishers, 1954.

WILLIAMS, HIRAM D., *Notes for a Young Painter.* Englewood Cliffs, N. J.: Prentice-Hall, Inc., 1963.

WÖLFFLIN, HEINRICH, *The Sense of Form in Art: A Comparative Psychological Study.* New York: Chelsea Publishing Company, 1958.

ZEVI, BRUNO, *Architecture as Space.* New York: American Heritage Publishing Co., Inc., 1957. Horizon Books.

ZUCKER, PAUL, *Styles in Painting.* New York: The Viking Press, Inc., 1950.

Italic page numbers indicate black and white illustrations.
Plate (Pl.) numbers refer to color reproductions.